# Real-World iOS

## by Tutorials

by Renan Dias, Aaqib Hussain & Josh Steele

# Real-World iOS by Tutorials

Renan Dias, Aaqib Hussain & Josh Steele

Copyright ©2022 Razeware LLC.

## Notice of Rights

All rights reserved. No part of this book or corresponding materials (such as text, images, or source code) may be reproduced or distributed by any means without prior written permission of the copyright owner.

## Notice of Liability

This book and all corresponding materials (such as source code) are provided on an "as is" basis, without warranty of any kind, express of implied, including but not limited to the warranties of merchantability, fitness for a particular purpose, and noninfringement. In no event shall the authors or copyright holders be liable for any claim, damages or other liability, whether in action of contract, tort or otherwise, arising from, out of or in connection with the software or the use of other dealing in the software.

## Trademarks

All trademarks and registered trademarks appearing in this book are the property of their own respective owners.

ISBN: 978-1-950325-60-3

# Table of Contents

# Book License

By purchasing *Real-World iOS by Tutorials*, you have the following license:

- You are allowed to use and/or modify the source code in *Real-World iOS by Tutorials* in as many apps as you want, with no attribution required.

- You are allowed to use and/or modify all art, images and designs that are included in *Real-World iOS by Tutorials* in as many apps as you want, but must include this attribution line somewhere inside your app: "Artwork/images/designs: from *Real-World iOS by Tutorials*, available at www.raywenderlich.com".

- The source code included in *Real-World iOS by Tutorials* is for your personal use only. You are NOT allowed to distribute or sell the source code in *Real-World iOS by Tutorials* without prior authorization.

- This book is for your personal use only. You are NOT allowed to sell this book without prior authorization, or distribute it to friends, coworkers or students; they would need to purchase their own copies.

All materials provided with this book are provided on an "as is" basis, without warranty of any kind, express or implied, including but not limited to the warranties of merchantability, fitness for a particular purpose and noninfringement. In no event shall the authors or copyright holders be liable for any claim, damages or other liability, whether in an action of contract, tort or otherwise, arising from, out of or in connection with the software or the use or other dealings in the software.

All trademarks and registered trademarks appearing in this guide are the properties of their respective owners.

# Before You Begin

This section tells you a few things you need to know before you get started, such as what you'll need for hardware and software, where to find the project files for this book, and more.

# What You Need

To follow along with the tutorials in this book, you'll need the following:

- A Mac running macOS Monterey or later. You'll need this to be able to install the latest version of Xcode and use Xcode previews.

- **Xcode 13 or later**. Xcode is the main development tool for iOS. You'll need Xcode 13 or later for the tasks in this book. You can download the latest version of Xcode from Apple's developer site here: https://developer.apple.com/develop/

- Basic knowledge of Swift and iOS development.

If you want to try things out on a physical iOS device, you'll need a developer account with Apple, which you can obtain for free. However, all the sample projects in this book will work just fine in the iOS Simulator bundled with Xcode, so the developer account is completely optional.

# Book Source Code & Forums

## Where to download the materials for this book

The materials for this book can be cloned or downloaded from the GitHub book materials repository:

- https://github.com/raywenderlich/rwi-materials/tree/editions/1.0

## Forums

We've also set up an official forum for the book at https://forums.raywenderlich.com/c/books/real-world-ios-by-tutorials. This is a great place to ask questions about the book or to submit any errors you may find.

"To my wife, Emily, and my sons, Noah and Daniel - you are my reason for being, and you drive me to succeed every day. To my dad, Robert, and my mom, Julie - thank you for the repeated reminders to do what I love and what comes naturally. Finally, thanks to the wonderful team at raywenderlich.com - you are the best!"

— *Josh Steele*

"To my mother, Luciane, who always cared for me and did everything she could to ensure my well-being and happiness. To my father, Julio Cesar, who always told me I could do anything as long as I put my mind to it. To my brother, Otávio, who's always taking care of me in his own way. To my partner, Nathália, for the unbelievable patience withstanding long nights while I was writing this book, but never stopped giving me love and support. To my good friend, Victor, for being an unbelievable companion and always being by my side. And finally, to the entire Real-World iOS by Tutorials team, who helped get this book done and never stopped supporting me. Without them, this book would not be possible."

— *Renan Dias*

"To my parents, specially my mother for all her prayers and wishes. My wife, for supporting me throughout the journey and bringing me tea from time to time. :)"

— *Aaqib Hussain*

# About the Authors

 Josh is an author of this book. He spends his days mostly working in Java, creating scientific applications for the Space and Health industries, helping researchers visualize complicated data sets. He also teaches iOS, both here at raywenderlich.com and in a graduate school class. In his copious spare time, he enjoys watching football and baseball (especially his son's baseball games), playing board games, and keeping up with the latest Marvel movies with his boys.

 Renan Dias is an author of this book. He is an iOS software engineer in love with Swift. Renan is always trying to learn more about new technologies. When not studying, you can find him playing video games, watching Disney/Pixar movies or reading manga.

 Aaqib is one of the co-authors of this book. He is an enthusiastic programmer. He loves writing code in Swift and exploring new technologies and platforms. He focuses on writing clean code and following best architectural practices. He also has his own blog kodesnippets.com where he often writes. When he is not writing code, he spends his time exploring new places and doing photography. He loves to try out new restaurants and different cuisines with his wife.

# About the Editors

Pinal Naik is a tech editor of this book. She lives in Bangalore, India. After more than a decade in regular corporate life, she chose to start working on her own to pursue her passions. She loves to create iOS apps from scratch to finish, using advanced technologies like Machine Learning and is the owner of the apps Xplooor and Alt-Selfie. Her latest creation is available at: https://apps.apple.com/app/id1542732315. When not coding, you'll find her immersed in a book, traveling or spending time with her husband and her two super-energetic boys. She appreciates the unconditional support of her husband, kids, mother-in-law, mother, her late father and her team in making this book a reality. She hopes to inspire a lot more women to become developers and app creators.

Kenny is a single dad and experienced iOS Developer. He currently works with several talented iOS and Android Developers, managing releases for the adaptive fitness app, JRNY. He also currently works as a Tech Editor for the Server-Side Swift team here at raywenderlich.com. Kenny previously assisted various private clients through freelance contracts - sometimes developing apps from start to release, sometimes adding new features, and always wanting to refactor! In his spare time, he strums his guitar, tinkers with his 3d printers, and plays on his Playstation 5.

April is a former high school English and theater teacher and director. When not volunteering at her daughters' schools, she usually spends her time being asked to pretend to be a unicorn, zombie princess or superhero. In her spare time, she enjoys reading, making pasta and exploring the Gulf Coast with her family.

Libranner is the final pass editor of this book. He's a software engineer with more than 14 years of experience, basketball fan and player, and a decent dancer. He loves learning and teaching at all levels. You can follow him on Twitter as @libranner (https://twitter.com/Libranner).

# Section I: Designing Real World Apps

For an app to be successful, it needs to be planned out. This means understanding the requirements, how they translate to code, and how to best structure your code to be flexible but powerful.

This section describes how up-front design helps drive your model and data layers, and how features in Swift and iOS help developers bring the design to life.

# Chapter 1: Introduction

By Josh Steele

When Steve Jobs introduced the iPhone in 2007, it didn't come with a developer-facing SDK. There were no third-party native apps available. Instead, Apple directed developers to make web apps for Safari. Fast forward 14 months later, and in response to intense feedback from developers, Apple released the first iOS SDK in March 2008.

Since then, Apple has released over a dozen versions of iOS. Over that time, the following also took place:

1. **iOS Framework Additions**: The development teams introduced many frameworks such as SiriKit, Game Center, CoreML and ARKit. These technologies and their associated documentation continue to grow in number each year. OK, the documentation may not grow as quickly as one would like.

2. **Objective-C to Swift**: Apple migrated from Objective-C to Swift as the primary language supported by Apple for iOS development.

3. **UIKit to SwiftUI**: Apple started promoting SwiftUI over UIKit for user interface development.

4. **Xcode Releases**: Xcode has also grown over the years to keep up with the frameworks, devices and languages developers use to develop iOS apps.

Apps need to reach the public to be successful. In 2008, Apple announced the App Store, and at the time, it contained 500 apps. Today, over five million apps are available to users worldwide.

To support releasing apps to the App Store, Apple released App Store Connect, originally part of iTunes Connect, in 2018. Since then, Apple added features such as managing app prices, creating and managing in-app purchases, analyzing sales and trends and managing beta testers through TestFlight.

As you can imagine, iOS developers need to be familiar with many technologies, best practices and techniques to release an app today. This book doesn't delve deep into any technology. Instead, this book helps you by providing an overview of the **end-to-end** processes involved in releasing an iOS app. In other words, breadth, not depth.

# What is this book about?

This book has to cover *a lot* of topics to address the needs of a successful, real-world iOS app. They fall into the following sections:

- **Designing Real World Apps**: Software engineering principles state that up-front design is vital to create code that is easy to understand and maintain, and designing for iOS is no exception.

- **Building App Features**: Once a foundation is in place, you can build features from the foundation up to the user interface, where applicable. These features ideally exist independently but may send information to other features through foundation layer components.

- **Modularizing Your App**: Taking features a step further, you can extract features from your main project into standalone projects and import them via tools such as CocoaPods or Swift Package Manager.

- **Enhancing the User Interface & Experience**: Developing an *intuitive* user interface is vital for any successful app. Developing a *unique* user experience to keep the user engaged and returning to your app is even more important.

- **App Privacy, Maintenance & Deployment**: Respecting user data privacy is a requirement for iOS apps imposed by Apple and can prompt a user to choose your app over others on the App Store. Once your app deploys, learning how to maintain your code and quickly push new releases to the store is essential to prevent your app's ratings from plummeting.

While learning how to implement specific techniques is important - you wouldn't have an app without implementation - this book strives to convey the "why" behind those implementations. By the end of the book, you'll find yourself going **beyond the code** to have a better understanding of the techniques developers learn over time.

You'll solve real-world problems with best practices and techniques throughout the book as you develop a single iOS app. As you implement parts of the app, you may discover that a particular technique may not be the best approach for the problem at hand. You'll also learn what makes that approach better or worse than others.

You may realize a different approach to solving a problem or totally disagree with the presented technique. That's good! There are usually many ways to approach and solve a problem. This book simply provides **a** set of best practices and techniques, not **the** set of best practices and techniques. What's important here is that you get familiar with these practices and use them - or a variation of them - as you develop your next iOS app.

## Who is this book for?

This book is useful for developers of all levels. The content assumes foundational knowledge of the following topics:

- **Swift**: Apple's leading language for iOS development.

- **SwiftUI**: The declarative and reactive framework for user interface development.

- **Networking**: The basics of networking with `URLSession` and its related framework classes and methods.

- **Core Data**: How to create database entities and attributes as well as fetch and save data.

- **Accessibility**: Designing for VoiceOver and Apple Human Interface Guidelines (HIG) best practices.

- **Unit Testing**: Xcode Unit Testing and Test Driven Development.

- **Deployment**: Testflight beta testing and App Store deployment.

> **Note**: If you need to fill in gaps in your knowledge, raywenderlich.com
> provides a variety of books to help. To brush up on Swift and SwiftUI, Swift
> Apprentice (https://www.raywenderlich.com/books/swift-apprentice) and
> Swift UI Apprentice (https://www.raywenderlich.com/books/swiftui-
> apprentice), are great places to start. Core Data by Tutorials (https://
> www.raywenderlich.com/books/core-data-by-tutorials) takes you through the
> entire Core Data stack. iOS Animations by Tutorials (https://
> www.raywenderlich.com/books/ios-animations-by-tutorials) gives you the
> basics to keep your app lively for your user. With iOS Test-Driven
> Development by Tutorials (https://www.raywenderlich.com/books/ios-test-
> driven-development-by-tutorials), you can learn techniques to keep your app
> bug-free. Finally, iOS App Distribution and Best Practices (https://
> www.raywenderlich.com/books/ios-app-distribution-best-practices) provides
> the best techniques for getting your app to the App Store.

As mentioned earlier, this book covers a wide breadth of topics and doesn't go too
deep into them. Instead, the focus is on why you should use these techniques and
best practices to make your app successful.

# The sample project

Throughout this book, you'll work on improving a sample project called **PetSave**.
PetSave is an adoption and fostering app that searches for animals available to you
in your area. It takes into account the pet's medical history along with your personal
preferences to return results.

Open the **final** folder of the **final chapter's** sample project to get an idea of what the app will be able to do:

*The PetSave Animals Near You Results Page.*

The features you'll work on developing or incorporating are:

- **Animals Near You**: This feature uses your current location to see which pets are up for adoption near you.

- **Search**: This feature lets you refine your search to particular pets or attributes you're looking for when adopting.

- **Onboarding**: On first launch, the onboarding feature will introduce the user to PetSave's features.

While you implement those features, you'll use iOS development best practices such as:

- **Low Coupling and High Cohesion**: Designing your code to be highly cohesive **within** code elements while minimizing coupling **between** elements helps promote reuse and makes future maintenance easier.

- **Proper code structure**: Structuring code elements into conceptual layers and segments helps you understand the purpose of each set of code, how they relate to one another and how you can use them when implementing parts of your app.

- **Persistence**: Keeping a copy of network data on device prevents the app from reaching back out to get that data repeatedly which saves valuable resources such as the user's data plan.

- **Modular App Features**: Isolate your features into modules that can be tested and maintained separately from your main app to promote reuse and decrease the likelihood of bugs.

- **Animations and Custom Controls**: Lively animations and custom controls help make a user's experience a memorable one and keeps them coming back to use your app in the future.

- **Accessibility**: Dynamic Text, proper use of colors and preparing your code for VoiceOver helps make your app accessible to a wider audience.

- **Localization**: To reach a worldwide audience, you need to prepare your app for the various locales in which you'll release it.

- **App Privacy**: Asking for permission to use certain device features and advertising what user data your app collects are both required by Apple when developing an iOS app.

Now since you know what the app will look like when you finish the book, it's time to see what you'll start with. Open this chapter's **starter** project. Build and run.

You'll see an almost blank screen under the **Animals Near You** and **Search** tabs. You'll populate those screens throughout the book using best practices in iOS development.

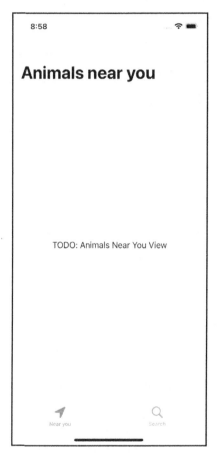

*An Empty Starter Project.*

PetSave uses the online **Petfinder** API from Purina. This API gives developers the ability to search for pets that need new homes. The main Petfinder website (http://www.petfinder.com) has information on shelters and adoption agencies across the United States. If you're looking for a new pet, you should check them out!

# Signing up for an API Key

To access the Petfinder database, you must sign up for one of their free API keys. Go to the Petfinder developer website (https://www.petfinder.com/developers/) and **sign up** for an account:

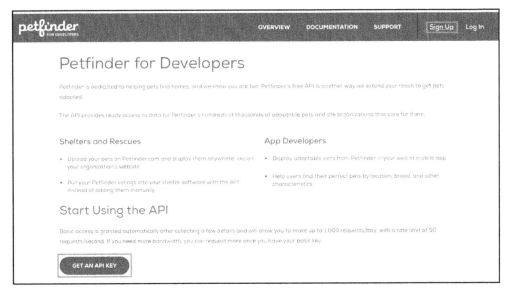

*The Petfinder Signup Page.*

After that, go back to the developer web page and click **GET AN API KEY** at the bottom of the page. Follow the steps to get both the API key and its corresponding secret.

Open **Core/data/api/APIConstants.swift** and set the `clientId` and `clientSecret` properties with the key and secret, respectively:

```
enum APIConstants {
  static let host = "api.petfinder.com"
  static let grantType = "client_credentials"
  static let clientId = "YourKeyHere"
  static let clientSecret = "YourSecretHere"
}
```

Don't forget to copy over the key and secret if you use the chapter's starter project as you progress through future chapters.

Check out the Petfinder API documentation here (https://www.petfinder.com/developers/v2/docs/).

## Key points

- In this book you'll learn techniques to create a real-world iOS app from scratch.

- Petfinder provides an API to search for pets around you. You'll use this API to create the **PetSave** iOS app throughout the coming chapters.

- You'll solve real-world problems with best practices and techniques throughout the book.

## Where to go from here?

You've taken a look at how the project will start and how it looks in its final form. Now you're ready to start adding everything that comes in between.

But, you're not ready to start writing code yet. Before you open Xcode, it's important to understand the purpose of the app. Moreover, you need to devise a good battle plan. You need to answer questions like "What architectures should I use?", "How should I organize my code?" and "What features should I include in the app?" *before* you start writing your code. In the next chapter, you'll start to answer those questions.

# Chapter 2: Laying Down a Strong Foundation

By Renan Benatti Dias

Last chapter, you got a glimpse of PetSave and what you'll build in this book. Now, you'll start your journey by laying down a strong foundation while learning multiple topics to keep in mind while developing your apps.

In this chapter, you'll learn about the many design decisions you may face while developing an iOS app and why it's essential to think about how architecture affects your app as it grows.

More specifically, you'll learn:

- How to organize your project and use a layered architecture using **feature grouping**.

- Why it's key to ensure your code has **high cohesion** and **low coupling**.

- How **SOLID** principles and **design patterns** can help you write better code.

- What PetSave's **domain** is and what the **domain layer** is for.

- How to identify **app features** and devise a plan of attack.

By the end of this chapter, you'll create domain models that represent the foundation of PetSave's features.

# Feature grouping

Open the starter project and expand the **PetSave** group. You'll notice a few groups already in the project:

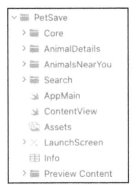

*Project Navigator with PetSave groups*

These groups define the scope of each part of the app and have everything that relates to it inside them.

- **Core**: Contains shared code between all features. It may contain views, business logic and data used on each part of PetSave.

- **AnimalDetails**: Holds the views and view model that compose a pet's details.

- **AnimalsNearYou**: Contains the views and view model for listing animals near the user's location.

- **Search**: A group for the models, view model and views to search for a pet.

By grouping your files like that, you create vertical layers that contain most of the code the enclosed feature needs. Making them primarily independent from other parts of your code.

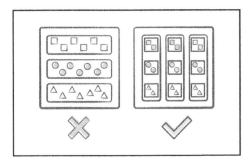

*Diagram showing horizontal grouping and another diagram showing vertical grouping*

This diagram shows the difference between the horizontal and vertical grouping. In the first approach, you have pieces of code grouped by their likenesses. For example, code for the network layer is together, and code for the model layer is together.

The second diagram shows code grouped by their use. So, you group code related to each other together. This type of organization, known as **feature grouping**, defines the borders of each part of the app, so you have the right code at the right place. It has a few advantages:

- It becomes easier to navigate and find code as the group's name already tells you what to expect from it.

- You create groups with high cohesion by only including code related to the same purpose.

- Makes it easier to create modular code.

As your project grows, it may become difficult to maintain code and find each part of the app. That's why it's essential to consider the project's organization early on. Following an organizational pattern like this helps mitigate problems and keeps code with high cohesion and low coupling.

But what does it mean to have a code with high cohesion and low coupling? In the next section, you'll learn why this is important and how using principles like **SOLID** and **Protocol Oriented Programming (POP)** helps you write better and more reusable code.

## Software isn't written in stone

Requirements change. You might be working with agile frameworks or more traditional methods, but the requirements of software change one way or the other.

Changes might happen during development or even after releasing the app. It might happen because a feature doesn't quite work as you expected or the users want something else. When users and stakeholders get hands-on with your app, ideas come up, features change and requirements are removed or added.

App development is an iterative process: You release a version and gather feedback. Developers must always be open to change and listen to the stakeholders and their needs.

Creating code that is flexible will help you when requirements change. Keep this in mind while designing a system, and you'll save tons of time later. High cohesion and low coupling are two concepts you should take into account to write software that's easy to maintain.

## High cohesion

**High cohesion** refers to the ability to keep related components of your code together. That means writing code that fits well together and follows the same purpose or domain.

For instance, consider an enum that's responsible for the API's paths:

```
enum APIRouter {
  case animalsNearYou
  case search

  var path: String {
    "/v2/animals"
  }
}
```

APIRouter contains only a single path that addresses both endpoints, animalsNearYou and search.

Imagine that from now on, the web API requires you to generate a token to make requests. You would need to update APIRouter to add this new path:

```
enum APIRouter {
  case animalsNearYou
  case search

  // New route
  case token

  var path: String {
    switch self {
    case .animalsNearYou,
      .search:
      return "/v2/animals"
    // New path
    case .token:
      return "/v2/token"
    }
  }
}
```

This code might not seem like much, but `APIRouter` now handles two different paths with different purposes. One deals with the animal's requests, while the other deals with authentication.

This enum would keep growing out of proportion with every new feature. Not only would it not make sense anymore, but it would also be tough to maintain and lack focus.

Instead of having a single enum that handles all routes, splitting it into two enums with a single domain makes it easier to change and understand the responsibility of each:

```
enum AnimalsRouter {
  case animalsNearYou
  case search

  var path: String {
    "/v2/animals"
  }
}

enum AuthRouter {
  case token

  var path: String {
    "/v2/token"
  }
}
```

Now, each enum has its purpose, making your code more cohesive and organized. Maintaining code with high cohesion reduces complexity and increases maintainability and reusability.

## Low coupling

**Low coupling** code, or even **completely decoupled** code, can work by itself, in any situation, without depending on other components. Take a look at the following class:

```
class AnimalsNearYouViewModel {
  let service = Service()

  func fetchAnimals() {
    service.fetchAnimals()
  }
}
```

AnimalsNearYouViewModel uses a service to fetch animals to display them in a list. This class depends on Service.

But, what would happen if requirements changed and you had to use the user's location to fetch animals? You would have to rewrite Service to add this functionality or create a new Service for this feature. Even so, AnimalsNearYouViewModel is still dependent on a concrete type.

Instead of doing that, you can use Protocols to create an abstraction for AnimalsNearYouViewModel that can accept any type, as long as it conforms to that protocol:

```
protocol AnimalFetcher {
  func fetchAnimals()
}

class AnimalsNearYouViewModel {
  let service: AnimalFetcher

  init(service: AnimalFetcher) {
    self.service = service
  }

  func fetchAnimals() {
    service.fetchAnimals()
  }
}
```

AnimalsNearYouViewModel now depends on AnimalFetcher. It takes any type that conforms to this protocol instead of a concrete type.

You also create an initializer that expects a type that conforms to AnimalFetcher. This way, you can pass any type that conforms to the protocol instead of instantiating a concrete type as a property.

Following these practices is known as **Protocol Oriented Programming (POP)**.

This abstraction lets you use this class in different contexts with different purposes. You can make it even easier to test AnimalsNearYouViewModel by creating a mock type, also known as a spy, that conforms to AnimalFetcher.

# Using design patterns and software principles

Following **Protocol Oriented Programming**, **SOLID** principles and design patterns is a great way to keep high cohesion and low coupling.

Even though you should strive to follow best practices, it's important to understand when to use them. Otherwise, you might over-engineer your code. Understanding why these practices exist and how they can help with different problems will help you know when to use them and when not to.

Created by Robert C. Martin, also known as Uncle Bob, **SOLID** is an acronym for these five principles:

1. **Single Responsibility Principle**: A module, class or function should be responsible for a single purpose, focusing on a single task. This single focus helps create code that doesn't grow out of proportion by solving the entire problem.

2. **Open/Closed Principle**: Define modules, classes and functions open for extension but closed for modification. In other words, you extend its behavior without modifying its implementation.

3. **Liskov Substitution Principle**: Replace classes with their subclasses without breaking the code. You can also apply this idea in Swift by using protocols where you can use another type as long as it conforms to the same protocol.

4. **Interface Segregation Principle**: A module shouldn't depend on requirements that it doesn't use. Instead of creating a protocol that defines the whole behavior of a type, creating a different protocol that covers other use cases helps modules use only what they need.

5. **Dependency Inversion Principle**: A module shouldn't depend on external dependencies, but the module should define its requirements. It states that your modules should depend on abstractions, not other modules. For example, by following this principle, you'll be able to test your networking module in isolation without having to depend on concrete implementation of other parts of the app.

These principles are the foundation of many design patterns and software architectures. Having a good understanding of them helps you better understand why some architectures are the way they are.

**Note**: If you want to learn more about **SOLID principles**, check out SOLID Principles for iOS Apps (https://www.raywenderlich.com/21503974-solid-principles-for-ios-apps). To read more about **Protocol Oriented Programming**, check out Chapter 25, Protocol-Oriented Programming (https://www.raywenderlich.com/books/swift-apprentice/v7.0/chapters/27-protocol-oriented-programming) of our book **Swift Apprentice**.

Understanding these principles will help you handle any software challenge you may face. But, they're not enough to create a great app. While they'll help engineer code, you still have to understand *what* you're building.

That's where the **domain** comes in.

# The app's domain

Before coding any features, you first have to understand what kind of app PetSave is: its purpose, features and users. Essentially, the **domain** defines what kind of app you're building.

The domain is a set of business logic and rules your app follows.

Usually, you would gather requirements for PetSave at the beginning of the software development cycle. Project stakeholders define these requirements that you then translate into features.

Understanding the app's domain is key to building a successful app. When you understand the user's problems, it's easier to build features that solve them. When users feel understood, and your app is valuable, they're more likely to use it again.

## Understanding the domain layer

Business logic is an integral part of app development. It defines and drives features and the way your app behaves.

As your app becomes larger, decoupling your business logic into a separate layer can help keep your project tidy. The domain layer removes business logic code from views, leaving only layout building and presentation logic.

Since the domain defines models that most features share, you'll find most of them in the **Core** group.

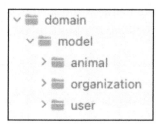

*Project Navigator with the domain layer groups*

This is the first part of PetSave you'll work on. Later, you'll create your first model and prepare its mock data. But before that, you'll lay out a plan on how to tackle PetSave required features.

# Planning the app

It's time to take a closer look at each feature. Don't worry: You don't have to think of every single detail now. But it's essential to plan things like how you're going to build each feature, the UI's design and which feature you're going to build first.

You'll start by understanding what each feature tries to do. Then, you'll lay out a simple UI and plan how data flows in that feature.

You'll also use **SwiftUI**, Apple's latest UI framework. It'll help you build and iterate fast over user interface development.

## Devising a plan of attack

There's no single way to plan features. Planning a feature is all about understanding what problem you're trying to fix. If the feature doesn't help your user, it really might not be a feature.

You learned the importance of writing software that's easy to change and scale. Now, you're going to learn that planning a feature is just as important.

# Identifying app features

To start, you need to identify the features you'll build. PetSave has a closed scope, so you'll work with features with defined requirements that won't change as you develop the app.

Those features are:

1. **Animals Near You**: The app displays a collection of pets for adoption near the user's location.

2. **Search**: Aside from browsing pets, users can also search pets by name and filter the results by age and type.

3. **Onboarding**: A simple introduction to the app's features. This is an essential feature because it's the first thing users see when they open the app for the first time.

After you understand those features, you'll layout a UI and the workflow of each feature.

Before you start planning those features, there's one last thing to consider: how your app's data flow will work.

# Understanding view models

To follow best practices and keep views clear from presentation logic, you'll use **View Models** to store view state and handle events from the user.

You learned that having a domain layer helps you keep domain-specific business logic decoupled from your views. View Models will help you bridge the view with your domain layer.

A **View Model** is a model that represents a view. It contains properties and methods to respond to all the data your view needs and handles presentation logic and data transformation. View Model is an excellent pattern for extracting events and states from views, letting them focus on UI building.

**Model-View-ViewModel (MVVM)** architecture relies heavily on using view models for presentation logic. It acts as an intermediate between the view and the data, fetching and transforming data to present in views.

PetSave follows most MVVM principles. By combining MVVM with SwiftUI's state management, you get an architecture where views have a model to drive their state.

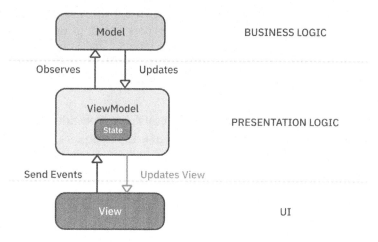

*Diagram showing data flow between view, view model and model.*

This architecture extracts dependencies from the view into a single source of truth, making your views clear of presentation logic so they can focus on UI building. It also makes testing state and data easier since view models are just regular objects.

Now, with the knowledge you've gained about view models and devising a plan of attack, you'll break down the first feature, **Animals Near You**.

# Animals Near You

This feature lets users scroll through a collection of nearby animals that are up for adoption. The Petfinder API takes the user's latitude and longitude to fetch pets near them.

You'll add the user's real location later, in Chapter 12, "App Privacy". For now, think about how to display a collection of pets that users can scroll through and tap over to see more information.

## Animals Near You: Designing the UI

Right now, AnimalsNearYouView is empty with a TODO text. You'll build each part of this feature later, in Chapter 5, "Building Features – Locating Animals Near You". But it's important to start thinking about *how* this feature will work.

SwiftUI is great for creating simple and efficient UI. It helps you build simple features faster so you can focus on your app's cool and exciting features.

Displaying a collection of animals with SwiftUI is straightforward, so listing animals in a row seems like a great way to show the users pets for adoption.

Each row will show an animal with a picture, name, breed, type, gender and age to get users interested in that pet. This gives enough information upfront to hook the user into opening the details of that animal.

Now, this data has to come from somewhere, in this case, Petfinder's API. That means users may have to wait a while for the request to complete. Users might get confused if they open the app and see a blank screen, so a loading indicator that says the app is fetching animals is essential to tell users the app is loading data.

Those are the basic ideas of how the UI should behave. In later chapters, you'll learn about the SwiftUI views you'll use to create this UI.

## Animals Near You: Using view models

Now that you have an idea of the UI, you also have to think about how you'll orchestrate fetching data and updating your views.

Here, you'll use a view model to store the view state when the view is loading or if there are more animals to fetch. It'll also respond to the user's actions like refreshing and fetching animals when the view first appears.

> **Note:** To learn more about using MVVM with SwiftUI, take a look at MVVM with Combine Tutorial for iOS (https://www.raywenderlich.com/4161005-mvvm-with-combine-tutorial-for-ios).

## Searching animals

Aside from listing animals near you, you'll also get to build a search feature. Even though scrolling through animals might seem like a good idea while browsing for your next pet, some people might want to search for particular types of animals. They might want to find pets of a certain age, type or even name.

Giving multiple ways to find and search animals will help users on their quest to find their next best friend.

## Searching animals: Designing the UI

In the starter project, SearchView is also empty with a TODO text.

A field where users can type a name and ask the app to search Petfinder's API for animals with that name should be enough to help users search for animals. They'll then see the results in a list, much like **Animals Near You**. This is the perfect opportunity to use SwiftUI's greatest strength, reusing views. Later, in Chapter 6, "Building Features - Search", you'll learn to refactor code from AnimalsNearYouView to reuse it inside SearchView.

Also, you'll build a small form where users can select the animal's age and type. They can select from a close range of types so they can find a specific type of animal, like **Cats**, **Dogs** or even **Horses**. Also, users can try to find pets of a certain age like **baby**, **young**, **adult** or **senior**. You'll have to add another field for users to select this.

While this already helps users find pets, this view might feel a bit empty when the user isn't searching for anything. They might also not understand that they can search animals by type and age. So you'll also build a view for suggesting types of animals the user may want to find.

Finally, if Petfinder's API can't find any animal with the requested name, type and age, you have to display a message to the user informing them.

## Searching animals: Using view models

You'll also use a view model to store the name users type and the type and age they select. Then you'll take this information and search Petfinder's API with it. The view model will also help you store the view state and handle all user interactions.

# Onboarding

As for the onboarding flow of the app, you'll build this feature in Chapter 7, "Multi-Module App". In that chapter, you'll learn about the benefits of modularizing by building a framework to manage the onboarding process of PetSave. You'll also get to learn about the different dependency managers you can use while building an iOS app, like Swift Package Manager, and how to publish your framework in a remote repository to be later reused in different projects.

# Understanding an offline-first approach

Besides all the functionality of both features, you'll also implement an **offline-first** approach to fetching, storing and displaying data.

Instead of fetching data each time the user opens the app and waits for the request to finish, you'll display data cached with **CoreData**. This cached data creates a pleasant user experience where users can see animals even while the app is still loading new data.

You'll work on this in Chapter 4, "Defining the Data Layer - Databases".

For now, you'll set up a foundation for building these features.

# Modeling domain models

Now that you understand what you're building, you'll start by modeling **Animal**, a key model in PetSave.

To start, take a look at the JSON that represents a single animal in the Petfinder API:

```
{
  "id": 52432090,
  "organization_id": "PA174",
  "type": "Cat",
  "species": "Cat",
  "age": "Adult",
  "gender": "Female",
  "size": "Medium",
  "coat": "Short",
  "name": "Kiki",
  // Other properties...
}
```

The PetFinder API provides several properties you may use in your app. You map those models from the API model to one of your domain's models. You'll find these models inside **Core ▸ domain ▸ model**.

Most of the time, apps have backend web services to handle data. Matching the backend models is usually enough for you to transform them from JSON to your domain.

Now, you'll create a model that defines an animal in the project.

# Creating the animal model

Inside **Core**, open the **domain** folder. Then expand **model**. Create a new Swift file inside the **animal** folder and name it **Animal**. Add the following code to the file:

```swift
struct Animal: Codable {
  var id: Int?
  let organizationId: String?
  let url: URL?
  let type: String
  let species: String?
  var breeds: Breed
  var colors: APIColors
  let age: Age
  let gender: Gender
  let size: Size
  let coat: Coat?
  let name: String
  let description: String?
  let photos: [PhotoSizes]
  let videos: [VideoLink]
  let status: AdoptionStatus
  var attributes: AnimalAttributes
  var environment: AnimalEnvironment?
  let tags: [String]
  var contact: Contact
  let publishedAt: String?
  let distance: Double?
  var ranking: Int? = 0
}
```

This model defines a type that represents an animal in your app's domain. It has a couple of primitive properties for storing its traits, like name and species. The model also has a couple of custom types like Breed, which defines the animal's breed, and PhotoSizes, to store URLs of each size of the animal picture.

You also use enums, like Coat, to store data. It can be one of the seven values:

```swift
enum Coat: String, Codable {
  case short = "Short"
  case medium = "Medium"
  case long = "Long"
  case wire = "Wire"
  case hairless = "Hairless"
  case curly = "Curly"
  case unknown = "Unknown"
}
```

Enums are great for enforcing type-safety when mapping values from JSON. Instead of mapping strings of the animal coat, you create an enum with pre-defined values.

You might have noticed that all models conform to the Codable protocol, even the enums. The Codable protocol is a typealias of Decodable and Encodable. Decodable lets you decode objects from other types of data representation, like JSON, to your models. Encodable lets you encode the models back into data.

You'll use this to map the Petfinder API's response to the domain models.

## Value types vs reference types

Notice that most of the models are structs, and they are simple representations of data from Petfinder's API. That's because structs are **value types**.

Structs are very lightweight, so you can use structs to pass values around for a low memory cost. Each instance of a value type is a unique copy of that data, and Swift creates a copy of the value whenever you manipulate it.

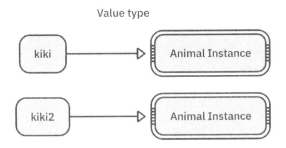

*Object Kiki pointing to a value of Animal. Another object, Kiki2, pointing to another value of Animal.*

On the other hand, classes are **reference types**. Class instances maintain a reference to their data in memory, propagating changes to this data to other references.

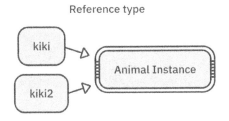

*Both objects, Kiki and Kiki2, pointing to the same Animal instance.*

Since models are simple representations of data, you'll use structs to create them. **Value types** are great for this.

> **Note**: Reference and Value types are a relatively advanced Swift topic. To learn more about it, check out Chapter 24, Value Types & Reference Types (https://www.raywenderlich.com/books/swift-apprentice/v7.0/chapters/25-value-types-reference-types) of our book **Swift Apprentice**.

# Preparing mock data for the animal model

Before you move on to the data layer and start fetching data, there's one last piece of work to do. You need to set up mock data for the animal model.

During development, you might want to run your app without depending on external data, test business logic or even iterate view design. Mocking data is a way to mitigate this dependency. It's also great for creating unit tests for specific use cases.

You'll use this data in your unit tests in later chapters like Chapter 4, "Defining the Data Layer - Databases". When building UI, you'll also use this data with **CoreData** to drive **Xcode Previews**.

For now, you'll create an extension of `Animal` to load animals from a JSON file.

Inside the **animal** group, create a new file and name it **AnimalsMock.swift**. Add this code to the new file:

```swift
// 1
private struct AnimalsMock: Codable {
  let animals: [Animal]
}

// 2
private func loadAnimals() -> [Animal] {
  guard let url = Bundle.main.url(
    forResource: "AnimalsMock",
    withExtension: "json"
  ), let data = try? Data(contentsOf: url) else { return [] }
  let decoder = JSONDecoder()
  // 3
  decoder.keyDecodingStrategy = .convertFromSnakeCase
  let jsonMock = try? decoder.decode(AnimalsMock.self, from:
data)
  return jsonMock?.animals ?? []
}
```

```
// 4
extension Animal {
  static let mock = loadAnimals()
}
```

This code:

1. Creates `AnimalsMock` that represents a response from the Petfinder API and makes it conform to `Codable`.

2. Creates a function that loads **AnimalsMock.json** and tries to decode it to an object of `AnimalsMock`. Then it returns the array of animals inside that object.

3. Automatically converts keys stored in the API as snake_case into camelCase. This way the properties in the struct will match the name of the ones in the JSON.

4. And finally, creates an extension of `Animal` to expose this mocked data to the rest of the project.

Take a look inside of **Preview Content**. In there, you'll find a JSON file, **AnimalsMock.json**, with a mocked response from the PetFinder's API. This group is a special group inside the Xcode project that allows you to add mocked code and data to be used inside Xcode Previews. When you later compile the app, Xcode doesn't include the content of this group in the build. That way, you can store development assets inside the project, like images and other data, and you don't have to worry about them cluttering your app.

With that, you finished working on the first model of the app's domain. PetSave is taking shape.

# Key points

- It's important to plan when designing and architecting your apps.

- **Feature Grouping** helps you create **highly cohesive** and **loosely coupled** code while still making it easy to identify the scope of each feature.

- Understanding the app's **domain** helps you identify new features and think like the users. Without the domain, you don't know what you're building.

- It's essential to understand where the **domain layer** falls in the architecture, its responsibilities and its role.

- Following design patterns and software principles is great, but it's essential to understand these principles and where and when to use them.

- You can create models of your domain and use the `Codable` protocol to map external objects.

# Where to go from here?

If you're interested in learning more about iOS architectures and MVVM, check out raywenderlich.com's book Advanced iOS App Architecture ([https://www.raywenderlich.com/books/advanced-ios-app-architecture](https://www.raywenderlich.com/books/advanced-ios-app-architecture)).

Also, check out Design Patterns by Tutorials ([https://www.raywenderlich.com/books/design-patterns-by-tutorials](https://www.raywenderlich.com/books/design-patterns-by-tutorials)) to learn more about design patterns.

Next, you'll learn about the **data layer** and how to fetch data from the Petfinder API. Buckle up, because you're just getting started. :]

# Chapter 3: Data Layer - Networking

By Aaqib Hussain

In the previous chapter, you learned the app's basic structure and identified the features you'll implement. You also familiarized yourself with high cohesion, loosely coupled code and the JSON structure that the Petfinder API provides.

In this chapter, you'll build on what you learned in the previous chapter. You'll create a networking layer and implement it following the principles of high cohesion so that you can reuse it for future projects.

Along the way, you'll learn what a **data layer** is and how to:

- Implement the networking side of a data layer and use it to fetch data.

- Write asynchronous code with the `async/await` API.

- Display fetched data using SwiftUI.

- Implement a token refresh mechanism.

# Getting started

Open **starter** project and build and run. You'll see:

*Starter app with empty data.*

By the end of this chapter, you'll create a network layer and render Petfinder API data. Your goal is to reach here:

*Final app with animal list.*

Before you jump into writing code, take a moment to learn about data layers and their responsibilities.

# Demystifying the data layer

A **data layer** is responsible for interactions with the data sources. A **data source** can be any particular database, file or data set hosted physically or digitally somewhere. Two examples of data sources are Petfinder's API and Core Data.

A data layer acts as a layer of abstraction between the consumer of the data and the data sources, so the consumer doesn't have to worry about the complexities of manipulating the data.

With a data layer, it's easier to change the data sources without affecting or breaking anything else. For example, say you previously used Core Data in the app and now want to replace it with Realm. You can do that without breaking a sweat!

The data layer also provides data to the domain layer for further processing.

In this chapter, you'll implement the networking side of the data layer. You'll implement the persistence part of the data layer in Chapter 4, "Defining the Data Layer - Databases".

Now, it's time to start setting up the network layer.

## Creating the request

First, you need to set up the central part of the network layer: the request for the network call.

Navigate to **Core/data/api** and create a group called **request**. Then create a file and name it **RequestProtocol.swift**.

Add this code:

```
protocol RequestProtocol {
  // 1
  var path: String { get }

  // 2
  var headers: [String: String] { get }
  var params: [String: Any] { get }

  // 3
```

```
    var urlParams: [String: String?] { get }

    // 4
    var addAuthorizationToken: Bool { get }

    // 5
    var requestType: RequestType { get }
}
```

You'll use this protocol as a template for all your requests. Here's what each property does:

1.  This property is the endpoint usually attached at the end of the base url.

2.  These are the headers and params you want to send with the request. The content of params will act as the request's body.

3.  You'll use this dictionary to attach query params in the URL.

4.  This boolean represents if your request needs to add the authorization token.

5.  By adding this, you make all the requests specify their type using RequestType.

## Adding request types

Inside the **request** group, create a file named **RequestType.swift**. Then add:

```
enum RequestType: String {
  case GET
  case POST
}
```

There are five REST API request types: POST, GET, PUT, PATCH and DELETE. You only need POST and GET for this app.

## Giving a default implementation to RequestProtocol

You don't need all the properties for every request. You'll define a default implementation of the RequestProtocol to simplify things.

In **RequestProtocol.swift**, create the following extension:

```
extension RequestProtocol {
  // 1
```

```
    var host: String {
      APIConstants.host
    }
    // 2
    var addAuthorizationToken: Bool {
      true
    }
    // 3
    var params: [String: Any] {
      [:]
    }

    var urlParams: [String: String?] {
      [:]
    }

    var headers: [String: String] {
      [:]
    }
  }
```

Here's what's going on:

1.  This is the app's base URL. Since there is only one, there's no need to add the protocol definitions.

2.  By default, every request has an authorization token.

3.  Some requests don't require `params`, `urlParams` and `headers`, so they have a default value of an empty dictionary.

Still in the same extension, add this method:

```
// 1
func createURLRequest(authToken: String) throws -> URLRequest {
  // 2
  var components = URLComponents()
  components.scheme = "https"
  components.host = host
  components.path = path
  // 3
  if !urlParams.isEmpty {
    components.queryItems = urlParams.map {
      URLQueryItem(name: $0, value: $1)
    }
  }

  guard let url = components.url
  else { throw NetworkError.invalidURL }

  // 4
```

```
  var urlRequest = URLRequest(url: url)
  urlRequest.httpMethod = requestType.rawValue
  // 5
  if !headers.isEmpty {
    urlRequest.allHTTPHeaderFields = headers
  }
  // 6
  if addAuthorizationToken {
    urlRequest.setValue(authToken,
      forHTTPHeaderField: "Authorization")
  }
  // 7
  urlRequest.setValue("application/json",
    forHTTPHeaderField: "Content-Type")
  // 8
  if !params.isEmpty {
    urlRequest.httpBody = try JSONSerialization.data(
      withJSONObject: params)
  }

  return urlRequest
}
```

In this method, you:

1. Use RequestProtocol.createURLRequest(authToken:) to create the request with an authorization token which throws an error in case of failures like an invalid URL.

2. You set up the base components of the URL by setting scheme, host and path.

3. Then you add urlParams to url components if it's not empty.

4. Create an URLRequest using url.

5. If you need to add any headers to the request, add them to the allHTTPHeaderFields.

6. Add an authorization token to the request if addAuthorizationToken is true.

7. The Petfinder API expects data to be of type JSON. So, set the request's content type to application/json.

8. Finally, you add non-empty parameters to the request as data in the httpBody. Since Petfinder API works with JSON, you serialize the params using NSJSONSerialization.data(withJSONObject:options:).

> **Note**: When you conform to a protocol, you can also overwrite its default implementations if you need to do something other than the default behaviors.

You completed the request part. Before you create the network call, there's a concept you need to learn: **async/await**.

# async/await

Apple introduced **async/await** with iOS 15 in Swift, but with the release of Xcode 13.2, it's also backward compatible starting with iOS 13. Swift now lets you write asynchronous code without using a completion handler. Say *bye* to completion handlers and *Hello* to async/await.

Writing asynchronous code can be cumbersome and a bit difficult to manage. It can also cause some unwanted errors. With async/await, you can write structured code and keep errors to a minimum.

Unlike a typical method, an `async` method suspends execution when waiting for a response. Other than waiting for a response, it works like a typical method. You can call methods with `await` when you want your method to suspend and wait for the response.

With async/await, you can achieve structured concurrency, which means you're aware of the order of execution of your statements. Unlike the completion handler, every statement depends on the statement above it, making it a linear code execution.

So how does this work? How can you write an `async` method? Take a look at the following code syntax:

```
func name(parameters) async throws -> type {
    return type
}
```

> **Note**: `throws` isn't part of the method syntax. You use this keyword when you need to throw an error from the method. You'll learn about it later in the chapter.

Following the above syntax, here's an example of writing a method for performing a network request:

```
func perform(_ request: URLRequest) async throws -> Data {
  let (data, response) =
    try await URLSession.shared.data(for: request)
  return data
}
```

Here's a code breakdown:

In the method signature, you indicate `async`. Inside, you call `URLSession.data(for:delegate:)` and use `try await` to tell the system this is an asynchronous operation, and it should suspend it. You use `try` because it can throw an error. Once the request finishes, it returns `Data` and `URLResponse` objects. It stores both in `data` and `response` correspondingly. Finally, it returns `data`.

In case of failure, `perform(_:)` throws an error.

Here you can see an example of how you'll use the above method to get data from a request:

```
guard let url = URL(string: "<--some-url-->") else {
  return
}

// 1
let urlRequest = URLRequest(url: url)
// 2
Task {
  do {
    // 3
    let data = try await perform(urlRequest)
    // do operations on data
  } catch { // 4
    print(error.localizedDescription)
  }
}
```

Here you:

1.  Create the `URLRequest` with the URL.

2.  A `Task` creates an asynchronous environment for `async` methods to execute in. You use `Task` to provide an asynchronous container for `perform(_:)`. This isn't necessary inside an `async` method.

3. Using `urlRequest`, you initialize the request. Every method marked with an `async` must use `await` while calling it. The method either returns the data or throws an error.

4. If there's an error, its description prints in the console.

That's the advantage you get with async/await.

If you were to write something similar with a completion handler, you would get something like this:

```
func perform(_ request: URLRequest,
  completionHandler: @escaping (Result<Data, Error>) -> ()) {
  // 1
  URLSession.shared.dataTask(with: request) {
    data, response, error in
    // 2
    if let err = error {
      completionHandler(.failure(err))
      return
    }
    // 3
    guard let data = data,
          let response = response as? HTTPURLResponse,
          response.statusCode == 200 else {
            return
          }
    // 4
    completionHandler(.success(data))
  }.resume()
}
```

Here's a code breakdown:

1. You use the `URLSession` to fetch the data.

2. If there's an error, you call the failure completion handler.

3. The `guard` statement checks if data is there and the status is 200 from the response.

4. The completion handler takes this object and returns it to the caller.

Here's a representation of how you'd call the request method if it were with a completion handler:

```
guard let url = URL(string: "<--some-url-->") else {
  return
}
let urlRequest = URLRequest(url: url)
```

```
perform(_ request: urlRequest) { response in
  switch response {
    case .success(let data):
      // do some operations on data
    case .failure(let error):
      print(error.localizedDescription)
  }
}
```

Observe the differences in these pieces of code. The `async/await` is much cleaner and easier to understand. It also requires the least amount of error handling.

That's not the case with the completion handler. As you can see, you have to handle all errors manually in `perform(_:)` with the completion handler.

Several interdependent tasks using completion handlers will quickly turn your code into a pyramid of doom. In contrast, async/await keeps your code structured and makes it easier to read and understand.

Now that you understand how to use async/await, you'll use it to create the networking.

## Creating the networking brain

When it comes to networking, having a single point for making a network request or having a layer of abstraction can save you time and make your code easier to maintain. To make requests, you'll use `URLSession`.

`URLSession` provides an API to download or upload data to the network on a defined endpoint. You can read more in its official documentation (https://developer.apple.com/documentation/foundation/urlsession).

Instead of writing a method and using `URLSession.shared` to make network calls directly inside it, you'll write a layer on top of `URLSession` to make network calls to achieve less coupling and high cohesion. It'll also be easy to change it if such requirements arise.

Time to create your first layer! Under **Core/data/api/network**, create a file named **APIManager.swift**. Then, create this protocol:

```
protocol APIManagerProtocol {
  func perform(_ request: RequestProtocol, authToken: String)
async throws -> Data
}
```

This protocol has one requirement, the implementation of `perform(_:authToken:)`. This method expects an object that conforms to `RequestProtocol`, an authentication token and returns `Data`. If the request fails, it throws an error.

Except for the authentication request, all the network calls for Petfinder API require a token. So you ask for `authToken`, too.

Still in the same file, add the following class:

```
// 1
class APIManager: APIManagerProtocol {
  // 2
  private let urlSession: URLSession

  // 3
  init(urlSession: URLSession = URLSession.shared) {
    self.urlSession = urlSession
  }
}
```

This class:

1. Indicates `APIManager` must conform to `APIManagerProtocol`.

2. Creates a private variable to store the `URLSession`.

3. Passes in the initializer the default shared `URLSession`. `shared` provides a singleton that returns a `URLSession`.

For most use cases, like this app, using `URLSession.shared` is enough. But keep in mind that you shouldn't do things like customizing the cache, cookie storage or credential storage when using `shared`. For that, create a `URLSessionConfiguration` object.

> **Note**: Read more about `URLSessionConfiguration` in the official documentation (https://developer.apple.com/documentation/foundation/urlsessionconfiguration).

Still inside `APIManager`, add the method below:

```
func perform(_ request: RequestProtocol,
  authToken: String = "") async throws -> Data {
  // 1
  let (data, response) = try await urlSession.data(for:
request.createURLRequest(authToken: authToken))
  // 2
  guard let httpResponse = response as? HTTPURLResponse,
    httpResponse.statusCode == 200
  else {
    // 3
    throw NetworkError.invalidServerResponse
  }
  return data
}
```

Here's a code breakdown:

1.  `URLSession.data(for:)` uses async/await to process a request and return data and an `URLResponse`. Here you used `try` because it can also throw an error.

2.  You check if the response code is `200`. If this condition passes, `data` is returned.

3.  If their response isn't successful, you return `invalidServerResponse`. `NetworkError` is a custom error enumeration and part of the starter project. A custom error enumeration makes it easier to customize the thrown error with meaningful messages.

## Layering on top of the brain

While most people love spaghetti, they usually don't want their code to look like it. To keep classes and network layers loosely coupled, you'll implement another class on top of `APIManager` to implement data parsing and token handling.

Under **network**, create a new file named **RequestManager.swift** and add:

```
protocol RequestManagerProtocol {
  func perform<T: Decodable>(_ request: RequestProtocol) async
  throws -> T
}
```

This method is similar to what you wrote in `APIManagerProtocol`, but with a slight difference. This method uses a generic of a type conforming to `Decodable`. It also takes in a request and returns either an error or an object of type `Decodable`.

perform(_:) expects to return the value in a type of object conforming to Decodable, and that type should be explicitly mentioned next to the variable declaration.

Confused? Well, don't worry. Everything will start to make sense soon enough.

Now, create a class named RequestManager. Conform to RequestManagerProtocol and implement the method perform like this:

```
class RequestManager: RequestManagerProtocol {
  let apiManager: APIManagerProtocol
  let parser: DataParserProtocol
  // 1
  init(
  apiManager: APIManagerProtocol = APIManager(),
  parser: DataParserProtocol = DataParser() // 2
  ) {
    self.apiManager = apiManager
    self.parser = parser
  }

  func perform<T: Decodable>(
    _ request: RequestProtocol) async throws -> T {
      // 3
      let data = try await apiManager.perform(data, authToken:
  """)
    }
  }
}
```

You probably see an error here: Missing return in instance method expected to return 'T'. Don't worry about that. You'll fix it later on.

For now, focus on the code breakdown:

1.  You set up the initializer and set apiManager with a default value.

2.  Navigate to **Core/data/api/parser**, and you'll see DataParser. It conforms to a protocol DataParserProtocol that implements a method that takes in Data and returns a generic Decodable. Then it uses JSONDecoder to decode Data into a Decodable. Here you simply give the object a default value.

3.  Implement perform(_:). Inside it, you call perform from APIManager to make a network call.

# Fetching the authentication token

Now that you've completed the fetching and parsing parts, you can use it to fetch the authentication token to work with the APIs. The Petfinder API provides an endpoint /v2/oauth2/token for fetching the authentication token. You also need to send credentials along with it as a POST request:

```
{
  "grant_type": "client_credentials",
  "client_id": "CLIENT-ID",
  "client_secret": "CLIENT-SECRET"
}
```

You can read more about it at petfinder's documentation (https://www.petfinder.com/developers/v2/docs/).

## Authentication token request

To fetch a token, first, you'll create a request.

Under **Core/data/api/request**, create a group called **auth**. Inside the new group, create a file named **AuthTokenRequest.swift**.

> **Note**: You can use a `struct`, `class` or enum to create a request. For this app, you'll use enums.

When creating requests, you'll conform to `RequestProtocol`. In **AuthTokenRequest.swift**, add:

```swift
// 1
enum AuthTokenRequest: RequestProtocol {
  case auth
  // 2
  var path: String {
    "/v2/oauth2/token"
  }
  // 3
  var params: [String: Any] {
    [
      "grant_type": APIConstants.grantType,
      "client_id": APIConstants.clientId,
      "client_secret": APIConstants.clientSecret
    ]
  }
}
```

```
    // 4
    var addAuthorizationToken: Bool {
      false
    }
    // 5
    var requestType: RequestType {
      .POST
    }
  }
```

Here, you:

1.  Declare an enum called `AuthTokenRequest` that conforms to `RequestProtocol` and has one case `auth`.

2.  Add `path`, which returns the endpoint to fetch the token.

3.  Implement `params` and assign a key-value with the credentials to make the request. Make sure to update `clientId` and `clientSecret` in **APIConstants.swift** with your keys.

4.  Since it's the authentication token fetch request itself, `addAuthorizationToken` is `false`.

5.  For this request, `requestType` needs to be `POST`.

The Petfinder API returns authentication token's JSON that looks like this:

```
{
  "token_type": "Bearer",
  "expires_in": 3600,
  "access_token": "..."
}
```

Navigate to **api/model** and open **APIToken.swift**. The `APIToken` struct maps to the JSON above.

Now that you've written the request for an authentication token, you can write the method for fetching.

Open **APIManager.swift** and update the protocol with this code:

```
protocol APIManagerProtocol {
  func perform(_ request: RequestProtocol, authToken: String)
async throws -> Data
  func requestToken() async throws -> Data
}
```

This newly introduced method returns you the authentication token data. Now implement it in `APIManager` class like this:

```
func requestToken() async throws -> Data {
  try await perform(AuthTokenRequest.auth)
}
```

Here, you use the same perform method you declared above and the `AuthTokenRequest` enum request you just created.

## Creating the authentication token call

Now that you've set up everything to fetch a token, you'll create the authentication token call. Open **RequestManager.swift** and add this method to `RequestManager`:

```
func requestAccessToken() async throws -> String {
  // 1
  let data = try await apiManager.requestToken()
  // 2
  let token: APIToken = try parser.parse(data: data)
  // 3
  return token.bearerAccessToken
}
```

Here, you:

1. Fetch the token based on the `AuthTokenRequest`. It returns either a `Data` object or throws an `Error`.

2. Parse the token and map it to `APIToken`.

3. Return the authentication token.

Now update your `perform(_:)` implementation in `RequestManager` with:

```
func perform<T: Decodable>(_ request: RequestProtocol)
  async throws -> T {
    // 1
    let authToken = try await requestAccessToken()
    // 2
    let data = try await apiManager.perform(request,
      authToken: authToken)

    // 3
    let decoded: T = try parser.parse(data: data)
    return decoded
}
```

Once you update this, the error in this method disappears. Now take a look at the code:

1. You get the authentication token and store it in `authToken`.

2. Then, you pass the authentication token to the `perform(_:)` of the `APIManager` object to add it to the `URLRequest`.

3. You decode and return the result of parsing `data` into the specific `T` type.

For now, it's OK to fetch the token each time. Later, you'll use the existing `AccessTokenManager` under **api/token** to persist the token locally.

# Animals fetching request

The Petfinder API lets you fetch animals depending on your location. You can also query by name, age or type of the animal. Check out the entire list of fields that you can query at Petfinder's official documentation ([https://www.petfinder.com/developers/v2/docs/#get-animals](https://www.petfinder.com/developers/v2/docs/#get-animals)).

Now you'll write the request to fetch the animals from the Petfinder API. First, create an **animals** group under **Core/data/api/request**.

Inside **animals**, create a file called **AnimalsRequest.swift** and add:

```
// 1
enum AnimalsRequest: RequestProtocol {
  case getAnimalsWith(
    page: Int, latitude: Double?, longitude: Double?)
  case getAnimalsBy(name: String, age: String?, type: String?)
  // 2
  var path: String {
    "/v2/animals"
  }
  // 3
  var urlParams: [String: String?] {
    switch self {
    case let .getAnimalsWith(page, latitude, longitude):
      var params = ["page": String(page)]
      if let latitude = latitude {
        params["latitude"] = String(latitude)
      }

      if let longitude = longitude {
        params["longitude"] = String(longitude)
      }
      params["sort"] = "random"
```

```
      return params

    case let .getAnimalsBy(name, age, type):
      var params: [String: String] = [:]
      if !name.isEmpty {
        params["name"] = name
      }

      if let age = age {
        params["age"] = age
      }

      if let type = type {
        params["type"] = type
      }
      return params
    }
  }
  // 4
  var requestType: RequestType {
    .GET
  }
}
```

This code:

1.  Creates an enum called `AnimalsRequest` that conforms to `RequestProtocol`. This enum has two cases: `getAnimalsWith(page:latitude:longitude:)` and `getAnimalsBy(name:age:type:)`.

2.  Makes `path` return the endpoint to fetch animals from the Petfinder API.

3.  `urlParams` creates the query parameters depending on the current case. For the first case, it adds page to the query parameters and the latitude and longitude if it exists. For the latter case, it adds `name` along with `age` and `type` if it's not `nil`. You also pass `random` to the `sort` param so that you can get random results with that location.

4.  `requestType` is `GET` since this is a request to *get* data from the API.

## Adjusting domain models

Before you test it, there's one thing more you need to do. The current domain models can't work as they are right now. The Petfinder API returns data like this:

```
{
  "animals": [
    // animals
```

```
    ],
    "pagination": {
        // pagination data
    }
}
```

The list of animals isn't directly part of the body; it's inside a key called `animals`. You need to create another model to work with the Petfinder API JSON.

Navigate to **Core/domain/model/animal** and create a file named **AnimalsContainer.swift**. Inside it, add

```
struct AnimalsContainer: Decodable {
    let animals: [Animal]
    let pagination: Pagination
}
```

You created a structure that works with the corresponding returned data. Now the animal list and the pagination data can be mapped appropriately.

## Fetching and presenting animals

Time for you to use the newly created request to display the animals list. Open **AnimalsNearYouView.swift** and add this line at the top, inside `AnimalsNearYouView`:

```
private let requestManager = RequestManager()
```

This code creates an instance of `RequestManager`.

Then, at the bottom add this:

```
func fetchAnimals() async {
    do {
        // 1
        let animalsContainer: AnimalsContainer =
            try await
requestManager.perform(AnimalsRequest.getAnimalsWith(
            page: 1,
            latitude: nil,
            longitude: nil))
        // 2
        self.animals = animalsContainer.animals
        // 3
        await stopLoading()
    } catch {}
}
```

This code:

1. Calls `perform(_:)` and stores the result in `animalsContainer`. Since this method uses generics, you need to indicate the type, in this case, `AnimalsContainer`. You pass 1 to the page as an argument and `nil` to `latitude` and `longitude` because you won't work with location or pagination in this chapter.

2. Stores the list of animals returned by the request in `animals`.

3. Calls `stopLoading()`.

Then, in the body of `AnimalsNearYouView`, replace the current `NavigationView` implementation with:

```
NavigationView {
  // 1
  List {
    ForEach(animals) { animal in
      AnimalRow(animal: animal)
    }
  }
  // 2
  .task {
    await fetchAnimals()
  }
  .listStyle(.plain)
  .navigationTitle("Animals near you")
  // 3
  .overlay {
    if isLoading {
      ProgressView("Finding Animals near you...")
    }
  }
}.navigationViewStyle(StackNavigationViewStyle())
```

Here's what this code does:

1. Sets up a `List` with a `ForEach` that creates an `AnimalRow` for each animal.

2. Uses `task(priority:_:)` to call `fetchAnimals()`. Since this is an asynchronous method, you need to use `await` so the system can handle it properly.

3. Adds an `overlay(alignment:content:)` that will show a `ProgressView` when `isLoading` is true.

There's another `View` that can be helpful when handling external requests: `AsyncImage`. Open **AnimalRow.swift**. You'll see the following code inside:

```
AsyncImage(
  url: animal.picture,
  content: { image in image
    .resizable()
  }, placeholder: {
    Image("rw-logo")
      .resizable()
      .overlay {
        if animal.picture != nil {
          ProgressView()
            .frame(maxWidth: .infinity,
              maxHeight: .infinity)
            .background(.gray.opacity(0.4))
        }
      }
  })
  .aspectRatio(contentMode: .fit)
  .frame(width: 112, height: 112)
  .cornerRadius(8)
```

What is `AsyncImage`? `AsyncImage` is a view that loads and displays images asynchronously. It makes it easier to download images without blocking the UI. In this case, it displays an image using `animal.picture`, which contains the URL for the Pet's photo.

> **Note**: To read more about `AsyncImage` visit Apple's official documentation (https://developer.apple.com/documentation/swiftui/asyncimage).

Finally, build and run. You'll see the list of animals, although your list might have different animal names:

*List of animals from network.*

Wooohoooo!!! Your app is already using the networking layer.

# Using AccessTokenManager to persist token

To avoid re-fetching the token before it expires, you need to tweak your RequestManager a bit. Open **RequestManager.swift** and update like this:

```
class RequestManager: RequestManagerProtocol {
  let apiManager: APIManagerProtocol
  let parser: DataParserProtocol
  let accessTokenManager: AccessTokenManagerProtocol

  init(
    apiManager: APIManagerProtocol = APIManager(),
    parser: DataParserProtocol = DataParser(),
    accessTokenManager: AccessTokenManagerProtocol =
AccessTokenManager()
  ) {
    self.apiManager = apiManager
    self.parser = parser
    self.accessTokenManager = accessTokenManager
```

```
    }
    // ...
```

Here, you add `accessTokenManager` and update the initializer.

Now, update `requestAccessToken` with:

```
func requestAccessToken() async throws -> String {
  // 1
  if accessTokenManager.isTokenValid() {
    return accessTokenManager.fetchToken()
  }
  // 2
  let data = try await apiManager.requestToken()
  let token: APIToken = try parser.parse(data: data)
  // 3
  try accessTokenManager.refreshWith(apiToken: token)
  return token.bearerAccessToken
}
```

Here's what you did:

1. If the saved token is valid, `isTokenValid` returns `true`.

2. If there is no saved token, it fetches the token again.

3. Then, it refreshes the authentication token stored in `UserDefaults`.

To test this, place a breakpoint at `return accessTokenManager.fetchToken`. Keep a close eye on Xcode's variables view.

Finally, build and run. The app needs to save the token once to return it on the next run. Then build and run again. The app will return the already saved token.

*Breakpoint at accessTokenManager.fetchToken*

That's awesome, right? You've finally done it, so it's time to move on to the next stage.

# Writing unit tests

Tests are an essential part of an app. When writing unit tests that involve network calls, you use mock data rather than making an actual network call. That's going to be the case here. For writing tests, you'll use the existing mock data you have in **Preview Content/AnimalsMock.json**.

Before you write any tests, you need to do some initial setup, some mocking, to be precise.

To keep the tests' files organized in a structure, start by creating a few groups. First create this group structure: **PetSaveTests/Tests/Core/data/api**.

Then create two more groups under **api**: **mock** and **helper**.

Your groups will look like this:

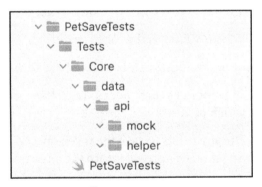

*Group structure*

Now, create **APIManagerMock.swift** under **mock**. Add this code:

```
// 1
@testable import PetSave

// 2
struct APIManagerMock: APIManagerProtocol {
  // 3
  func perform(_ request: RequestProtocol, authToken: String)
async throws -> Data {
    return try Data(contentsOf: URL(fileURLWithPath:
request.path), options: .mappedIfSafe)
```

```
    }
    // 4
    func requestToken() async throws -> Data {

    }
}
```

Here's what you did:

1.  Import PetSave using @testable attribute. @testable compiles the module with testing enabled. In this module, the public class or struct and its members now behave like they are open and the ones marked with an internal behave like they are public.

2.  Create APIManagerMock and make it conform to APIManagerProtocol.

3.  Since request is of type RequestProtocol, it has a property path. path will contain the location of the mock file. This function uses this information to get the file and convert its content to Data.

4.  You return a dummy token from here. Leave it empty for now.

Then, under **helper**, create a file named **AccessTokenTestHelper.swift**. Add this code:

```
@testable import PetSave

enum AccessTokenTestHelper {
  // 1
  static func randomString() -> String {
    let letters = "abcdefghijklmnopqrstuvwxyz"
    return String(letters.shuffled().prefix(8))
  }
  // 2
  static func randomAPIToken() -> APIToken {
    return APIToken(tokenType: "Bearer", expiresIn: 10,
      accessToken: AccessTokenTestHelper.randomString())
  }
  // 3
  static func generateValidToken() -> String {
    """
    {
      "token_type": "Bearer",
      "expires_in": 10,
      "access_token": \"\(randomString())\"
    }
    """

  }
}
```

Here's a code breakdown:

1. Returns a random string of length eight.

2. Returns a random `APIToken` using `randomString`.

3. Generates random token data similar to the one the apps received from the Petfinder API.

Now, go back to **APIManagerMock.swift** and update the `requestToken()` method like this:

```
func requestToken() async throws -> Data {
  Data(AccessTokenTestHelper.generateValidToken().utf8)
}
```

Here you return the dummy token you created in the form of string json as `Data`.

Create a file named **AnimalsRequestMock.swift** under **mock**. Add:

```
@testable import PetSave

enum AnimalsRequestMock: RequestProtocol {
  case getAnimals
  // 1
  var requestType: RequestType {
    return .GET
  }
  // 2
  var path: String {
    guard let path = Bundle.main.path(
      forResource: "AnimalsMock", ofType: "json")
    else { return "" }
    return path
  }
}
```

This code:

1. Sets the `requestType`. For this case, it could be anything since this is a mock.

2. Reads the path for `AnimalsMock.json` in `Bundle.main` if available. If not, it sets it to an empty string.

You've completed the setup. Now, you can start writing tests.

First, you'll write tests for `RequestManager` to check if the data is parsing correctly. To do this, navigate to **api** and create **RequestManagerTests.swift**. Then, add:

```
import XCTest
@testable import PetSave

class RequestManagerTests: XCTestCase {
  private var requestManager: RequestManagerProtocol?

  override func setUp() {
    super.setUp()
    // 1
    guard let userDefaults = UserDefaults(suiteName: #file) else
{
      return
    }

    userDefaults.removePersistentDomain(forName: #file)

    // 2
    requestManager = RequestManager(
      apiManager: APIManagerMock(),
      accessTokenManager: AccessTokenManager(userDefaults:
userDefaults)
    )
  }
}
```

This code:

1. Gets a reference to a `UserDefaults` instance and removes all its content. It returns early in case of any errors.

2. Initializes `requestManager` with mock objects.

This code will execute before each test, so you'll get a fresh instance of `RequestManager` every time.

Finally, add the following test:

```
func testRequestAnimals() async throws {
  // 1
  guard let container: AnimalsContainer =
    try await requestManager?.perform(
      AnimalsRequestMock.getAnimals) else {
      XCTFail("Didn't get data from the request manager")
      return
    }

  let animals = container.animals

  // 2
  let first = animals.first
  let last = animals.last
```

```
// 3
XCTAssertEqual(first?.name, "Kiki")
XCTAssertEqual(first?.age.rawValue, "Adult")
XCTAssertEqual(first?.gender.rawValue, "Female")
XCTAssertEqual(first?.size.rawValue, "Medium")
XCTAssertEqual(first?.coat?.rawValue, "Short")

XCTAssertEqual(last?.name, "Midnight")
XCTAssertEqual(last?.age.rawValue, "Adult")
XCTAssertEqual(last?.gender.rawValue, "Female")
XCTAssertEqual(last?.size.rawValue, "Large")
XCTAssertEqual(last?.coat, nil)
}
```

This test:

1. Fetches animals from the local JSON. guard checks that some data is returned and fails the test if any errors occur.

2. To keep it simple, tests the first and last animal object.

3. Tests if objects are the same as you expected.

Build and run the test. You'll see the test pass.

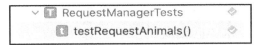

*Test Results - testRequestAnimals.*

# Challenge

It's time you take control and create tests yourself.

Create tests for `AccessTokenManager`. Cover the following scenarios:

1. Test that when you call `AccessTokenManager.fetchToken()` it returns a non-empty value. Call this test `testRequestToken()`.

2. Using a previously stored token, check that the code returns the same token if you call `AccessTokenManager.fetchToken()` again. Call this test `testCachedToken()`.

3. Test if you can refresh the token and get a new one using `AccessTokenManager.refreshWith(apiToken:)`. Call this test `testRefreshToken()`

So, how do you do that? Here are some hints that might help.

- Create a file called **AccessTokenManagerTests.swift**. Initialize the object with `UserDefaults` like you did in `RequestManagerTests`. In the test class's setup method, persist a dummy token and an expiry date to that `UserDefaults` object.

- For writing `testRefreshToken()`, you need to use a combination of methods that includes both `fetchToken()` and `refreshWith(apiToken:)` from the `AccessTokenManager` object.

- You'll need help from `AccessTokenTestHelper` when writing these tests.

Give it a try! Check the solution in the **challenge** folder if you get stuck.

# Key points

- A **data layer** provides a layer of abstraction. It may consist of data from different providers.

- Data layers process data and then hand it to the domain layer.

- **async/await** helps you write asynchronous code without using completion handlers. Async/await makes your code readable by using structured concurrency.

- `AsyncImage` is a view that lets you render images from the network using a URL without blocking the main thread.

- Protocols help with testing and make mocking of classes and structs easier. They also help with abstraction.

- Use mocks to make your tests fast and reliable.

# Where to go from here?

Good job! You implemented your very first Network layer. With this, you reach the end of this chapter. This chapter was loaded with new concepts. You worked on the data layer and networking. You learned about the importance of high cohesion and how it leads you to write testable code.

If you want to learn more about concurrency, including async/await and Task, check out our book Modern Concurrency in Swift (https://www.raywenderlich.com/books/modern-concurrency-in-swift).

You can also check out the official documentation on Concurrency (https://docs.swift.org/swift-book/LanguageGuide/Concurrency.html) and Task (https://developer.apple.com/documentation/swift/task) if you need more details.

In the next chapter, you'll learn about the other part of the data layer, databases. You'll persist the data you get from the remote server using **Core Data**.

# Chapter 4: Defining the Data Layer - Databases

By Josh Steele

In the last chapter, you learned how to fetch data from the Petfinder API and convert that data into objects in your model. To this point, the model objects, represented as structs in the code, exist in memory only. Unfortunately, when the user closes the app, any data the app has in memory gets released.

In this chapter, you'll learn about **data persistence** in iOS apps. In the broadest sense, persistence involves storing data on the user's device to prevent the app from having to download the data again in the future, at least in its entirety.

Some of the native persistence frameworks in iOS are User Defaults, Core Data and CloudKit, and of course, writing directly to the file system. You can also use third-party frameworks, such as those in Google Firebase.

Your focus for this chapter is **Core Data**, Apple's framework for working with databases. It's time to *persist* information and understand why persistence is a good standard practice in real-world iOS development.

> **Note**: There are other iOS libraries that support persistence via databases. This book stays with the native framework, Core Data, to take advantage of tight integration with other frameworks such as SwiftUI. You'll see this later in the chapter, and later in the book.

# The benefits of persistence

Persistence is a must-have feature in *most* modern-day mobile apps. Here are some reasons why you should consider persistence early on in your design process.

## Saving resources

One of the guiding principles in developing mobile apps is to be considerate of the device resources your app uses. For example, a call to the network touches on the following resources:

- **Power**: The device's antenna requires power to communicate with the network.

- **Data plan**: Communication with the network may also use the user's data plan if they are on a cellular network.

Repeated calls to the network can spend these resources at a higher rate than normal, especially if the app downloads the same data over and over again. If the app uses persistence, it can focus on only retrieving new data from the network, saving on valuable device resources.

## Your app is always available, immediately

Once data is on a device, your app no longer *needs* network access to get data. Even though it may be stale, the onboard data can populate your app's views until the networking layer can fetch new data. Without persistence, your views would remain unpopulated, which would make for a poor user experience.

## Your app can maintain user state

Persistence isn't only for data retrieved from the network. It can also store lightweight items such as user preferences inside **User Defaults**. The ability to store the user state of the app lets the user continue where they left off the last time they used the app.

## Your app can live on many devices

If your app syncs data to **iCloud** via **CloudKit**, the user can also continue their session on their other devices. Recent changes to the CloudKit framework make cloud sync as easy as changing a few lines of code.

Now with a better understanding of why persistence is valuable in your app, it's time to add it to the project!

> **Note:** The starter project for this chapter will *not* compile! You'll fix this as you add some code later on.

# Defining a database schema

Earlier in the book, you set up structs to represent the various domain objects from the Petfinder API. Now you need to map those domain objects into something that Core Data can understand. You do this with a database schema.

## Updating the database schema

In the starter project for this chapter, open **Core/data/coreData**. You'll find a mostly completed **PetSave.xcdatamodeld** that contains the schema for the project:

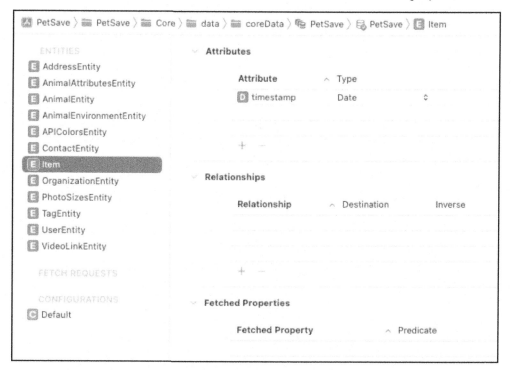

*PetSave database schema*

You're missing one entity in the schema - the pet's breed! Add `BreedEntity` and the following attributes:

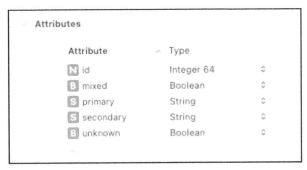

*Newly added breed entity*

The attributes are:

1. **id**: Although entities have a built-in unique id, the entities here have their own id to help better translate between struct and classes. You'll read more on using this later.

2. **mixed**: A Boolean which states if the pet is a mixed breed.

3. **primary** and **secondary**: Strings that describe the pet's primary and secondary breeds.

4. **unknown**: A Boolean that describes if the breed is unknown. This attribute is useful if that data isn't retrieved from the API.

Core Data synthesizes classes behind the scenes for each of the entities in the schema by default. You can add extra functionality to the classes via extensions, which you'll learn about later in this chapter.

## Special case: enums

Many of the types in the project are **enum**s, which don't map to any of the types available in the schema. But enums in Swift can have associated values which means built-in Swift types can represent the enums in the database schema.

One of `AnimalEntity`'s properties is a `String` that describes the pet's age called
`ageValue`. You must store it as a string since you can't store enums in the schema.
But to take advantage of Swift's type safety features, you *should* use the enum when
dealing with that value for the animal's age elsewhere in the code.

Open **Core/data/coreData/extensions/**. Then open **Animal+CoreData.swift**. Find
the extension to the **AnimalEntity**, and declare a computed property for the age:

```swift
extension AnimalEntity {
  var age: Age {
    //1
    get {
      guard let ageValue = ageValue,
            let age = Age(rawValue: ageValue) else {
        return Age.unknown
      }
      return age
    }
    //2
    set {
      self.ageValue = newValue.rawValue
    }
  }
  //......
}
```

In this computed property:

1.  get uses a pair of guard  let statements to do some checks. First, it makes sure
    that a current value for the age exists. Second, it ensures that it's convertible to
    an Age enum with the Age(rawValue:) initializer. If the guard fails, it returns
    Age.unknown. Otherwise, it returns the Age enum.

2.  set only deals with the string you store in the entity, so it sets ageValue to the
    newValue.rawValue property.

# Defining relationships

So far, the entities you've defined have been basic building blocks for the bigger `Animal` entity you need to build. The starter project includes many of the relationships that you'll need. Here's the current state of the `AnimalEntity` in the schema:

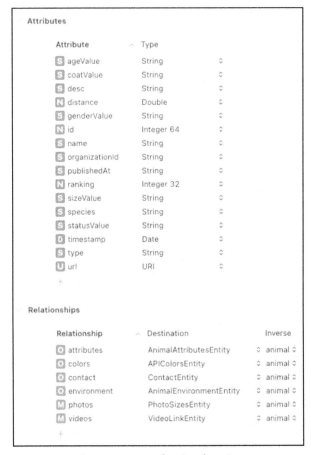

*Current state of animal entity*

`AnimalEntity` connects to other entities in the schema by way of relationships. As you can see at the bottom of the image above, the entity stores relationships below the attributes. Some of the relationships are One-to-One, denoted by the red **O**, and others are One-to-Many, denoted by the red **M**.

To finish setting up `AnimalEntity`, first select the newly created `BreedEntity` and add a One-to-Many `animal` relationship.

*One-to-Many relationship in BreedEntity*

**Note**: At first, the Inverse part of the relationship will be set to **No Inverse**. This will look like the screenshot after the step below, once you set the other part of the relationship.

Then, select `AnimalEntity` and add the `breeds` relationship, which is a One-to-One relationship:

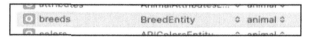

*One-to-One relationship in AnimalEntity*

**Note**: Even though you call the relationship `breeds`, it's only a One-to-One relationship. The pet may be a mix of many breeds, and the entity captures that in the breed's `primary` and `secondary` properties.

OK, that completes your schema. So, how do you use it?

# The Persistence class

Xcode projects set up to use Core Data include **Persistence.swift**. This file sets up the Core Data Stack and in-memory and on-disk stores, which act as scratch pads for your work until you persist them to the database. As part of this setup, it has access to the entities you declared in the schema earlier.

## In-Memory store

**Persistence.swift** sets up two distinct stores for your app. The first is for in-memory objects. Near the top of the file you'll find:

```
static var preview: PersistenceController = {
  let result = PersistenceController(inMemory: true)
  let viewContext = result.container.viewContext
  for _ in 0..<10 {
    let newItem = Item(context: viewContext)
    newItem.timestamp = Date()
  }
  //.......
```

The code currently uses the default `Item` entity that comes with the Core Data-based project template. Later, you'll change this to use `AnimalEntity`, which will provide a set of data to your view previews, so you don't have to rely on an on-disk database.

## On-Disk store

For the on-disk store, there's a much simpler declaration near the top of **Persistence.swift**:

```
struct PersistenceController {
  static let shared = PersistenceController()
  //...
```

This code provides access to a singleton of `PersistenceController`, which lets you access the database from anywhere in your project.

To aid you in saving the context, add a static method to **Persistence.swift**:

```
static func save() {
  // 1
  let context =
    PersistenceController.shared.container.viewContext
  // 2
  guard context.hasChanges else { return }

  // 3
  do {
    try context.save()
  } catch {
    fatalError("""
      \(#file), \
      \(#function), \
      \(error.localizedDescription)
```

```
         """)
    }
  }
}
```

This code does a few simple things:

1. You get a reference to the Core Data Context. In this case, using the on-disk store.

2. You don't need to save unless there are pending changes, so return if `hasChanges` is false.

3. The call to `context.save()` can throw, so wrap it in a do/catch. Any errors get their information sent to a `fatalError` call.

The latter half of **Persistence.swift** initializes the `NSPersistentContainer` and attempts to load the persistent stores.

There's a place to handle errors encountered when loading the persistent stores. Typically, they only happen during development, but it may be worth alerting the user if the app encounters a disk space error.

> **Note**: For much more on the Core Data stack, be sure to check out Core Data by Tutorials (https://www.raywenderlich.com/books/core-data-by-tutorials)

# Swift structs and Core Data classes

As you learned when working with entities in **PetSave.xcdatamodeld** earlier, Core Data works with classes. The PetSave app, up to this point, uses structs for the data model objects. Here's how you can add some code to convert from the structs to Core Data classes and back again.

## Implementing a CoreDataPersistable protocol

If you've had any experience with Core Data in the past and have had to worry about converting back and forth between structs and classes, you know there's a *lot* of boilerplate code. Consider an example `Person` struct, which has a corresponding `PersonEntity` Core Data entity.

Here's the code that you need to handle converting back and forth between struct and class:

```
struct Person {
  var age: Int
  var gender: Gender
  var height: Double
  var weight: Double
  //....
}

extension Person {
  init(managedObject: PersonEntity) {
    self.age = managedObject.age
    self.gender = Gender(rawValue: managedObject.gender)
    self.height = managedObject.height
    self.weight = managedObject.weight
    //...
  }
}

extension PersonEntity {
  init (valueObject: Person) {
    self.setValue(valueObject.age, forKey: "age")
    self.setValue(
      valueObject.gender.rawValue, forKey: "gender")
    self.setValue(valueObject.height, forKey: "height")
    self.setValue(valueObject.weight, forKey: "weight")
    //...
  }
}
```

This amount of code seems manageable for one class, but what if you have ten or twenty, or more, entities in your schema or many more properties? This creates a lot of code for each struct. On the surface, that code does the same thing: converting between structs and classes. You can reduce this boilerplate code by defining some protocols and default implementations.

First, add a new file in **Core/data/coreData/extensions** called **CoreDataPersistable.swift**. Here, add import CoreData and the following protocol, UUIDIdentifiable, that adopts Identifiable:

```
import CoreData

protocol UUIDIdentifiable: Identifiable {
  var id: Int? { get set }
}
```

This code ensures that each of the data model objects is identifiable by an Integer id.

Next, add a `CoreDataPersistable` protocol that adopts `UUIDIdentifiable`. Add the following initializers and methods:

```
protocol CoreDataPersistable: UUIDIdentifiable {
  //1
  associatedtype ManagedType

  //2
  init()

  //3
  init(managedObject: ManagedType?)

  //4
  var keyMap: [PartialKeyPath<Self>: String] { get }

  //5
  mutating func toManagedObject(
  context: NSManagedObjectContext) -> ManagedType

  //6
  func save(context: NSManagedObjectContext) throws
}
```

Here's a breakdown of this protocol:

1.  This protocol uses generics and has an **associated type**. Associated types are placeholders for the concrete types you'll pass in later when you adopt this protocol, which will let you bind a value type, struct, with a class type, `ManagedType`, at compile time.

2.  This initializer sets up the object's basic state.

3.  This initializer takes in the `ManagedType` object as a parameter. The initializer's body will handle the conversion from class to struct.

4.  To set values from the managed object to the struct, you need to map key paths in the struct to keys in the managed object. This array stores that mapping.

5.  `toManagedObject(context:)` saves the struct-based object to the Core Data store.

6.  `save(context:)` saves the view context to disk, persisting the data.

## Using KeyPaths to make initializers

With the protocol defined, it's time to add some default method implementations. By doing this inside a **protocol extension**, you let the actual type extensions be as small as possible. Under the protocol definition, add the following protocol extension:

```
//1
extension CoreDataPersistable
  where ManagedType: NSManagedObject {
  //2
  init(managedObject: ManagedType?) {
    self.init()
    //3
    guard let managedObject = managedObject else { return }

    //4
    for attribute in managedObject.entity.attributesByName {
      if let keyP = keyMap.first(
          where: { $0.value == attribute.key })?.key {
        let value =
      managedObject.value(forKey: attribute.key)
        storeValue(value, toKeyPath: keyP)
      }
    }
  }
}
```

For this method:

1. Only types where `ManagedType` inherits from `NSManagedObject` can use this extension.

2. The initializer takes in an optional `ManagedType` and calls the class's default initializer.

3. A guard statement checks to confirm the passed in `managedObject` isn't `nil`.

4. For each attribute of the `managedObject`, the struct stores each KeyPath-Value pair via the `storeValue(_: toKeyPath:)`. This only gets attributes, not relationships.

Now add this after the previous code:

```
private mutating func storeValue(_ value: Any?,
  toKeyPath partial: AnyKeyPath) {
  switch partial {
  case let keyPath as WritableKeyPath<Self, URL?>:
```

```
      self[keyPath: keyPath] = value as? URL
  case let keyPath as WritableKeyPath<Self, Int?>:
      self[keyPath: keyPath] = value as? Int
  case let keyPath as WritableKeyPath<Self, String?>:
      self[keyPath: keyPath] = value as? String
  case let keyPath as WritableKeyPath<Self, Bool?>:
      self[keyPath: keyPath] = value as? Bool
  default:
    return
  }
}
```

This method takes in a value and a **KeyPath**, specifically, an AnyKeyPath. You then use a switch to check for the real form of the AnyKeyPath. In this case, the KeyPath is some flavor of WritableKeyPath. WritableKeyPath lets you store the value in the struct. Note here that you have to specify *each* basic type that you could potentially handle. For example, there's no handling of Double values here.

**Note**: Curious why you have to jump through all these hoops? Structs in Swift don't have the same methods available that classes do when accessing their properties. It's one of the downsides of using structs instead of classes. Hopefully, Apple will provide better APIs in future versions of Swift.

## Using the Mirror API to store values

Now you have to convert the struct objects to Core Data managed objects. Add the following implementation for toManagedObject(context:):

```
//1
mutating func toManagedObject(context: NSManagedObjectContext =
    PersistenceController.shared.container.viewContext
) -> ManagedType {
  let persistedValue: ManagedType
  //2
  if let id = self.id {
    let fetchRequest = ManagedType.fetchRequest()
    //3
    fetchRequest.predicate = NSPredicate(
      format: "id = %@", id as CVarArg)
    if let results = try? context.fetch(fetchRequest),
      let firstResult = results.first as? ManagedType {
      persistedValue = firstResult
    } else {
      persistedValue = ManagedType.init(context: context)
      self.id = persistedValue.value(forKey: "id") as? Int
    }
```

```
    } else {
      //4
      persistedValue = ManagedType.init(context: context)
      self.id = persistedValue.value(forKey: "id") as? Int
    }

    return setValuesFromMirror(persistedValue: persistedValue)
  }
```

In this method:

1. `toManagedObject(context:)` is mutating because the `id` gets saved back in the struct when creating the managed object. This lets you check for existing entries in the database.

2. This `if` block checks to see if the struct has a non-nil `id` value. If so, the code within the `if` block attempts to fetch that entry from the database. If successful, `persistedValue` is set to that object. Otherwise, the initializer makes a new object and sets it to `persistedValue`.

3. This is where you set the predicate for the fetch request. This uses a string with substitution variables and a variadic list of values that replace those arguments. Here, the `id` is cast to a `CVarArg` and replaces the `%@` in the string.

4. If the struct's `id` is `nil`, the initializer makes a new object and sets the struct's `id` to the managed object's `id`.

Below the previous code, add code using **Mirror** to help assign values to the managed object:

```
private func setValuesFromMirror(persistedValue: ManagedType) ->
ManagedType {
  //1
  let mirror = Mirror(reflecting: self)
  //2
  for case let (label?, value) in mirror.children {
    //3
    let value2 = Mirror(reflecting: value)
    //4
    if value2.displayStyle != .optional || !
value2.children.isEmpty {
      //5
      persistedValue.setValue(value, forKey: label)
    }
  }

  return persistedValue
}
```

The Mirror API performs some introspection on the struct. The goal here is to map the values at the struct's keyPaths to those in the managed object. Unfortunately, there isn't a straightforward way to get a hold of the values at the key paths, so one has to resort to using `Mirror` to look inside.

Here's what this code does:

1.  Create a mirror of the current struct, `self`.

2.  Loop over each of the (`label`, `value`) pairings in the mirror's `children` property.

3.  Make a mirror object for the current value in the loop.

4.  Check to make sure the child value isn't optional, and ensure that the child value's `children` collection isn't empty.

5.  If you make it this far, set the (`label`, `value`) pair on the managed object via its `setValue(_:, forKey:)`.

Finally, add:

```
func save(context: NSManagedObjectContext =
  PersistenceController.shared.container.viewContext) throws {
    try context.save()
}
```

This method saves the managed object context to disk. You implement it here in `CoreDataPersistable`, so you don't have to duplicate it in every structure that extends `CoreDataPersistable`.

That's a lot of code to transform back and forth between structs and Core Data classes. Was it worth it? Time to make a concrete implementation and find out.

## Making a concrete implementation

Open **Core/data/coreData/extensions**. You'll find many implementations of this protocol already in place. Create a new file, **Breed+CoreData.swift**, and add:

```
import CoreData

//1
extension Breed: CoreDataPersistable {
  //2
  var keyMap: [PartialKeyPath<Breed>: String] {
    [
      \.primary: "primary",
```

```
        \.secondary: "secondary",
        \.mixed: "mixed",
        \.unknown: "unknown",
        \.id: "id"
    ]
  }

  //3
  typealias ManagedType = BreedEntity
}
```

Here's a breakdown of this default implementation:

1. This is an extension of the `Breed` struct and adopts `CoreDataPersistable`.

2. This is the key map connecting those keyPaths in `Breed` with the keys from the managed object.

3. The managed type for `Breed` is `BreedEntity`.

That's it! With this simple extension on the data model types, you can now convert back and forth between struct and Core Data class. Next, you'll look at how to use this functionality to add data to the database.

# Storing data

Storing, deleting and fetching data are three common interactions with the Core Data database. Here's how easy it is to store data and test your methods.

## Saving entities

You've seen that `toManagedObject(context:)` gives you a flexible way to save the struct-based data model objects as Core Data entities. With this functionality in place, you can now start to convert the structs from the data model into Core Data objects.

In **Persistence.swift**, replace the contents of the `for` loop near the top with:

```
for i in 0..<10 {
  var animal = Animal.mock[i]
  animal.toManagedObject(context: viewContext)
}
```

This code initializes entries into the in-memory store. It grabs the ith entry from the mock `Animal` array and uses `toManagedObject(context:)` to persist it to Core Data which will come in handy when previewing views later.

## Converting model objects from the network

The project so far only has one place that uses the data from the network API. Open **AnimalsNearYouView.swift** and replace `fetchAnimals` with:

```swift
func fetchAnimals() async {
  do {
    // 1
    let animalsContainer: AnimalsContainer = try await
    requestManager.perform(
      AnimalsRequest.getAnimalsWith(
        page: 1,
        latitude: nil,
        longitude: nil
      )
    )

    for var animal in animalsContainer.animals {
      // 2
      animal.toManagedObject()
    }

    await stopLoading()
  } catch {
    print("Error fetching animals...\(error)")
  }
}
```

Here's what's happening:

1. `perform(_:)` connects to the Petfinder API and gets the animals in a structure.

2. Iterate over each animal and call `toManagedObject(context:)` to convert it from the structure to a Core Data object.

Since you're transitioning to using `AnimalEntity` instead of `Animal`, update the type of the `animals` property at the top of the struct:

```swift
@State var animals: [AnimalEntity] = []
```

Then update the previews struct to match this new property type:

```swift
struct AnimalsNearYouView_Previews: PreviewProvider {
  static var previews: some View {
```

```
      if let animals = CoreDataHelper.getTestAnimalEntities() {
        AnimalsNearYouView(animals: animals, isLoading: false)
      }
    }
  }
}
```

This code uses a helper method in **CoreDataHelper.swift** to get an array of entities to test with from the in-memory database.

**AnimalRow.swift** should also use `AnimalEntity`, so change the type of the `animal` property accordingly:

```
let animal: AnimalEntity
```

Since the entity's name property may be `nil`, update the `Text` view that displays the animal's name:

```
Text(animal.name ?? "No Name Available")
```

Finally, update the previews struct to use a test `AnimalEntity` using a helper method from `CoreDataHelper`:

```
struct AnimalRow_Previews: PreviewProvider {
  static var previews: some View {
    if let animal = CoreDataHelper.getTestAnimalEntity() {
      AnimalRow(animal: animal)
    }
  }
}
```

Preview the `AnimalRow` in the preview canvas. You'll see it's identical to the view from the last chapter, possibly with a different name, but now populated with an `AnimalEntity`:

*A single animal row. It's OK if yours is populated with a different name.*

# Testing storing data

One way to test that structs are getting converted to entities correctly is to write unit tests.

Go to **PetSaveTests/Tests/Core/data/coreData** and open **CoreDataTests.swift**. Add a new test method called `testToManagedObject()`:

```
func testToManagedObject() throws {
  //1
  let previewContext =
    PersistenceController.preview.container.viewContext

  //2
  let fetchRequest = AnimalEntity.fetchRequest()
  fetchRequest.fetchLimit = 1
  fetchRequest.sortDescriptors =
    [NSSortDescriptor(keyPath: \AnimalEntity.name,
    ascending: true)]
  guard let results = try? previewContext.fetch(fetchRequest),
    let first = results.first else { return }

  //3
  XCTAssert(first.name == "CHARLA", """
    Pet name did not match, was expecting Kiki, got
    \(String(describing: first.name))
    """)
  XCTAssert(first.type == "Dog", """
    Pet type did not match, was expecting Cat, got
    \(String(describing: first.type))
    """)
  XCTAssert(first.coat.rawValue == "Short", """
    Pet coat did not match, was expecting Short, got
    \(first.coat.rawValue)
    """)
}
```

Here's what's happening in this test code:

1. This test method takes advantage of the in-memory store, which has a fixed set of pets already persisted.

2. The `fetchRequest` on `AnimalEntity` generates a fetch request. `fetchLimit` limits the fetch to one result, and a `guard` checks for a valid result.

3. If the result is valid, a series of `XCTestAsserts` test various fields of the result against the expected value from `AnimalsMock.json`.

Run the test. As expected, the testToManagedObject passes.

```
func testToManagedObject() throws {
    let previewContext = PersistenceController.preview.container.viewContext
    let fetchRequest = AnimalEntity.fetchRequest()
    fetchRequest.fetchLimit = 1
    fetchRequest.sortDescriptors = [NSSortDescriptor(keyPath: \AnimalEntity.name, ascending: true)]
    guard let results = try? previewContext.fetch(fetchRequest),
      let first = results.first else { return }

    XCTAssert(first.name == "CHARLA", """
      Pet name did not match, was expecting Kiki, got
      \(String(describing: first.name))
      """)
    XCTAssert(first.type == "Dog", """
      Pet type did not match, was expecting Cat, got
      \(String(describing: first.type))
      """)
    XCTAssert(first.coat.rawValue == "Short", """
      Pet coat did not match, was expecting Short, got
      \(first.coat.rawValue)
      """)
}
```

*As expected, test toManagedObject passes.*

Previewing views is another way to test the toManagedObject(context:). In fact, you did that in the last section! Great job! You were testing and you didn't even realize it!

# Deleting data

Deleting data from the Core Data store doesn't use the CoreDataPersistable protocol. **CoreDataHelper.swift** contains an extension on the Collection type you can use to delete a collection of NSManagedObjects.

```
extension Collection where Element == NSManagedObject, Index ==
Int {
  func delete(at indices: IndexSet,
      inViewContext viewContext: NSManagedObjectContext =
      CoreDataHelper.context) {
        indices.forEach { index in
          viewContext.delete(self[index])
        }

    do {
      try viewContext.save()
    } catch {
      fatalError("""
        \(#file), \
        \(#function), \
        \(error.localizedDescription)
        """)
```

```
      }
    }
  }
```

This method removes the objects at the provided `indices` from the data store. It does so by calling `viewContext.delete(_:)` over each element. It then calls `viewContext.save` to push the changes to the database.

## Testing deletion

To test object deletion, go back to **CoreDataTests.swift** and add:

```
func testDeleteManagedObject() throws {
  let previewContext =
    PersistenceController.preview.container.viewContext

  let fetchRequest = AnimalEntity.fetchRequest()
  guard let results = try? previewContext.fetch(fetchRequest),
    let first = results.first else { return }

  let expectedResult = results.count - 1
  previewContext.delete(first)

  guard let resultsAfterDeletion = try?
previewContext.fetch(fetchRequest)
    else { return }

  XCTAssertEqual(expectedResult, resultsAfterDeletion.count, """
    The number of results was expected to be \(expectedResult)
after deletion, was \(results.count)
    """)
}
```

This test again uses the `previewContext` but removes the first entry from the database, which causes the number of entries in the database to reduce by one. Run the test in Xcode. It passes! The deletion operation is working now.

```
⊘     func testDeleteManagedObject() throws {
```

*As expected, the testDeleteManagedObject method passes.*

**Note**: Throughout the book, tests will focus on the bigger features of the app, instead of attempting to attain a high level of test coverage. iOS Test-Driven Development by Tutorials (https://www.raywenderlich.com/books/ios-test-driven-development-by-tutorials) is a great resource to learn more about testing your iOS apps.

# Fetching data

Now with data stored in the Core Data database, you need to be able to fetch it to use it in your views. There are three ways to do this, the first of which is NSFetchRequest.

## Fetching from Core Data with NSFetchRequest

NSFetchRequest can fetch data from a Core Data store. For example, **CoreDataHelper.swift** has this method:

```
// 1
static func getTestAnimalEntities() -> [AnimalEntity]? {
  // 2
  let fetchRequest = AnimalEntity.fetchRequest()
  // 3
  guard let results = try? previewContext.fetch(fetchRequest),
      !results.isEmpty else { return nil }
  return results
}
```

Here's what's going on:

1. The method may return nil if no objects in the database match the request.

2. Each entity has a fetchRequest that returns an NSFetchRequest for that entity. If necessary, you can use sortDescriptors and predicate properties to customize the returned results.

3. A compound guard statement checks that a non-nil set of results comes back, and if so, it isn't empty. If the guard fails, the method returns nil. Otherwise, the method returns the results.

NSFetchRequest is powerful, but Apple started to add some Core Data features to SwiftUI, starting with @FetchRequest.

## Using @FetchRequest

iOS 14 introduced the @FetchRequest property wrapper, which gets entries from a Core Data store and provides them to a SwiftUI view. When the database changes, views with @FetchRequest properties update automatically. This behavior is like the view having an @ObservedObject property. Those properties respond to changes in the @Published items of the ObservableObject.

With @FetchRequest, you can also perform operations on the data before the property returns values to the view, including sorting with SortDescriptors and filtering data with NSPredicates.

You may be thinking to yourself, "Self, won't this possibly break patterns like MVVM that I may use when making my features?" Well, you'd be right.

In the AnimalsNearYouView you updated earlier, replace the animals property with:

```
@FetchRequest(
  sortDescriptors: [
    NSSortDescriptor(
      keyPath: \AnimalEntity.timestamp, ascending: true)
  ],
  animation: .default
)
var animals: FetchedResults<AnimalEntity>
```

This code now binds the fetch request in the property wrapper with the animals property. Like @State and other state-related property wrappers, @FetchRequest will cause the body of the view to refresh if the underlying database data changes.

Notice how you added an NSSortDescriptor. It'll order the results by timestamp in an ascending manner. It also has an animation property you can use to indicate how the result should be animated when displayed.

Don't forget to also update the previews struct since you're no longer passing in a collection of animals and are instead letting the database get them for you:

```
static var previews: some View {
  AnimalsNearYouView(isLoading: false)
    .environment(\.managedObjectContext,
      PersistenceController.preview.container.viewContext)
}
```

To make this work, you need to inject the view context into the SwiftUI Environment.

Open **ContentView.swift**. Add the following modifier to the AnimalsNearYouView and SearchView views:

```
.environment(\.managedObjectContext, managedObjectContext)
```

At the top of **ContentView.swift**, define the managedObjectContext property:

```
let managedObjectContext =
  PersistenceController.shared.container.viewContext
```

As you build out features later in the book, these views will fetch data with @FetchRequests.

So is @FetchRequest in your view better than NSFetchRequest in your view model?

Pros:

1. **UI updates**: SwiftUI updates the UI for you behind the scenes.

2. **Code savings**: You potentially save on code you may have written to keep the data structures up-to-date.

Cons:

1. **Testing**: You lose the ability to do model-based testing on the code that fetches from the database.

2. **Data manipulation**: You lose the ability to perform other methods on your data before the view can display it.

Which is better? It depends on how integrated you are with SwiftUI. Deep integration is the direction Apple is going since they introduced an improvement to @FetchRequest in iOS 15.

## Using @SectionedFetchRequest

In iOS 15, Apple introduced a new twist on @FetchRequest:
@SectionedFetchRequest. Open AnimalsNearYouView.swift and replace the @FetchRequest at the top with this @SectionedFetchRequest below:

```
@SectionedFetchRequest<String, AnimalEntity>(
  sectionIdentifier: \AnimalEntity.animalSpecies,
  sortDescriptors: [
    NSSortDescriptor(keyPath: \AnimalEntity.timestamp,
                     ascending: true)
    ],
  animation: .default
) private var sectionedAnimals:
    SectionedFetchResults<String, AnimalEntity>
```

Besides sortDescriptors and an animation parameter, which were possible with @FetchRequest, you now can specify a sectionIdentifier that uses a keyPath from the fetched type to group the fetched results by section. Views, such as Lists, use this sectioned data to help users organize the data they're viewing.

Replace the existing `ForEach` in the `List` with:

```
ForEach(sectionedAnimals) { animals in
  Section(header: Text(animals.id)) {
    ForEach(animals) { animal in
      NavigationLink(destination: AnimalDetailsView()) {
        AnimalRow(animal: animal)
      }
    }
  }
}
```

This code iterates through each section, generates a header from the section's id and builds an `AnimalRow` for each animal in the section. `AnimalRow` is now inside a `NavigationLink` that will push an `AnimalDetailsView` when the user taps over a row. You'll work on this view in a later chapter.

Build and run the app.

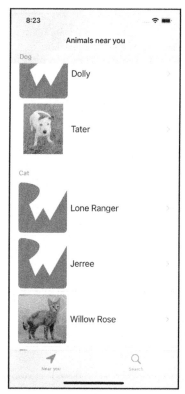

*New in iOS 15 - Sectioned Fetch Request*

# Enabling CloudKit support

Many users have different devices - an iPhone, an iPad or even a Mac - that may have the ability to run your app. They're also logged into those devices with their Apple ID, which lets them share data across those devices if the app supports it.

Luckily it's easy to add that support, so you'll make those changes in PetSave next.

## Updating the persistent container

It's *really* simple to add support for CloudKit, at least when syncing data with your app's private cloud database. In **Persistence.swift**, change NSPersistentContainer to NSPersistentCloudKitContainer:

```
let container: NSPersistentCloudKitContainer

init(inMemory: Bool = false) {
  container = NSPersistentCloudKitContainer(name: "PetSave")
  if inMemory {
    container.persistentStoreDescriptions
      .first?.url = URL(fileURLWithPath: "/dev/null")
  }
  //...
```

That's it! Your app's Core Data database will sync with the app's private cloud instance as long as:

- **iCloud capability**: Your project has the iCloud capability enabled. You can find this in your project's "Signing and Capabilities" tab.

- **Apple ID**: Your user signs in with their Apple ID when using your app.

# Challenge

You've been testing NSFetchRequest while testing saving and deleting. For a challenge, add a new test method for fetch. Here's a list of general steps you'll need to complete this challenge:

1. Use the previewContext.

2. Make a fetch request for AnimalEntity.

3. Limit the number of results to one.

4. Only accept results with the name "Ellie".

5. Assert that your results have the correct name.

Check out the project in the **challenges** folder for the solution.

# Key points

- **Persistence** is vital to many modern-day mobile apps.

- Persistence lets your app **have data when offline** and helps **maintain user state** between sessions.

- Swift structs and Core Data classes don't mix, but techniques like **default protocol implementations**, **generics** and **key paths** can help go back and forth between the two.

- **In-memory stores** are useful for testing, especially with previews, while your deployed app uses **an on-disk store**.

- `@FetchRequest` and `@SectionedFetchRequest` are SwiftUI property wrappers that help keep your views up-to-date as the database changes underneath.

# Where to go from here?

Congratulations, you learned a lot about using **Core Data** to implement persistence in your app! But you've only scratched the surface. There's a lot more to discover about the concepts in this chapter.

Check out the tutorial on Core Data with SwiftUI (https://www.raywenderlich.com/9335365-core-data-with-swiftui-tutorial-getting-started) that touches on properties like `@FetchRequest`, and several tutorials on CloudKit (https://www.raywenderlich.com/13219461-getting-started-with-core-data-and-cloudkit), where you can learn how to see your database in CloudKit Dashboard (https://www.raywenderlich.com/4878052-cloudkit-tutorial-getting-started).

Finally, you can learn more about Core Data with the Core Data by Tutorials (https://www.raywenderlich.com/books/core-data-by-tutorials/v7.0/) book!

By finishing this chapter, you've also finished the first section of the book! Give yourself a pat on the back. When you're ready, head on over to the next chapter, where you'll start putting some of the techniques from this section into practice.

# Section II: Building App Features

Using layers to logically organize your code is only part of the answer when it comes to structuring your app's features. The user interface is the main connection between your user and your lower level layers, so it's important to pick a proper architecture that you can easily keep up to date when you build your features.

In this section, you'll go over the upper-level architecture for the app, while building out two new features. For this, you'll use capabilities such as SwiftUI, Combine and async/await.

# Chapter 5: Building Features - Locating Animals Near You

By Renan Benatti Dias

Great job getting through Section I of this book! By now, you have a good grasp of how the app's foundation works and how you'll leverage those components to build features.

You'll get to the meat of the app in this chapter by building PetSave's first feature, **Animals Near You**. Since this is the app's main feature, you'll spend some careful time improving the UI and refactoring some of the code you wrote so far.

More specifically, you'll learn how to:

- Use **view models** to decouple code from your views.

- Leverage SwiftUI **property wrappers** to handle the state of your views.

- Use **services** to fetch and store animals using asynchronous code.

- Fetch more animals at the bottom of the list.

- Polish UI to improve usability.

Additionally, you'll write **unit tests** to test the behavior of your new view model. By implementing unit tests as you develop new features, you'll have more confidence when refactoring them down the line.

# Building Animals Near You

Animals Near You is PetSave's core feature. It helps users browse pets for adoption that might fit their profile.

Using the data you learned how to fetch and store from the previous chapter, you'll populate a list of animals that users can scroll through to find their perfect pet.

Right now, the app shows a simple list of pets that the user can scroll.

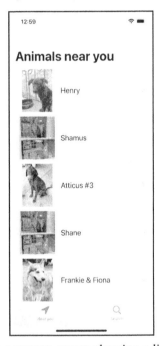

*Animals near you screen showing a list of pets*

The user can already scroll through animals, but nothing happens when they reach the end of the list. Even though Petfinder's API has a lot of pets to adopt, the app only shows a handful.

APIs, like Petfinder's API, **paginate** their results to give the app small amounts of data to prevent requests from being heavy and slow. That way, the app can request more data on demand.

If the app were to fetch all the data upfront, the user might not even see it, and the app would seem slow or unresponsive. Pagination lets you implement a feature known as infinite scrolling. Your favorite social media app likely does something similar to prevent your device from downloading your entire feed at once!

Also, the list's row is a little too simple right now. It only shows a picture and the pet's name. With so little information, users may not feel like opening the details view to check out more data about that pet.

To improve their user experience and make it more likely that they'll want to learn more about a pet that catches their eye, you'll add more information to each row by including labels for the pet's breed, age, gender and a short description.

At the end of this chapter, PetSave will look like this:

*Final version of the near you screen*

# Using View Models

Right now, animals fetched from the API are stored in CoreData, so `AnimalsNearYouView` can fetch pets from the locally persisted database to show on the screen. Not only that, but the view also uses an `@State` variable to show a loading indicator.

As your project grows, you'll have to add a state property for fetching more animals when the user reaches the bottom of the list and another for keeping track of the API's page.

Before you know it, your view class could be gigantic. That's not good. You want to keep your views as loosely coupled as possible, focusing on layout building and user interaction.

You'll create a **view model** to handle user events and the view's state.

> **Note**: Usually, in an MVVM architecture, the view model is responsible for fetching data and handling user interaction as well as transforming and passing data down to the view. However, since you're using CoreData and Apple has a nice property wrapper, @FetchRequest, that works great with SwiftUI, you'll only use view models to handle input from the user and fetching data.

## Creating your first view model

Open the starter project of this chapter and find **AnimalsNearYou** group. Inside it, create a new group named **viewModels**.

Next, inside the new group, create a new file named **AnimalsNearYouViewModel.swift**. Add the following code to this file:

```
final class AnimalsNearYouViewModel: ObservableObject {

}
```

This class will be the view model for AnimalsNearYouView. You'll use it to store it's state and handle requests and user interaction.

Marking the class as final provides a couple of benefits. First, it prevents the class from being overridden by disallowing subclassing. Second, it's a compiler optimization that can speed up build times.

In addition, you made it conform to the ObservableObject protocol.

## Understanding the ObservableObject protocol

The protocol ObservableObject lets you store your data outside the view while still updating the UI when that data changes.

AnimalsNearYouViewModel will house the state and handle the events of Animals Near You. It's the source of truth for AnimalsNearYouView, responsible for data that drives the UI. Any changes to this object updates the view.

# Refactoring code from the view to the view model

Now that you have a view model for `AnimalsNearYouView`, you must remove the state property and the code that fetches and stores animals.

Back inside **AnimalsNearYouView.swift**, remove these two properties:

```
@State var isLoading = true
private let requestManager = RequestManager()
```

You'll add a variable for loading and a `RequestManager` inside the view model later.

Next, remove:

```
func fetchAnimals() async {
  do {
    let animalsContainer: AnimalsContainer = try await
requestManager.perform(
      AnimalsRequest.getAnimalsWith(
        page: 1,
        latitude: nil,
        longitude: nil
      )
    )
    for var animal in animalsContainer.animals {
      animal.toManagedObject()
    }
    await stopLoading()
  } catch {
    print("Error fetching animals...\(error)")
  }
}

@MainActor
func stopLoading() {
  self.isLoading = false
}
```

You'll see a couple of compilation errors in Xcode. Don't worry about them. You'll fix them shortly.

Go back to **AnimalsNearYouViewModel.swift** and add this to the class:

```
// 1
@Published var isLoading: Bool

// 2
```

```
private let requestManager = RequestManager()

// 3
init(isLoading: Bool = true) {
  self.isLoading = isLoading
}
```

This code:

1.  Adds isLoading, a **published** property for tracking if the view is loading.

2.  Adds requestManager, you'll use it to request data to the API.

3.  Creates a initializer that sets isLoading to true by default.

You'll use these properties to add and remove a loading indicator and populate the local database with animals.

## Updating the UI with Published properties

You may have noticed the @Published annotation on the isLoading property. SwiftUI uses this property wrapper to **observe** changes in an ObservableObject. You can use @Published on any type, even custom types. Whenever published properties change, observers of the object receive a notification of that change. SwiftUI uses this to update any view that is dependent on that property.

@Published and @ObservableObject use Swift's **Combine** framework under the hood to publish changes to that property's observers.

Here, you'll use @Published to publish the view's state changes to update the AnimalsNearYouView UI.

AnimalsNearYouView observes changes of the property isLoading inside AnimalsNearYouViewModel and adds a loading indicator when the value is true.

## Fetching and storing animals inside the view model

Still inside **AnimalsNearYouViewModel.swift**, add:

```
// 1
func fetchAnimals() async {
  do {
    // 2
    let animalsContainer: AnimalsContainer = try await
```

```
        requestManager.perform(
          AnimalsRequest.getAnimalsWith(
            page: 1,
            latitude: nil,
            longitude: nil
          )
        )

      // 3
      for var animal in animalsContainer.animals {
        animal.toManagedObject()
      }

      // 4
      isLoading = false
    } catch {
      // 5
      print("Error fetching animals...\
(error.localizedDescription)")
    }
  }
}
```

Here, you:

1. Define a method called `fetchAnimals()` to fetch and store animals. The `async` keyword indicates this method is asynchronous.

2. Start an asynchronous HTTP request using `requestManager` to fetch animals from the API.

3. Iterate over the objects from the response and convert them to entities to save in CoreData.

4. Update the property `isLoading` to `false` to remove the loading indicator.

5. Catch any error that fetching from the API may throw and print a localized description.

Now that your view model is ready to fetch and store animals, it's time to update the views to use the view model.

In **AnimalsNearYouView.swift**, add:

```
@ObservedObject var viewModel: AnimalsNearYouViewModel
```

This line adds a property to the view for observing changes to the view model's state.

# Understanding @ObservedObject

Since the view model conforms to @ObservableObject, you use @ObservedObjectto tell SwiftUI it should observe changes to the object's state and updates the view where it uses that data. It lets the view stay up to date with its source of truth. In this case, that's AnimalsNearYouViewModel.

# Updating the body to use the view model

Next, you'll update the body property of the view to use the view model's properties.

Still inside **AnimalsNearYouView.swift**, find:

```
await fetchAnimals()
```

And replace it with:

```
await viewModel.fetchAnimals()
```

Then, find this line:

```
if isLoading && animals.isEmpty {
```

And change it to:

```
if viewModel.isLoading && animals.isEmpty {
```

Now, AnimalsNearYouView uses the state of AnimalsNearYouViewModel to show the loading indicator and fetch animals when the view appears.

Also inside **ContentView.swift**, update:

```
AnimalsNearYouView()
```

To:

```
AnimalsNearYouView(viewModel: AnimalsNearYouViewModel())
```

This updates ContentView to pass a new instance of AnimalsNearYouViewModel to the view.

# Updating the preview

Before you build and rerun the app, you have to update the preview code for
`AnimalsNearYouView` to use the view model.

Inside **AnimalsNearYouView.swift**, at the bottom of the file, find:

```
AnimalsNearYouView(isLoading: false)
```

Update it with:

```
AnimalsNearYouView(viewModel: AnimalsNearYouViewModel())
```

In Xcode, resume the preview by clicking **resume** at the top right corner of the
preview canvas. Or use the shortcut **Command-Shift-P** to resume the preview.

> **Note**: If you don't see the preview canvas at the right or bottom of Xcode, at
> the top right, click **Adjust Editor Options** and select Canvas. Or, use the
> shortcut **Command-Option-Return** to open the canvas.

*Animals near you screen showing a list of pets in Xcode Preview*

Fantastic! To see the app running on the simulator, build and run.

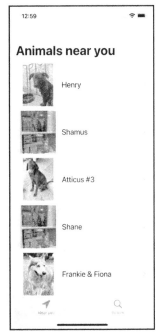

*Animals near you screen showing a list of pets*

Success! The app still works as expected, but you removed the code to fetch and handle state from the view.

However, you may notice a **purple warning** on Xcode's issue navigator.

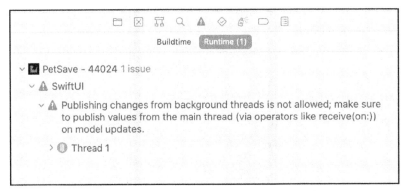

*Xcode's issue navigator showing some warnings*

## Publishing changes and threads

When you call perform(:_), Swift **suspends** fetchAnimals() and starts an HTTP request using URLSession. By default, URLSession uses a background thread to make HTTP requests.

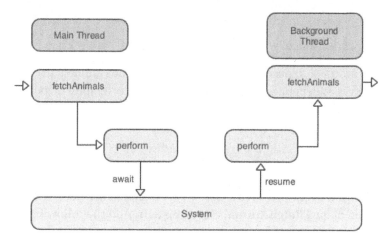

*How the system handles asynchronous code*

When the response arrives, fetchAnimals() resumes execution but outside the main thread. When updating the UI outside the main thread, Xcode warns you because doing so can causes performance issues and/or unexpected behavior.

You could fix this by adding the code to update isLoading inside an async call from the main dispatch queue:

```
DispatchQueue.main.async {
    self.isLoading = true
}
```

This updates isLoading on the main thread. AnimalsNearYouView also receives this update inside the main thread.

However, **Swift 5.5** has a new way of handling async calls and managing updates outside the main thread.

You'll fix this issue in a moment. But first, you'll create a **Service** to fetch animals from the API. That way you remove the code to fetch and store animals from your view model, decoupling code and separating concerns from your view model.

# Creating AnimalFetcher

In **AnimalsNearYouViewModel.swift**, at the top of the file, add:

```
protocol AnimalsFetcher {
  func fetchAnimals(page: Int) async -> [Animal]
}
```

This code defines a protocol with the requirement to fetch animals.

You'll use this protocol to decouple the object that fetches animals from the view model. This enforces dependency inversion, a software principle introduced in Chapter 2 "Laying Down a Strong Foundation", to create lowly coupled code. You'll see how this aids in unit testing later in the chapter.

## Creating your first service

Now, inside **AnimalsNearYou**, create a new group named **services**. Inside **services**, create a new file named **FetchAnimalsService.swift**. Add the following code to the new file:

```
struct FetchAnimalsService {
  private let requestManager: RequestManagerProtocol

  init(requestManager: RequestManagerProtocol) {
    self.requestManager = requestManager
  }
}
```

This code creates a new struct with a request manager to fetch animals.

Next, create the following extension below:

```
// MARK: - AnimalFetcher
extension FetchAnimalsService: AnimalsFetcher {
  func fetchAnimals(page: Int) async -> [Animal] {
    let requestData = AnimalsRequest.getAnimalsWith(
      page: page,
      latitude: nil,
      longitude: nil
    )
    do {
      let animalsContainer: AnimalsContainer = try await
        requestManager.perform(requestData)
      return animalsContainer.animals
    } catch {
      print(error.localizedDescription)
```

```
        return []
    }
  }
}
```

This creates an extension of `FetchAnimalsService` to conform to `AnimalsFetcher` and add the code to fetch animals from the API, which asynchronously returns an array of `Animal`.

## Updating View Model to use FetchAnimalsService

Back in **AnimalsNearYouViewModel.swift**, replace:

```
private let requestManager = RequestManager()
```

With:

```
private let animalFetcher: AnimalsFetcher
```

Also, replace the initializer with:

```
init(isLoading: Bool = true, animalFetcher: AnimalsFetcher) {
  self.isLoading = isLoading
  self.animalFetcher = animalFetcher
}
```

This new initializer has two parameters: `isLoading` that by default is set to `true` and `animalFetcher` that expects any object that conforms to `AnimalsFetcher`.

Next, change `fetchAnimals()` to use this object to fetch animals from the API and store them in CoreData. Replace everything with:

```
let animals = await animalFetcher.fetchAnimals(page: 1)
for var animal in animals {
  animal.toManagedObject()
}
isLoading = false
```

Inside **ContentView.swift**, find:

```
AnimalsNearYouView(viewModel: AnimalsNearYouViewModel())
```

And replace it with:

```
AnimalsNearYouView(
  viewModel: AnimalsNearYouViewModel(
    animalFetcher: FetchAnimalsService(requestManager:
RequestManager())
  )
)
```

Now, when instantiating an `AnimalsNearYouViewModel`, you also pass an instance of `FetchAnimalsService`.

To build and run, you'll also have to update the preview for `AnimalsNearYouView`.

Inside **services**, create a new file called **AnimalsFetcherMock.swift** and add:

```
struct AnimalsFetcherMock: AnimalsFetcher {
  func fetchAnimals(page: Int) async -> [Animal] {
    Animal.mock
  }
}
```

This code creates a mock object to feed mock data to your view previews. When previewing data, you don't want to wait for a network request to finish.

Back in **AnimalsNearYouView.swift**, at the bottom of the file in the preview code, replace:

```
viewModel: AnimalsNearYouViewModel()
```

With:

```
viewModel: AnimalsNearYouViewModel(
  animalFetcher: AnimalsFetcherMock()
)
```

Here, you update the preview's view model to use your newly created `AnimalFetcherMock()`, thereby skipping the load from the API.

Build and run.

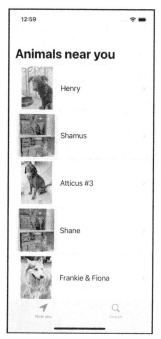

*Animals near you screen showing a list of pets*

The app continues to run as expected, but Xcode still shows a purple warning.

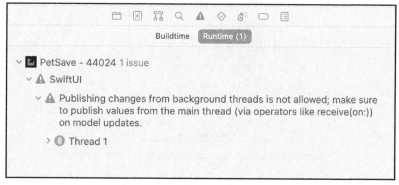

*Xcode's issue navigator showing some warnings*

That's because `FetchAnimalsService` runs outside the main thread. To fix this, you have to set the execution of `AnimalsNearYouViewModel` to the main thread.

## Using @MainActor

Inside **AnimalsNearYouViewModel.swift**, add the following line at the top before the class declaration:

```
@MainActor
```

The @MainActor annotation makes sure all code executed in this class is inside the main thread. When you receive the result back from FetchAnimalsService, the execution changes back to the main thread so you can update any publishing property without the fear of updating the UI outside the main thread.

Build and run again.

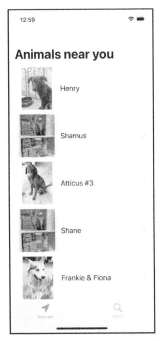

*Animals near you screen showing a list of pets*

Now the purple warning should be gone.

### Understanding actors

An **actor** is a type in Swift that runs concurrent code while protecting its state from data races. You create actors to run code asynchronously that performs a task and changes state, without worrying about other parts of your code accessing and modifying that data while the task is running.

You've already used @MainActor to change the state of the view and show the loading indicator.

If you want to learn more about actors, check out chapter 8 "Getting Started With Actors" from **Modern Concurrency in Swift**.

# Creating a service for storing animals

To make your view model even slimmer and follow another principle introduced in Chapter 2 "Laying Down a Strong Foundation", the single responsibility principle, you'll also create a service for storing animals.

Inside **AnimalsNearYouViewModel.swift** add the following protocol at the top of the file:

```
protocol AnimalStore {
  func save(animals: [Animal]) async throws
}
```

Create a new file inside **services** and name it **AnimalStoreService.swift**. Add:

```
import CoreData

struct AnimalStoreService {
  private let context: NSManagedObjectContext

  init(context: NSManagedObjectContext) {
    self.context = context
  }
}
```

AnimalStoreService takes a NSManagedObjectContext object for saving fetched animals to CoreData. Keep in mind that this context must be a **background context** because you'll use this service to manage CoreData objects fetched from the API by a method running on a background thread. Using viewContext instead would intermittently result in a crash or poor performance, since it runs in the main thread.

Next, add the following extension to convert objects fetched from the API into managed objects and save new ones:

```
// MARK: - AnimalStore
extension AnimalStoreService: AnimalStore {
  func save(animals: [Animal]) async throws {
    // 1
    for var animal in animals {
      // 2
      animal.toManagedObject(context: context)
    }
    // 3
    try context.save()
  }
}
```

Here's a code breakdown:

1.  You iterate over the animals fetched from the API.

2.  Then, you transform your animal object into CoreData entities, passing the background context from the service. You must do this because you're saving animals in the **background context** and using CoreData to merge changes to the **view context**.

3.  You save the context to persist your changes.

Back in `AnimalsNearYouViewModel`, add:

```
private let animalStore: AnimalStore
```

Also, change the init to:

```
init(
  isLoading: Bool = true,
  animalFetcher: AnimalsFetcher,
  animalStore: AnimalStore
) {
  self.isLoading = isLoading
  self.animalFetcher = animalFetcher
  self.animalStore = animalStore
}
```

This code adds a new property for receiving an object that conforms to `AnimalsStore` to store animals from the API request.

Inside `fetchAnimals()`, replace the **for-in** loop with:

```
do {
  try await animalStore.save(animals: animals)
} catch {
  print("Error storing animals... \
(error.localizedDescription)")
}
```

Here, you remove the code that saves the animals from the view model and call `save(animals:)` from `AnimalStore` to do this job.

Next, open **ContentView.swift** and replace the initializer for `AnimalsNearYouViewModel` with:

```
AnimalsNearYouView(
  viewModel: AnimalsNearYouViewModel(
    animalFetcher: FetchAnimalsService(requestManager:
RequestManager()),
      animalStore: AnimalStoreService(
        context:
PersistenceController.shared.container.newBackgroundContext()
      )
  )
)
```

This code passes an instance of `AnimalStoreService` to the view model's initializer.

Finally, in **AnimalsNearYouView.swift**, inside the Preview Provider code, add the following parameter to the view model's initializer:

```
animalStore: AnimalStoreService(context:
CoreDataHelper.previewContext)
```

Here you create a new `AnimalStoreService` object with preview context, so this view can be rendered in Xcode Previews using in-memory store.

Build and run to make sure the app still fetches and stores animals.

*Animals near you screen showing a list of pets*

# Adding infinite scrolling

Great job refactoring the code to use a view model! This will help you implement new features in the future.

Speaking of new features, there's one that's still missing from Animals Near You: Infinite scrolling. Users already expect this behavior when scrolling through a list.

Petfinder's API has so many kinds of animals that it's impractical to fetch everything over a single HTTP request. The API paginates the result and returns a fixed number of animals.

With infinite scrolling, when the user reaches the bottom of the list, the app requests the next page from the API.

You'll implement this feature now.

Open **AnimalsNearYouViewModel.swift**, add this inside
`AnimalsNearYouViewModel`:

```
@Published var hasMoreAnimals = true
```

Next, at the end of `fetchAnimals()`, add:

```
hasMoreAnimals = !animals.isEmpty
```

`hasMoreAnimals` tracks if the API can return more animals on request. You'll use
this property to show a row at the end of the list indicating the app is fetching more
animals. If the response from Petfinder's API returns an empty array of animals,
you'll set this property to false, as that means the list has reached its end.

## Adding pagination

Still in `AnimalsNearYouViewModel`, to keep track of the page from the API, add:

```
private(set) var page = 1
```

Finally, add the following method:

```
func fetchMoreAnimals() async {
  page += 1
  await fetchAnimals()
}
```

`fetchMoreAnimals()` is a method that increments the current page by one and calls
`fetchAnimals()` to fetch the next page.

For this to work, find the following line inside `fetchAnimals()`:

```
let animals = await animalFetcher.fetchAnimals(page: 1)
```

And update it to use the new page property:

```
let animals = await animalFetcher.fetchAnimals(page: page)
```

This code keeps the current page up to date as you request more animals from the
API.

Return to **AnimalsNearYouView.swift**. In body, under the ForEach view, add:

```
if !animals.isEmpty && viewModel.hasMoreAnimals {
  ProgressView("Finding more animals...")
    .padding()
    .frame(maxWidth: .infinity)
    .task {
      await viewModel.fetchMoreAnimals()
    }
}
```

Here, you add a new ProgressView at the end of the list, indicating the app is fetching more animals. When it appears, the task(priority:_:) modifier calls fetchMoreAnimals() to asynchronously fetch more animals from the API.

Build and run the app. Scroll to the bottom of the list to see more animals from the API added to the list.

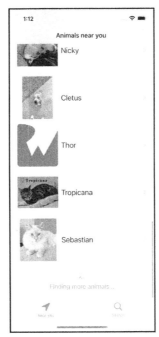

*Animals near you screen showing finding more animals indicator*

# Improving the UI

Animals Near You has all the functionality you planned for, but there's still something missing. The user might scroll through animals, but there's very little information upfront to hook them into viewing an animal's details. Each row only displays the animal's photo and name.

To get the user to view an animal's details, you'll add more information to each row, like gender, age and a short description.

## Adding more information to rows

Open **AnimalRow.swift** and add the following two computed properties:

```
var animalType: String {
  animal.type ?? ""
}

var animalBreedAndType: String {
  "\(animal.breed) \(animalType)"
}
```

You'll use these properties to display a label on `AnimalRow` for the animal's breed and type.

Under the `Text` for the animal name, insert:

```
Text(animalBreedAndType)
  .font(.callout)

if let description = animal.desc {
  Text(description)
    .lineLimit(2)
    .font(.footnote)
}
```

This code adds two `Text` one to display a string containing the animal breed and type, and another to display a description, this ones will only appear if `animal.desc` is not `nil`.

Build and run.

*Animals near you screen now with pet's breed, type and description*

## Adding labels for attributes

Now that the row has the animal breed, type and description, all that's left to add are age and gender.

Below the previous added code, insert:

```
HStack {
  Text(animal.age.rawValue)
    .padding(4)
    .background(animal.age.color.opacity(0.2))
    .cornerRadius(8)
    .foregroundColor(animal.age.color)
    .font(.subheadline)
  Text(animal.gender.rawValue)
    .padding(4)
    .background(.pink.opacity(0.2))
    .cornerRadius(8)
    .foregroundColor(.pink)
    .font(.subheadline)
}
```

Here, you add a new `HStack` view with two new `Text` labels: One for the animal's age and another for its gender.

Build and run.

*Animals near You screen with gender and age*

## Reducing repetition with View Modifiers

Notice both `Text` labels have the same view modifiers, except for changing the background and foreground color depending on the information it displays.

To avoid the code duplicate use **Custom View Modifiers**. Custom view modifiers help you create a view modifier that applies all those modifiers at once, so you don't have to do it for each text label.

Create a new file inside **views** and name it **AnimalAttributesCard.swift**. Add:

```swift
import SwiftUI

struct AnimalAttributesCard: ViewModifier {
  let color: Color
  func body(content: Content) -> some View {
    content
      .padding(4)
```

```
        .background(color.opacity(0.2))
        .cornerRadius(8)
        .foregroundColor(color)
        .font(.subheadline)
    }
}
```

This code creates a custom view modifier with all the common modifiers you're using for Text views.

Back in **AnimalRow.swift**, remove the modifiers from the age Text:

```
.padding(4)
.background(animal.age.color.opacity(0.2))
.cornerRadius(8)
.foregroundColor(animal.age.color)
.font(.subheadline)
```

And replace them with:

```
.modifier(AnimalAttributesCard(color: animal.age.color))
```

Next, remove the modifiers from the gender Text:

```
.padding(4)
.background(.pink.opacity(0.2))
.cornerRadius(8)
.foregroundColor(.pink)
.font(.subheadline)
```

And replace them with:

```
.modifier(AnimalAttributesCard(color: .pink))
```

Build and run to ensure everything still runs the same.

*Animals near you screen with gender and age*

# Testing your view model

Making sure your code is resilient is a key part of app development, because it's always in constant change. To help you accomplish this you need to add tests to your code. There are many types of software tests, for this project,  you'll use **Unit tests** to test your view model and make sure it behaves the way you expect.

**Unit tests** act as a safeguard for your codebase. This tests will catch breaking changes and any problems with your code when you introduce new features or changes to the existing ones.

# Writing test cases

Inside **PetSaveTests/Tests**, create a new group and name it **AnimalsNearYou**.

Next, create a new file named **AnimalsNearYouViewModelTestCase.swift**.

Add the following code to the new file:

```
import XCTest
@testable import PetSave

@MainActor
final class AnimalsNearYouViewModelTestCase: XCTestCase {
  let testContext =
PersistenceController.preview.container.viewContext
  // swiftlint:disable:next implicitly_unwrapped_optional
  var viewModel: AnimalsNearYouViewModel!

  @MainActor
  override func setUp() {
    super.setUp()
    viewModel = AnimalsNearYouViewModel(
      isLoading: true,
      animalFetcher: AnimalsFetcherMock(),
      animalStore: AnimalStoreService(context: testContext)
    )
  }
}
```

Here, you create a new test case class for testing `AnimalsNearYouViewModel`. It also overrides `setUp()` to set up the view model for each test.

Notice that when instantiating an `AnimalsNearYouViewModel`, you use `AnimalsFetcherMock` as the service to fetch animals. When testing the view model, it's always good to isolate and focus your tests on a specific test case. Since you're only testing the view model and don't want your tests to depend on external data, you'll use a mocked response from the API.

Next, you'll add the code to test if the view model updates the `isLoading` property as it fetches animals from the API. Add:

```
func testFetchAnimalsLoadingState() async {
  XCTAssertTrue(viewModel.isLoading, "The view model should be
loading, but it isn't")
  await viewModel.fetchAnimals()
  XCTAssertFalse(viewModel.isLoading, "The view model should'nt
be loading, but it is")
}
```

testFetchAnimalsLoadingState() tests if isLoading is true before the API response and if it's false when the response arrives.

Notice testFetchAnimalsLoadingState() is an async method. This is necessary because fetchAnimals() is also an async method, and you may only call it in an async context.

Build and run the tests.

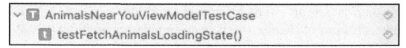

*testFetchAnimalsLoadingState test passed*

Now that you're testing the state for loading, it's time to test the pagination from the API.

Add the following code:

```
func testUpdatePageOnFetchMoreAnimals() async {
  XCTAssertEqual(viewModel.page, 1, "the view model's page
property should be 1 before fetching, but it's \
(viewModel.page)")
  await viewModel.fetchMoreAnimals()
  XCTAssertEqual(viewModel.page, 2, "the view model's page
property should be 2 after fetching, but it's \
(viewModel.page)")
}
```

This method tests if page is 1 before the user scrolls to the bottom of the list and requests more animals. Then, it tests if page changed to 2 once the request finishes.

Build and rerun the tests.

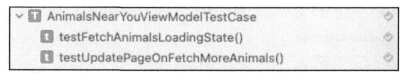

*testFetchAnimalsLoadingState and testUpdatePageOnFetchMoreAnimals passed*

Finally, you'll test when AnimalsNearYouViewModel receives an empty response.

To do this, you'll create a new struct that conforms to AnimalFetcher to mock an empty response from the API.

At the bottom of the file, add:

```
struct EmptyResponseAnimalsFetcherMock: AnimalsFetcher {
  func fetchAnimals(page: Int) async -> [Animal] {
    return []
  }
}
```

EmptyResponseAnimalsFetcherMock conforms to AnimalsFetch. However, instead of fetching animals from an external source or returning mock data, it immediately returns an empty array of Animal, mocking an empty response from the API.

Next inside AnimalsNearYouViewModelTestCase, add:

```
func testFetchAnimalsEmptyResponse() async {
  // 1
  viewModel = AnimalsNearYouViewModel(
    isLoading: true,
    animalFetcher: EmptyResponseAnimalsFetcherMock(),
    animalStore: AnimalStoreService(context: testContext)
  )
  await viewModel.fetchAnimals()
  // 2
  XCTAssertFalse(viewModel.hasMoreAnimals, "hasMoreAnimals
should be false with an empty response, but it's true")
  XCTAssertFalse(viewModel.isLoading, "the view model shouldn't
be loading after receiving an empty response, but it is")
}
```

Here you:

1. Instantiate a new view model, pass the EmptyResponseAnimalsFetcherMock and try to fetch more animals.

2. Then, you test if hasMoreAnimals is false and if isLoading is also false.

Build and run the test case.

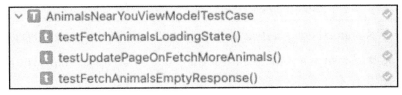

*All tests passed*

## Key points

- **View models** help you keep your view code clean and focused on layout building.

- You can easily update SwiftUI views by using `@Published` and `@ObservedObject` properties to observe state.

- **Actors** are great for protecting the state from data races and performing async tasks that don't block the main thread.

- You can create **Services** to decouple code and run tasks from your view model.

- **Software tests** can make your development **safer** and help you find possible bugs in your code.

## Where to go from here?

You've reached the end of the chapter, but there are still features PetSave needs. Animals Near You might be done, but the search for the perfect pet continues. In the next chapter, you'll implement the search feature, so that users can better find pets for them.

If you want to learn more about testing, check out our video tutorial about Testing in iOS (https://www.raywenderlich.com/25842120-testing-in-ios).

Also, check out our tutorial about Understanding Data Flow in SwiftUI (https://www.raywenderlich.com/11781349-understanding-data-flow-in-swiftui) to learn more about `@ObservedObjects`, `@State` and source of truth.

# Chapter 6: Building Features - Search

By Renan Benatti Dias

In the previous chapter, you learned how to create a list of animals with infinite scrolling using SwiftUI. You also learned about view models and how to decouple your view code from domain code.

In this chapter, you'll build a search feature for people that want to search Petfinder's API for a pet better suited to them.

More specifically, you'll learn how to:

- Use a new view modifier, introduced in iOS 15, to add a **search bar** to your view.

- Filter pets by **name**, **age** and **type**.

- Search animals on an external web service, **Petfinder's API**.

- Use Form and Picker views to create a filter view.

- Improve the UI to make it more approachable.

You'll also learn to leverage @ViewBuilders to **reuse** view code from Animals Near You inside Search.

# Building Search

Search is a feature that many apps have. While it's nice to scroll through a list of animals to find a pet you like, you might be scrolling through hundreds of animals.

This might get tedious when you have a large collection of data. If a user is looking to adopt an animal of a specific age or type, they should be able to search for an animal that way.

Right now, you can scroll through animals in Animals Near You, but you can't do anything in Search. It's just a blank screen.

You'll build a search view with a **search bar** and a filter for **age** and **type** to better filter results.

You'll start by listing all animals already stored. Then, you'll add a search bar so users can type a name and filter the results. Finally, you'll add a form for people to pick their preferred age and type.

At the end of this chapter, **Search** is going to look like this:

*Search screen showing search bar and browse by type*

# Building the base UI

Open **SearchView.swift** and add this declaration at the top:

```
@FetchRequest(
  sortDescriptors: [
    NSSortDescriptor(
      keyPath: \AnimalEntity.timestamp, ascending: true)
  ],
  animation: .default
)
private var animals: FetchedResults<AnimalEntity>
```

This code adds a property, `animals`, that's a `FetchedResults` of the current animals stored in the database. It's sorted by their `timestamp`. You'll filter these results by typing a name on the search bar. This gets data from Core Data thanks to `@FetchRequest`.

Next, replace the code inside `NavigationView` with:

```
List {
  ForEach(animals) { animal in
    NavigationLink(destination: AnimalDetailsView()) {
      AnimalRow(animal: animal)
    }
  }
}
.listStyle(.plain)
.navigationTitle("Find your future pet")
```

This code replaces the blank view and creates a list with `animals`. Build and run. Then click the Search tab.

*Search screen showing a list of animals*

This looks a lot like Animals Near You. It reuses the same row view you created in Chapter 5, "Building Features - Locating Animals Near You", and the code used to create the list is identical to the one in Animals Near You.

Before you add a search bar and start filtering animals, you'll create a new view to share this code in both features.

# Extracting Animal List view

The only difference between the code you just added for SearchView and the code for AnimalsNearYouView is that the list inside AnimalsNearYouView has a view at the bottom for loading more animals. The rest is pretty much the same. Both views use a List to place each animal in a row, and both rows take to the same AnimalDetailsView.

SwiftUI is great for creating views you can reuse in other views. Keeping both views as the same component has a couple of benefits:

1.  You ensure both views behave the same way. They're both Lists of animals.

2.  If you need to change the look of the list or the rows, you don't have to write code twice.

To avoid code repetition, you'll create a custom list view to use in both features, Animals Near You and Search.

# Using @ViewBuilders to build custom views

The main difference between the Lists inside AnimalsNearYouView and SearchView is the ProgressViewat the end. To create a view that takes any view at the bottom, or anywhere else, you'll have to use a SwiftUI feature, **View Builders**.

@ViewBuilder is a **result builder** introduced for SwiftUI. It uses result builders to create a DSL-like syntax for composing views from a closure. It lets you declare your views, one after the other, inside the body property.

> **Note:** You can also use @resultBuilder to compose other types. @ViewBuilder is just a specialization of a result builder for views.

You can also use @ViewBuilder to create custom views that encapsulate other views, like the VStack, HStack and List.

You'll use this to create a custom Animal List View to share code between Animals Near You and Search.

Inside **Core** create a group called **views**, then inside **views** create a new SwiftUI View and name it **AnimalListView.swift**. Replace the contents of the file with:

```swift
import SwiftUI

// 1
struct AnimalListView<Content, Data>: View
  where Content: View,
  Data: RandomAccessCollection,
  Data.Element: AnimalEntity {
  let animals: Data

  // 2
  let footer: Content

  // 3
  init(animals: Data, @ViewBuilder footer: () -> Content) {
    self.animals = animals
    self.footer = footer()
  }

  // 4
  init(animals: Data) where Content == EmptyView {
    self.init(animals: animals) {
      EmptyView()
    }
  }

  var body: some View {
    // 5
    List {
      ForEach(animals) { animal in
        NavigationLink(destination: AnimalDetailsView()) {
          AnimalRow(animal: animal)
        }
      }

      // 6
      footer
    }
    .listStyle(.plain)
  }
}

struct AnimalListView_Previews: PreviewProvider {
  static var previews: some View {
    NavigationView {
      AnimalListView(animals:
CoreDataHelper.getTestAnimalEntities() ?? [])
    }

    NavigationView {
```

```
    AnimalListView(animals: []) {
        Text("This is a footer")
      }
    }
  }
}
```

Here's a breakdown of `AnimalListView`:

1.  It defines a new view with the generic parameters `Content` and `Data`. Then, it defines constraints to those types, `Content` being a `View`, `Data` a `RandomAccessCollection` and `Data.Element` an `AnimalEntity`. Now, you can use `AnimalListView` with any type of collection, as long as it's a collection of `AnimalEntity`.

2.  A property for holding the list's footer view.

3.  An initializer that takes an array of animal entities and a view builder closure for the footer view.

4.  A second initializer that takes only an array of animal entities. This initializer uses an empty view for the list's footer.

5.  The body of the view, laying down a list with rows of animals.

6.  The footer view passed in the initializer, placed at the bottom of the list.

Back inside **SearchView.swift**, find:

```
List {
  ForEach(animals) { animal in
    NavigationLink(destination: AnimalDetailsView()) {
      AnimalRow(animal: animal)
    }
  }
}
.listStyle(.plain)
```

And replace it with:

```
AnimalListView(animals: animals)
```

Next, inside **AnimalsNearYouView.swift**, find:

```
List {
  ForEach(animals) { animal in
    NavigationLink(destination: AnimalDetailsView()) {
      AnimalRow(animal: animal)
```

```
    }
  }
  if !animals.isEmpty && viewModel.hasMoreAnimals {
    ProgressView("Finding more animals...")
      .padding()
      .frame(maxWidth: .infinity)
      .task {
        await viewModel.fetchMoreAnimals()
      }
  }
}
```

Replace it with:

```
AnimalListView(animals: animals) {
  if !animals.isEmpty && viewModel.hasMoreAnimals {
    ProgressView("Finding more animals...")
      .padding()
      .frame(maxWidth: .infinity)
      .task {
        await viewModel.fetchMoreAnimals()
      }
  }
}
```

Build and run to make sure everything still works like before.

*Near you screen showing a list of animals*

Now, it's time to add a search bar for searching animals by name.

# Filtering locally

Open **SearchView.swift** and add this to `SearchView`:

```
@State var searchText = ""
```

This line adds a new `@State` variable that keeps track of the text the user types.

Next, add the following modifier at the end of `AnimalListView`:

```
.searchable(
  text: $searchText,
  placement: .navigationBarDrawer(displayMode: .always)
)
```

This will add a search bar to you view. Build and run.

Tap **Search** and you'll something like this:

*Search screen with a search bar at the top*

# The new searchable Modifier

searchable(text:placement:prompt:), is a new view modifier added in iOS 15, adds a search bar to a NavigationView. You pass a Binding to a String and the placement of the search bar. The search bar then updates the Binding when the user types.

Still in **SearchView.swift**, add the following computed property:

```
var filteredAnimals: [AnimalEntity] {
  animals.filter {
    if searchText.isEmpty {
      return true
    }
    return $0.name?.contains(searchText) ?? false
  }
}
```

You use the computed property filteredAnimals to filter animals from core data with searchText. If searchText is empty, you return all the animals from core data. Otherwise, you match their name with the text the user typed.

Next, replace:

```
AnimalListView(animals: animals)
```

With:

```
AnimalListView(animals: filteredAnimals)
```

This code replaces AnimalListView's data source with your new property.

Build and run. Type the name of a pet in the search bar to see the result.

*Search screen with results of searching by name*

Success! SwiftUI filters the results from Core Data with the name you type.

However, you're only filtering locally stored animals, not the entire **Petfinder's API** database.

You'll add a request to search the API now.

# Searching Petfinder's API

You're going to search Petfinder's API and add network logic to this feature. To avoid making SearchView even bigger and adding domain logic to view code, create a new view model to handle this.

## Creating a View Model for searching

Create a new group inside **Search** and name it **viewModels**. Next, create a new file inside the new group and name it **SearchViewModel.swift**.

Add the following code to the new file:

```
final class SearchViewModel: ObservableObject {
  @Published var searchText = ""

  var shouldFilter: Bool {
    !searchText.isEmpty
  }
}
```

You declare a published variable called searchText that will contain the text typed by the user. You also use shouldFilter later to add and remove views if the search bar is empty.

Now, you'll create a new service for searching the API with a query and other filters you'll add later, like age and type.

## Creating the service for searching

Still inside **SearchViewModel.swift**, add the following protocol at the top of the file:

```
protocol AnimalSearcher {
  func searchAnimal(
    by text: String,
    age: AnimalSearchAge,
    type: AnimalSearchType
  ) async -> [Animal]
}
```

This protocol defines a service that searches for animals by text, age and type.

Next, inside the **Search** group, create a new group and name it **services**. Create a file and name it **AnimalSearcherService.swift**. Add the following code to this new file:

```
// 1
struct AnimalSearcherService {
  let requestManager: RequestManagerProtocol
}

// MARK: - AnimalSearcher
// 2
extension AnimalSearcherService: AnimalSearcher {
  func searchAnimal(
    by text: String,
    age: AnimalSearchAge,
    type: AnimalSearchType
  ) async -> [Animal] {
    // 3
    let requestData = AnimalsRequest.getAnimalsBy(
      name: text,
      age: age != .none ? age.rawValue : nil,
      type: type != .none ? type.rawValue : nil
    )
    // 4
    do {
      let animalsContainer: AnimalsContainer = try await
requestManager
        .perform(requestData)
      return animalsContainer.animals
    } catch {
      // 5
      print(error.localizedDescription)
      return []
    }
  }
}
```

Here's a breakdown of the struct you just added:

1. Here, you declare a new service, `AnimalSearcherService`, with a request manager to make requests to Petfinder's API.

2. Then, you extend `AnimalSearcherService` to conform to `AnimalSearcher`.

3. You create `requestData` passing the text, age and type. If age or type are not selected, you don't pass those values in the request.

4. Here, you make a request with the given data and return an array of animals.

5. If an error happens, you print the error the request thrown and return an empty array.

Next, back in **SearchViewModel.swift**, add this to `SearchViewModel`:

```
private let animalSearcher: AnimalSearcher
private let animalStore: AnimalStore

init(animalSearcher: AnimalSearcher, animalStore: AnimalStore) {
  self.animalSearcher = animalSearcher
  self.animalStore = animalStore
}
```

This adds two properties to your view model: `animalSearcher` to search animals and `animalStore` for storing the results in the database. You also add an initializer for injecting those properties.

Also, add:

```
func search() {
  Task {
    // 1
    let animals = await animalSearcher.searchAnimal(
      by: searchText,
      age: .none,
      type: .none
    )

    // 2
    do {
      try await animalStore.save(animals: animals)
    } catch {
      print("Error storing animals... \
(error.localizedDescription)")
    }
  }
}
```

Here's what's happening:

1. You start a request passing the text the user typed as a parameter. For now, you pass none for age and `type`. You'll add those filters later.

2. Save the results in Core Data and handle an error it may throw.

When typing on the search bar, you use this method for querying the API and saving results. Then, Core Data also updates the results and displays them on screen.

Now that your view model is complete, it's time to update the view to use it.

# Refactoring the view to use the view model

Inside **SearchView.swift**, replace searchText declaration with:

```
@StateObject var viewModel = SearchViewModel(
  animalSearcher: AnimalSearcherService(requestManager:
RequestManager()),
  animalStore: AnimalStoreService(
    context:
PersistenceController.shared.container.newBackgroundContext()
  )
)
```

Here, you add a StateObject variable for the view model you just created.
@StateObject makes this an observable object so your views can observe and react
to its changes.

Next, find filteredAnimals, and replace its code with:

```
guard viewModel.shouldFilter else { return [] }
return animals.filter {
  if viewModel.searchText.isEmpty {
    return true
  }
  return $0.name?.contains(viewModel.searchText) ?? false
}
```

This code updates filteredAnimals to use your new view model to filter animals
using the new searchText property. It returns an empty array if shouldFilter is
true.

Finally, find the text parameter of searchable(text:placement:):

```
text: $searchText,
```

And replace it with:

```
text: $viewModel.searchText,
```

This code binds searchText from your view model to the view's search bar.

Build and run to make sure everything still works.

*Search screen with results of searching by name*

Your view uses your view model to search locally. It's time to add a call to also search Petfinder's API.

## Searching the API

Still in **SearchView.swift**, under searchable(text:placement:), add:

```
// 1
.onChange(of: viewModel.searchText) { _ in
  // 2
  viewModel.search()
}
```

This is what's happening:

1.  onChange(of:perform:) is a modifier that observes changes to a type that conforms to Equatable, in this case viewModel.searchText.

2.  It then calls a closure with a new value whenever it changes, you put viewModel.search() so it gets called when the user types on the search bar.

Build and run. Type a name that isn't on the list.

*Search screen with results of searching by name*

At first, the app may not have the animal stored locally, but as the request to the API completes, the results are added to the list.

Finally, you'll fix Xcode previews for `SearchView`.

## Updating previews with mock data

Inside **Search/services**, create a new file and name it **AnimalSearcherMock.swift**. Add the following code:

```
struct AnimalSearcherMock: AnimalSearcher {
  func searchAnimal(
    by text: String,
    age: AnimalSearchAge,
    type: AnimalSearchType
  ) async -> [Animal] {
    var animals = Animal.mock
    if age != .none {
      animals = animals.filter {
        $0.age.rawValue.lowercased() ==
age.rawValue.lowercased()
      }
```

```
    }
    if type != .none {
      animals = animals.filter {
        $0.type.lowercased() == type.rawValue.lowercased()
      }
    }
    return animals.filter { $0.name.contains(text) }
  }
}
```

This creates a new mock object conforming to `AnimalSearcher` that mocks the result from the API for Xcode previews.

Back inside **SearchView.swift**, in the preview code at the bottom of the file, replace:

```
SearchView()
```

With:

```
SearchView(
  viewModel: SearchViewModel(
    animalSearcher: AnimalSearcherMock(),
    animalStore: AnimalStoreService(
      context:
PersistenceController.preview.container.viewContext
    )
  )
)
.environment(
  \.managedObjectContext,
  PersistenceController.preview.container.viewContext
)
```

This code adds a view model with your mock service for displaying a list of animals in Xcode previews.

Resume the preview by clicking **resume** at the top right corner of the preview canvas or use **Command-Option-P**. Activate live preview and type something in the search bar.

*Search screen in live preview*

# Handling empty results

Everything is working great so far, but if you search for an animal Petfinder's API doesn't have, the app simply shows a blank screen.

You'll fix that by adding a message explaining the app didn't find any results.

In **SearchView.swift**, at the bottom of `AnimalListView`, add the following modifier:

```
.overlay {
  if filteredAnimals.isEmpty && !viewModel.searchText.isEmpty {
    EmptyResultsView(query: viewModel.searchText)
  }
}
```

This code adds a new overlay with `EmptyResultsView`, a view in this chapter's starter project. This view displays a message explaining that the app didn't find any animals with that name. It only appears onscreen when the filtered results and search bar are empty.

Build and run. Search for a name that isn't on the list.

*Search screen showing a message when there aren't results available*

# Filtering animals by age and type

Now that you can filter animals by name, it's time to filter them by age and type to help users find suitable pets faster.

# Adding age and type to the view model

Open **SearchViewModel.swift** and add these two published properties to
SearchViewModel:

```
@Published var ageSelection = AnimalSearchAge.none
@Published var typeSelection = AnimalSearchType.none
```

You'll use them to keep track of the age and type the user selected. They both start
with none, in case the user doesn't want to use any filters.

Next, update shouldFilter with:

```
!searchText.isEmpty ||
  ageSelection != .none ||
  typeSelection != .none
```

This code updates this property to take into account the age and type the user
selects.

Next, add the following method at the end of the class:

```
func clearFilters() {
  typeSelection = .none
  ageSelection = .none
}
```

This method sets the selection of typeSelection and ageSelection back to none.

Inside search(), find and update the following two lines:

```
age: .none,
type: .none
```

With:

```
age: ageSelection,
type: typeSelection
```

Now, when the user searches an animal, it also sends the type and age that the user
picked.

You're done updating the view model. It's time to create a view for users to select the
animal's age and type.

# Building a picker view

To filter animals by age and type, you'll build a form view that lets you pick from the available options.

Inside **Search/views**, create a new SwiftUI View and name it **SearchFilterView.swift**.

Add the following properties:

```
@Environment(\.dismiss) private var dismiss
@ObservedObject var viewModel: SearchViewModel
```

dismiss is an environment value you access to dismiss the current presentation. You'll use it to dismiss SearchFilterView when the user finishes picking their preference.

You also added viewModel, which will contain a reference to your SearchViewModel.

Next, replace the contents of body with:

```
Form {
  Section {
    // 1
    Picker("Age", selection: $viewModel.ageSelection) {
      ForEach(AnimalSearchAge.allCases, id: \.self) { age in
        Text(age.rawValue.capitalized)
      }
    }
    // 2
    .onChange(of: viewModel.ageSelection) { _ in
      viewModel.search()
    }

    // 3
    Picker("Type", selection: $viewModel.typeSelection) {
      ForEach(AnimalSearchType.allCases, id: \.self) { type in
        Text(type.rawValue.capitalized)
      }
    }
    // 4
    .onChange(of: viewModel.typeSelection) { _ in
      viewModel.search()
    }
  } footer: {
    Text("You can mix both, age and type, to make a more
accurate search.")
  }
```

```
    // 5
    Button("Clear", role: .destructive, action:
viewModel.clearFilters)
    Button("Done") {
      dismiss()
    }
  }
}
.navigationBarTitle("Filters")
.toolbar {
    // 6
    ToolbarItem {
      Button {
        dismiss()
      } label: {
        Label("Close", systemImage: "xmark.circle.fill")
      }
    }
  }
}
```

Here's what this code builds:

1. First, it adds a `Picker` view for selecting the pet's age. This value can either be baby, young, adult or senior which are the cases for `AnimalSearchAge`.

2. Then it adds an `onChange(of:perform:)` view modifier that triggers a call to `viewModel.search` when an age is selected.

3. It adds another `Picker` view for selecting the pet's type. This value can be cat, dog, rabbit, smallAndFurry, horse, bird, scalesFinsAndOther or barnyard, which are the cases for `AnimalSearchType`.

4. Then it adds an `onChange(of:perform:)` view modifier that also triggers a call to `viewModel.search`, but this time, with the selected type.

5. It adds two buttons, one for clearing both filters and another for dismissing the view.

6. Finally, it adds a toolbar button for dismissing the view.

You'll use this `Form` view to select the animal's age and type. Before you do that, you'll fix Xcode previews for this form.

At the bottom of the file, inside `SearchFilterView_Previews`, update `previews` with:

```
let context =
PersistenceController.preview.container.viewContext
NavigationView {
  SearchFilterView(
```

```
    viewModel: SearchViewModel(
      animalSearcher: AnimalSearcherMock(),
      animalStore: AnimalStoreService(context: context)
    )
  )
}
```

This code adds a view model to the preview with a mocked service, so you can render this form in Xcode previews.

Run Xcode previews by pressing **Command-Option-P**.

*Search filter view*.

Now that you're done with SearchFilterView, you have to add a button for presenting this new form.

# Adding a button to open SearchFilterView

Back inside **SearchView.swift**, add:

```
@State var filterPickerIsPresented = false
```

You'll use this property to present `SearchFilterView`.

Next, below the `overlay(alignment:content:)` at the bottom of `AnimalListView`, add:

```
// 1
.toolbar {
  ToolbarItem {
    Button {
      filterPickerIsPresented.toggle()
    } label: {
      Label("Filter", systemImage: "slider.horizontal.3")
    }
    // 2
    .sheet(isPresented: $filterPickerIsPresented) {
      NavigationView {
        SearchFilterView(viewModel: viewModel)
      }
    }
  }
}
```

This code:

1.  Adds a new button in the top right corner of the toolbar.

2.  It presents `SearchFilterView` inside a `NavigationView` using `sheet(isPresented:onDismiss:content:)`. The modal will appear when `filterPickerIsPresented` is true.

Build and run. Open the new filter view and select an age and type.

*Filter view on top of Search View*

Even though you can select an age and a type, the app doesn't yet filter the results. To fix this, you'll use a feature added to Swift 5.2, **callAsFunction**.

## Using callAsFunction to filter animals

**callAsFunction** is a Swift feature that lets you call types as if they were functions. The type implements a method called `callAsFunction`. When you call the type, it forwards the call to this method.

`callAsFunction` is a nice feature for types that behave like functions.

You'll create a type to filter animals with the text from the search bar and the age and type selected.

Create a new file inside **Search/viewModels** and name it **FilterAnimals.swift**. Add the following code to this file:

```
import SwiftUI

// 1
struct FilterAnimals {
```

```swift
// 2
let animals: FetchedResults<AnimalEntity>
let query: String
let age: AnimalSearchAge
let type: AnimalSearchType

// 3
func callAsFunction() -> [AnimalEntity] {
  let ageText = age.rawValue.lowercased()
  let typeText = type.rawValue.lowercased()
  // 4
  return animals.filter {
    if ageText != "none" {
      return $0.age.rawValue.lowercased() == ageText
    }
    return true
  }
  .filter {
    if typeText != "none" {
      return $0.type?.lowercased() == typeText
    }
    return true
  }
  .filter {
    if query.isEmpty {
      return true
    }
    return $0.name?.contains(query) ?? false
  }
}
}
```

Here you:

1. Declare a regular struct and name it **FilterAnimals**.

2. Declare properties for the animals you want to filter, the query from the search bar and the age and type selected.

3. Implement a method called `callAsFunction` that Swift forwards whenever you call this type like a function.

4. Chain `filter(_:)` calls to filter animals by name, age and type. First by age, then by type and finally by name.

Now, inside **SearchView.swift**, add:

```swift
private var filterAnimals: FilterAnimals {
  FilterAnimals(
    animals: animals,
    query: viewModel.searchText,
```

```
      age: viewModel.ageSelection,
      type: viewModel.typeSelection
  )
}
```

This creates a new computed property that creates a new `FilterAnimals` instance with the current animals displayed, text from the search bar and age and type selection.

Next, replace the content of `filteredAnimals` with:

```
guard viewModel.shouldFilter else { return [] }
return filterAnimals()
```

Now, `filteredAnimals` use the new instance of `FilterAnimals` to filter them by name, age and type.

Build and run. Filter by name, age and type to see the results.

*Search view with results after filtering*

# Improving the UI

The search feature is done. And yet, this view feels a bit too blank. When the user isn't filtering, the view has no content to show.

You'll add a suggestions view for showing the possible types of animals users can search for.

Open **SearchViewModel.swift** and inside `SearchViewModel`, add:

```
func selectTypeSuggestion(_ type: AnimalSearchType) {
  typeSelection = type
  search()
}
```

This method sets `typeSelection` to a selected type and triggers a search to the API.

Back inside **SearchView.swift**, add another overlay right below the `List`'s `toolbar` modifier with:

```
.overlay {
  // 1
  if filteredAnimals.isEmpty && viewModel.searchText.isEmpty {
    // 2
    SuggestionsGrid(suggestions: AnimalSearchType.suggestions) {
suggestion in
      // 3
      viewModel.selectTypeSuggestion(suggestion)
    }
    .frame(maxWidth: .infinity, maxHeight: .infinity, alignment:
.top)
  }
}
```

This code:

1. Adds a new overlay to the view that appears when `filteredAnimals` is empty, and there isn't any text in the search bar, nor any age and type selected.

2. Creates a `SuggestionsGrid`. This is a view contained in this chapter's starter project that shows a grid of animal types users can tap to filter.

3. If a suggestion is selected, you call `selectTypeSuggestion(_:)` to update the view model and fire a search.

Build and run to see the suggestions grid on the search view.

*Search screen showing search bar and browse by type*

# Testing your view model

To close this chapter, you'll write unit tests for your filters.

## Setting up test cases

Inside **PetSaveTests/Tests**, create a new group and name it **Search**.

Inside **Search**, create a new Swift file and name it
**SearchViewModelTestCase.swift**. Add:

```
import Foundation
import XCTest
@testable import PetSave

final class SearchViewModelTestCase: XCTestCase {
  let testContext =
PersistenceController.preview.container.viewContext
  // swiftlint:disable:next implicitly_unwrapped_optional
```

```
    var viewModel: SearchViewModel!

    override func setUp() {
      super.setUp()
      viewModel = SearchViewModel(
        animalSearcher: AnimalSearcherMock(),
        animalStore: AnimalStoreService(context: testContext)
      )
    }
  }
```

This code creates a new test case for testing `SearchViewModel`. It set's up the view model with an `AnimalSearcherMock` and an `AnimalStoreService` with an in-memory context, so each test has mock animals and an empty database to run.

You'll start by testing `shouldFilter` and how `searchText`, `ageSelection` and `typeSelection` affect this computed property.

## Testing shouldFilter

Still inside `SearchViewModelTestCase`, add:

```
func testShouldFilterIsFalseForEmptyFilters() {
  XCTAssertTrue(viewModel.searchText.isEmpty)
  XCTAssertEqual(viewModel.ageSelection, .none)
  XCTAssertEqual(viewModel.typeSelection, .none)
  XCTAssertFalse(viewModel.shouldFilter)
}
```

`SearchViewModel` starts with all properties with empty values. `searchText` is an empty `String` and `ageSelection` and `typeSelection` are `.none`. That means the user just opened the view and didn't search for anything. In this test case, you expect `shouldFilter` to be false.

Build and run the test by clicking the diamond play button at the side of the test function.

**Note**: You can also run all tests of a test case by clicking the diamond play button at the side of the class declaration.

*Filter test passed*

Awesome! Next, you'll test if changing any of the three properties is enough to change `shouldFilter` to `true`.

Add the following three methods:

```
func testShouldFilterIsTrueForSearchText() {
  viewModel.searchText = "Kiki"
  XCTAssertFalse(viewModel.searchText.isEmpty)
  XCTAssertEqual(viewModel.ageSelection, .none)
  XCTAssertEqual(viewModel.typeSelection, .none)
  XCTAssertTrue(viewModel.shouldFilter)
}

func testShouldFilterIsTrueForAgeFilter() {
  viewModel.ageSelection = .baby
  XCTAssertTrue(viewModel.searchText.isEmpty)
  XCTAssertEqual(viewModel.ageSelection, .baby)
  XCTAssertEqual(viewModel.typeSelection, .none)
  XCTAssertTrue(viewModel.shouldFilter)
}

func testShouldFilterIsTrueForTypeFilter() {
  viewModel.typeSelection = .cat
  XCTAssertTrue(viewModel.searchText.isEmpty)
  XCTAssertEqual(viewModel.ageSelection, .none)
  XCTAssertEqual(viewModel.typeSelection, .cat)
  XCTAssertTrue(viewModel.shouldFilter)
}
```

Build and test again.

*Should filters tests passed*

## Testing clearing filters

Next, you'll test if clearing the filters also changes `shouldFilter` when the search text is empty and when it's not.

Add the following two test methods, right below the previous ones:

```swift
func testClearFiltersSearchTextIsNotEmpty() {
  viewModel.typeSelection = .cat
  viewModel.ageSelection = .baby
  viewModel.searchText = "Kiki"

  viewModel.clearFilters()

  XCTAssertFalse(viewModel.searchText.isEmpty)
  XCTAssertEqual(viewModel.ageSelection, .none)
  XCTAssertEqual(viewModel.typeSelection, .none)
  XCTAssertTrue(viewModel.shouldFilter)
}

func testClearFiltersSearchTextIsEmpty() {
  viewModel.typeSelection = .cat
  viewModel.ageSelection = .baby

  viewModel.clearFilters()

  XCTAssertTrue(viewModel.searchText.isEmpty)
  XCTAssertEqual(viewModel.ageSelection, .none)
  XCTAssertEqual(viewModel.typeSelection, .none)
  XCTAssertFalse(viewModel.shouldFilter)
}
```

First, you select the type cat, age baby and add a query for **Kiki**. Then you clear the filters and check if the view should still filter since seartchText isn't empty.

The second method does the same but with a searchText empty, so shouldFilter should be false after calling clearFilters().

Build and run the tests.

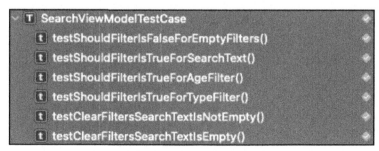

*Clear filters tests passed*

## Testing suggestion selection

All that's left is to test when the user selects a suggestion from `SuggestionGrid`.

Finally, still in **SearchViewModelTestCase.swift**, add the following test:

```swift
func testSelectTypeSuggestion() {
  viewModel.selectTypeSuggestion(.cat)

  XCTAssertTrue(viewModel.searchText.isEmpty)
  XCTAssertEqual(viewModel.ageSelection, .none)
  XCTAssertEqual(viewModel.typeSelection, .cat)
  XCTAssertTrue(viewModel.shouldFilter)
}
```

This method calls `selectTypeSuggestion(_:)` and checks if the only property that changed was `typeSelection`.

Build and run the test case.

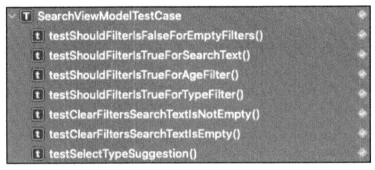

*All tests passed*

# Key points

- The new `searchable(text:placement:prompt:)` modifier adds a search bar that you can use to search with text.

- You can use view models to search data **locally** and make requests to an **external** web API.

- **Extracting** views to share code between features is easy with SwiftUI.

- You can use `@ViewBuilder` to create SwiftUI views that take other views in a closure.

- `callAsFunctions` is great for types that behave like functions.

# Where to go from here?

Nice work! You now have a complete search feature in PetSave. This is the second feature you've developed so far, you should be proud. In the next chapter, you'll learn about modularization and work on the onboarding feature for PetSave.

If you want to learn how to query Core Data using NSPredicate with a text from the search bar, checkout out our article Dynamic Core Data with SwiftUI Tutorial for iOS (https://www.raywenderlich.com/27201015-dynamic-core-data-with-swiftui-tutorial-for-ios).

To learn more SwiftUI views and `@ViewBuilders`, check out our book SwiftUI Apprentice (https://www.raywenderlich.com/books/swiftui-apprentice).

# Section III: Modularizing Your App

Don't reinvent the wheel. Modules that others have built and provided to the community can save you time. You can also make your own modules to use later in your development or make them available to the community.

Modules (and the features they come from) have some costs though, one of which is navigating between features. In this section, you'll explore how Xcode can help in not only the creation of, but the use of, modules in your app, and understand how features can be tied together with navigation.

# Chapter 7: Multi-Module App

By Aaqib Hussain

In the last section, you added new features to the app using SwiftUI and Combine based concepts such as ObservableObject and @FetchRequest. You used these concepts to implement features like Search and Locating animals near you. These features made the app more usable. But what about making our code more reusable?

In this section, you'll learn how to modularize the app and navigate between different modules. In this chapter, you'll learn about the benefits of modularization and what tools are at your disposal to support it.

More specifically, you'll learn about:

- Xcode support in the build process using **build targets** and **workspace compilation**.

- The different types of frameworks you can create for your apps.

- Some of the dependency management options available for iOS development

With the acquired skills, you'll create an onboarding framework for PetSave. So users can have a nice introduction to your app.

Onboarding screens welcome users the first time they launch your app. Since their first impression *could be* the last impression, it's *quite* important for the developers to get this right.

Are you excited to get onboarded? Here you go!

# Modularization

**Modularization** is a software design technique that lets you separate an app's features into many smaller, independent modules. To achieve modularization, one must think out of the box. You use encapsulation and abstraction by exposing the methods you want the app to use and hiding all the unnecessary or complex details.

## Benefits of modularization

Modularization comes with many benefits, including:

- Reusability

- Time and cost savings

- Community support

- Improved build time

Using modularization helps you write more robust and scalable code. Now, you'll go over each one of the benefits to understand what they can mean for your codebase.

### Reusability

Consider you develop an onboarding framework where you customize texts and images before showing them in the app. To create such a framework, you must implement it so it's independent of the app. Then, you share and reuse it in other projects.

### Time and cost savings

Reusability leads to time and cost savings. In the example of creating an onboarding module, you can easily integrate the onboarding module into a different project. It's like plug and play that saves you both time and development cost.

### Community support

By publishing the onboarding module as public on a platform like GitHub, you get support from the open-source community on fixing bugs you might have missed. Developers simply open a pull request for a bug fix or add a new feature.

# Build time

When you rebuild the project after changing the onboarding framework, Xcode won't recompile the entire app. Instead, it'll *only* compile the changed module. This results in faster build times and, in general, accelerated development. But for you to guarantee this, you have two know the different kinds of frameworks and the use case for each one, you'll go over that later in this chapter.

# Xcode support in the build process

While Xcode comes with many features, the two features you'll learn about in this chapter are **build targets** and **workspace compilation**.

# Build targets

A **target** is a modularized structure. A target takes its instruction through build settings and build phases. A project can contain more than one target, and one target can depend on another. These targets can be something like the watchOS version of your app or represent your app test suite.

If one target is dependent on another, and they're in the same workspace, Xcode automatically builds the one the other depends on first. For example:

Consider target A and target B. If B is dependent on A, then Xcode will build A first. Such a relationship is an **implicit dependency**.

Suppose two of your targets depend on a single dependency, and you want to link one target to a different version. In that case, you add an **explicit dependency** in the build settings to override the implicit dependency.

A typical Xcode project contains Main, Unit test and UI test targets. When you add a framework to your project, it's added as a separate target.

# Workspace compilation

A **workspace** combines projects and other documents under one roof so you can work on them together. It can have multiple projects or documents you want to work on. It also manages implicit and explicit dependencies among the included targets.

A workspace holds references to all the files included in each of its contained projects. Then, it handles tasks like indexing files, code completion and jump to definition.

You can refactor a piece of code in a framework and see the changes throughout the targets using it in one go. All the projects inside a workspace share the same build directory. Thus, all files are visible to each other. If two of your targets use the same dependency, you don't need to copy it in both projects. Xcode is intelligent enough to copy it *just* once.

> **Note**: Apple uses the term **framework** to refer to modules. You'll see the term **framework** instead of module throughout this chapter and later on.

# What is a framework?

A **framework** is a bundle that can contain resources of any type, such as classes, assets, nib files or localizable strings. Frameworks encapsulate and modularize code, making it reusable. Common iOS frameworks include **Foundation**, **UIKit** and **SwiftUI**.

## Types of Frameworks

There are two types of frameworks in iOS: **Static** and **Dynamic**. Take a moment to learn about these frameworks and how they differ.

## Static Framework

**Static** frameworks consist of code that doesn't change because it's linked at compile time. Static frameworks generate a **.a** extension. They *only* hold code and gets copied with the app's executable, making the executable size larger.

It has faster function calls, even when you need to call *just* one function the entire framework is present in the app. Thus, this type of framework guarantees its presence in the app. When you change the framework, the entire app recompiles.

The networking layer you built earlier in the book, *could be* considered a classic example of creating a static framework.

# Dynamic Framework

Unlike static frameworks, **dynamic** frameworks have a codebase that may change and contain other resources, like images. Dynamic frameworks generate the extension **.dylib**. It's not copied, but linked with the app's executable at runtime, thus, resulting in a smaller app size.

As the name suggests, these frameworks are dynamic, so the code only loads when it's needed. The system *usually* holds a single copy of the framework. The apps then share this common framework's copy.

Function calls are slower because the framework is located outside the app and shared. When you change it, you don't recompile the entire app. Instead, you only compile the framework.

To check the type of framework, open the **Final** project. In **Project target**, select **PetSaveOnboarding**. Go to **Build Settings ▸ Linking ▸ Mach-O Type**. Here, you'll see the framework is dynamic, but you could change it in the dropdown if you wanted to.

*Framework type in build settings.*

Resources are a classic example of creating a dynamic framework. Next, you'll create a dynamic onboarding framework.

> **Note**: Previously, Apple only supported static frameworks. With iOS 8+, Apple allowed the use of dynamic frameworks. You can read more about frameworks in the official documentation. (https://developer.apple.com/library/archive/documentation/MacOSX/Conceptual/BPFrameworks/Concepts/WhatAreFrameworks.html)

# Creating a dynamic onboarding framework

It's finally time to start coding your very first framework! Your goal is to reach this:

*Final app with onboarding framework.*

Open the **starter** project. Click **File ▸ New ▸ Target** in **iOS**. Then, in the filter, type **Framework**.

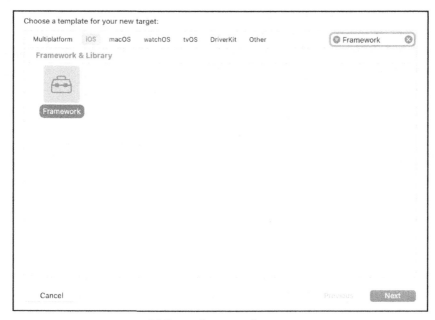

*Adding a framework target.*

Select **Framework** and click **Next**. Give the product name **PetSaveOnboarding**.Make sure to uncheck **Include Tests** and **Include Documentation** as you don't need them for this chapter. Then click **Finish**.

*Options for target.*

> **Note:** At the time of writing, the latest Xcode version was 13.2, which selects iOS 15.2 as the framework's deployment target by default. To avoid any future problems, change this target to iOS 15.0.

You'll see a **PetSaveOnboarding** in the project navigator:

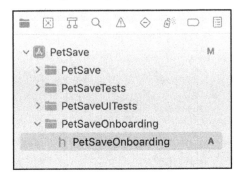

*PetSaveOnboarding listed on the project navigator.*

Next, create a group named **Resources** under **PetSaveOnboarding**. Then, in this chapter's materials, find the **assets** folder.

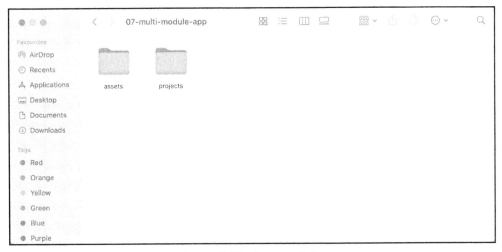

*Assets folder in materials.*

You'll see some pet and color resources. Drag and drop the contents of **assets** into **Resources**.

In **Add to targets**, choose **PetSave** and **PetSaveOnboarding**. Then click **Finish**.

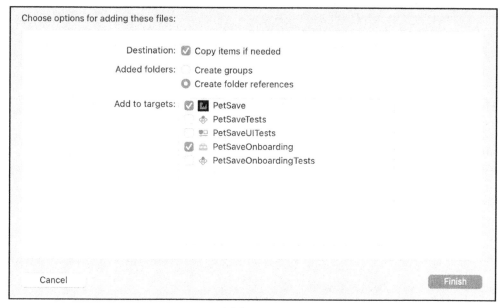

*Add targets.*

The project directory now looks like this:

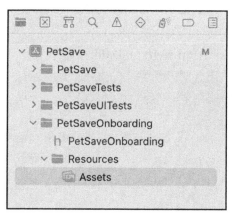

*Add assets contents into Resources.*

Still in **PetSaveOnboarding**, create a group named **Extensions**. Then create three files: **Bundle+Extension.swift**, **Color+Extension.swift** and **Image+Extension.swift**.

Open **Bundle+Extension.swift** and add:

```
extension Bundle {
  public static var module: Bundle? {
    Bundle(identifier: "com.raywenderlich.PetSaveOnboarding")
  }
}
```

This bundle refers to the framework using its identifier. It helps in accessing the assets.

Then, open **Color+Extension.swift** and add:

```
import SwiftUI

extension Color {

  static var rwGreen: Color {
    Color("rw-green", bundle: .module)
  }

  static var rwDark: Color {
    Color("rw-dark", bundle: .module)
  }
}
```

Here, you add the default theme colors that you'll use for styling the buttons and the page controls.

Finally, open **Image+Extension.swift** and add:

```
import SwiftUI

public extension Image {
  static var bird: Image {
    Image("creature-bird-blue-fly", bundle: .module)
  }

  static var catPurple: Image {
    Image("creature-cat-purple-cute", bundle: .module)
  }

  static var catPurr: Image {
    Image("creature-cat-purr", bundle: .module)
  }

  static var chameleon: Image {
    Image("creature-chameleon", bundle: .module)
  }
```

```swift
  static var dogBoneStand: Image {
    Image("creature-dog-and-bone", bundle: .module)
  }

  static var dogBone: Image {
    Image("creature-dog-bone", bundle: .module)
  }

  static var dogTennisBall: Image {
    Image("creature-dog-tennis-ball", bundle: .module)
  }
}
```

This extension refers to all the image assets from the assets you added.

Now, create a group named **Model**. Under it, create files named
**OnboardingModel.swift** and **Pet.swift**.

Open **OnboardingModel.swift** and add:

```swift
import SwiftUI

public struct OnboardingModel: Identifiable {
  public let id = UUID()
  // 1
  let title: String
  let description: String
  let image: Image

  // 2
  let nextButtonTitle: String
  let skipButtonTitle: String

  // 3
  public init(
    title: String,
    description: String,
    image: Image,
    nextButtonTitle: String = "Next",
    skipButtonTitle: String = "Skip") {
      self.title = title
      self.description = description
      self.image = image
      self.nextButtonTitle = nextButtonTitle
      self.skipButtonTitle = skipButtonTitle
  }
}
```

Here's a code breakdown:

1. Creates `title`, `description` and `image` to hold the data that appears on each page of the onboarding screen.

2. These properties hold the titles for the **Next** and **Skip** buttons shown on each page.

3. This is an initializer with default titles for the buttons.

Now, open **Pet.swift** and add:

```swift
import SwiftUI

// 1
struct Pet: Identifiable {
  let id = UUID()
  let petImage: Image
  let position: CGPoint
}

// 2
extension Pet {
  static let backgroundPets: [Pet] = {
    let bounds = UIScreen.main.bounds
    return [
      Pet(petImage: .bird,
        position: .init(x: bounds.minX + 50, y: 20)),
      Pet(petImage: .catPurple,
        position: .init(x: bounds.maxX, y: bounds.maxY / 2)),
      Pet(petImage: .catPurr,
        position: .init(x: bounds.maxX, y: bounds.maxY - 100)),
      Pet(petImage: .chameleon,
        position: .init(x: bounds.minX, y: bounds.maxY / 2)),
      Pet(petImage: .dogBoneStand,
        position: .init(x: bounds.minX, y: bounds.maxY / 1.5)),
      Pet(petImage: .dogBone,
        position: .init(x: bounds.maxX - 50, y: 50)),
      Pet(petImage: .dogTennisBall,
        position: .init(x: bounds.minX, y: bounds.maxY - 10))
    ]
  }()
}
```

Here's what you added:

1. This structure contains the pet's image and the position shown on the onboarding background view.

2. A list of pets with some tried and tested positions that look good on the view.

Now that the initial setup is complete, you'll add your first view to the framework.

Under **PetSaveOnboarding**, create a SwiftUI view named **OnboardingView.swift** and replace the default code with:

```
import SwiftUI

struct OnboardingView: View {
  // 1
  let onboarding: OnboardingModel

  var body: some View {
    ZStack {
      RoundedRectangle(cornerRadius: 12, style: .circular)
        .fill(.white)
        .shadow(radius: 12)
        .padding(.horizontal, 20)
      VStack(alignment: .center) {
        VStack {
          // 2
          Text(onboarding.title)
            .foregroundColor(.rwDark)
            .font(.largeTitle)
            .bold()
            .multilineTextAlignment(.center)
            .padding(.horizontal, 10)

          Text(onboarding.description)
            .foregroundColor(.rwDark)
            .multilineTextAlignment(.center)
            .padding([.top, .bottom], 10)
            .padding(.horizontal, 10)

          onboarding.image
            .resizable()
            .frame(width: 140, height: 140, alignment: .center)
            .foregroundColor(.rwDark)
            .aspectRatio(contentMode: .fit)
        }
        .padding()
      }
    }
  }
}
```

This is the base view of the onboarding screen. It:

1.  Holds the onboarding model's object.

2.  Sets the title, description and image from the model to the UI.

Then, add another SwiftUI view and call it **OnboardingBackgroundView.swift**. This
view acts as a background for the `OnboardingView`. Replace the code with:

```
import SwiftUI

struct OnboardingBackgroundView: View {
  // 1
  let backgroundPets = Pet.backgroundPets
  // 2
  var body: some View {
    ZStack {
      ForEach(backgroundPets) { pet in
        pet.petImage
          .resizable()
          .frame(width: 200, height: 200, alignment: .center)
          .position(pet.position)
      }
    }
  }
}
```

Here's a code breakdown:

1.  An array holding all pets displayed in the background.

2.  Displays each pet on a view.

Now, create another SwiftUI view named **PetSaveOnboardingView.swift** and add
the following code before body:

```
@State var currentPageIndex = 0
// 2
public init(items: [OnboardingModel]) {
  self.items = items
}
// 3
private var onNext: (_ currentIndex: Int) -> Void = { _ in }
private var onSkip: () -> Void = {}
// 4
private var items: [OnboardingModel] = []
// 5
private var nextButtonTitle: String {
  items[currentPageIndex].nextButtonTitle
}
private var skipButtonTitle: String {
  items[currentPageIndex].skipButtonTitle
}
```

Here's what you added:

1.  Holds the current index of the onboarding view.

2.  The initializer to read the onboarding model array.

3.  A completion handler for listening to Next and Skip button actions.

4.  Holds the array that contains all of the onboarding models.

5.  Titles for the Next and Skip buttons.

Now, replace body with:

```
public var body: some View {
  if items.isEmpty {
    Text("No items to show.")
  } else {
      VStack {
        TabView(selection: $currentPageIndex) {
          // 1
          ForEach(0..<items.count) { index in
            OnboardingView(onboarding: items[index])
              .tag(index)
          }
        }
        .padding(.bottom, 10)
        .tabViewStyle(.page)
        .indexViewStyle(.page(backgroundDisplayMode: .always))
        .onAppear(perform: setupPageControlAppearance)
        // 2
        Button(action: next) {
          Text(nextButtonTitle)
            .frame(maxWidth: .infinity, maxHeight: 44)
        }
        .animation(nil, value: currentPageIndex)
        .buttonStyle(OnboardingButtonStyle(color: .rwDark))

        Button(action: onSkip) {
          Text(skipButtonTitle)
            .frame(maxWidth: .infinity, maxHeight: 44)
        }
        .animation(nil, value: currentPageIndex)
        .buttonStyle(OnboardingButtonStyle(color: .rwGreen))
        .padding(.bottom, 20)
      }
      .background(OnboardingBackgroundView())
  }
}
```

Here is what this does:

1.  Creates `OnboardingView` to show each onboarding item in the array.

2.  Next and Skip buttons added to the view.

Right after body add this:

```
// 1
public func onNext(
    action: @escaping (_ currentIndex: Int) -> Void
) -> Self {
    var petSaveOnboardingView = self
    petSaveOnboardingView.onNext = action
    return petSaveOnboardingView
}

public func onSkip(action: @escaping () -> Void) -> Self {
    var petSaveOnboardingView = self
    petSaveOnboardingView.onSkip = action
    return petSaveOnboardingView
}

// 2
private func setupPageControlAppearance() {
    UIPageControl.appearance().currentPageIndicatorTintColor =
        UIColor(.rwGreen)
}

// 3
private func next() {
    withAnimation {
        if currentPageIndex + 1 < items.count {
            currentPageIndex += 1
        } else {
            currentPageIndex = 0
        }
    }
    onNext(currentPageIndex)
}
```

Here, you add:

1. Create `onNext(action:)` and `onSkip(action:)` to listen to the buttons' actions.

2. This method sets the selected page control indicator color.

3. Changes the index of the current onboarding view with animation.

At the end of the file, add this:

```
struct OnboardingButtonStyle: ButtonStyle {
    let color: Color
    func makeBody(configuration: Configuration) -> some View {
        configuration.label
            .background(color)
            .clipShape(Capsule())
            .buttonStyle(.plain)
```

```
        .padding(.horizontal, 20)
        .foregroundColor(.white)
    }
}
```

This is the custom style you used for the buttons on PetSaveOnboardingView.

> **Note**: When creating frameworks, the structures or classes can use a **public** access modifier so that other projects can call them.

To preview the views you created so far, create a private extension like this:

```
private extension PreviewProvider {
  static var mockOboardingModel: [OnboardingModel] {
    [
      OnboardingModel(
        title: "Welcome to\n PetSave",
        description:
          "Looking for a Pet?\n Then you're at the right place",
        image: .bird
      ),
      OnboardingModel(
        title: "Search...",
        description:
          "Search from a list of our huge database of animals.",
        image: .dogBoneStand,
        nextButtonTitle: "Allow"
      ),
      OnboardingModel(
        title: "Nearby",
        description:
          "Find pets to adopt from nearby your place...",
        image: .chameleon
      )
    ]
  }
}
```

Here, you initialize the mock onboarding model with the values shown on each page.

Then, replace PetSaveOnboardingView_Previews implementation with this:

```
struct PetSaveOnboardingView_Previews: PreviewProvider {
  static var previews: some View {
    PetSaveOnboardingView(items: mockOboardingModel)
  }
}
```

This code previews the view using mock data.

The preview on your canvas shows this:

*Onboarding preview.*

That's so cool!

Now it's time to use the framework you created in the app.

The onboarding screens for any app usually show up once, the first time the user launches the app. You'll now build this logic bysaving the app's state in `UserDefaults`.

Open **AppUserDefaultsKeys.swift** and add the following property to the already existing enum:

```
static let onboarding = "onboarding"
```

This key saves the state of each user's action to indicate if they're launching the app for the first time or a subsequent time.

Next, open **AppMain.swift** and import the `PetSaveOnboarding` framework:

```
import PetSaveOnboarding
```

In the existing structure, add:

```
// 1
@AppStorage(AppUserDefaultsKeys.onboarding)
  var shouldPresentOnboarding = true
// 2
var onboardingModels: [OnboardingModel] {
  [
    OnboardingModel(
      title: "Welcome to\n PetSave",
      description:
        "Looking for a Pet?\n Then you're at the right place",
      image: .bird
    ),
    OnboardingModel(
      title: "Search...",
      description:
        "Search from a list of our huge database of animals.",
      image: .dogBoneStand
    ),
    OnboardingModel(
      title: "Nearby",
      description:
        "Find pets to adopt from nearby your place...",
      image: .chameleon
    )
  ]
}
```

Here's what you added:

1. @AppStorage is a SwiftUI property wrapper that works hand-in-hand with UserDefaults. It saves the value of shouldPresentOnboarding in UserDefaults.

2. The model data to show the first time of app launch.

Next, update the body scene like this:

```
var body: some Scene {
  WindowGroup {
    ContentView()
    // 1
    .fullScreenCover(
      isPresented: $shouldPresentOnboarding, onDismiss: nil
    ) {
        // 2
        PetSaveOnboardingView(items: onboardingModels)
        .onSkip { // 3
          shouldPresentOnboarding = false
        }
```

```
        }
      }
   }
```

Here's a code breakdown:

1.  Shows the full-screen cover if `shouldPresentOnboarding` is `true`.

2.  Presents `PetSaveOnboardingView` with the model data.

3.  On Skip button tap, set `shouldPresentOnboarding` to `false` to avoid showing the onboarding again.

Finally, build and run. You'll see the onboarding screen looks like this:

*Final app preview.*

Nicely done, you deserve a pat on the back!

Now that you had developed a framework, you need to decide how to distribute it. There are multiple options for developers to manage and distribute their frameworks and libraries. Swift Package Manager is the de-facto choice for handling dependencies since Apple introduced it with Xcode 11.

In the remaining segments of this chapter, you'll go over the following tools and concepts:

- Cocoapods.

- Carthage.

- Swift packages.

- Differences between dependency managers.

- Creating and configuring a Swift package.

- Adding code and resources to the package.

- Publishing the package to GitHub.

- Replacing the PetSaveOnboarding framework with the published Swift package.

# What is Cocoapods?

Cocoapods is a dependency manager that supports publishing and maintaining libraries in Swift and Objective-C. You can use it to import multiple libraries in your project. It's built with Ruby, and you can use the default version of Ruby on Mac to install it.

## Using Cocoapods

There's a large variety of third-party libraries written with Cocoapods on GitHub. To consume these libraries, initialize Cocoapods in your project and put all your dependencies in a file called **Podfile**.

Once you install your dependencies using:

```
pod install
```

Cocoapods will create a **.xcworkspace** containing all your source code and dependencies.

> **Note**: To read in detail about Cocoapods visit the Cocoapods website (https://cocoapods.org/).

# What is Carthage?

Like Cocoapods, Carthage is a dependency manager. It's the first one to support Swift that was *also* written in Swift. It supports macOS and iOS applications.

You need to install Carthage and follow a similar process as the one you do for Cocoapods by indicating your dependencies in a file called **Cartfile**, then you run:

```
carthage update --use-xcframeworks
```

In your project, this command generates a file named **Cartfile.resolved** and a directory named **Carthage**. The **Carthage/Build** directory contains the built frameworks as an **.xcframework**.

> **Note:** This tutorial will help you get started with Carthage (https://www.raywenderlich.com/7649117-carthage-tutorial-getting-started). Carthage also has very detailed documentation on GitHub (https://github.com/Carthage/Carthage).

# What are Swift packages?

Swift Packages are repositories that enable developers to create, publish and maintain a package. Furthermore, they help to add, remove and manage Swift package dependencies. Besides Swift language, they allow porting of code from Objective-C, Objective-C++, C or C++.

Swift packages use the open-source project Swift Package Manager (https://github.com/apple/swift-package-manager) or SPM. The Swift team introduced SPM in Swift 3.0. They came up with a tool to manage the distribution of code. SPM downloads, compiles and links libraries. It's an integral part of the Swift build system and provides a good alternative to other package managers like CocoaPods.

When you create a Swift Package, it comes with a **Sources** folder and a manifest file called **Package.swift**.

**Package.swift** describes the package and contains configuration information such as the package name, libraries, executables, dependencies and targets.

# Differences between dependency managers

You've so far studied Cocoapods, Carthage and Swift Package. Here, you'll learn the basic differences between them:

| Properties | Cocoapods | Carthage | Swift Package |
|---|---|---|---|
| Agnostic of the project | ✗ | ☑ | ☑ |
| Easy to manage | ✗ | ✗ | ☑ |
| Supported by Apple | ✗ | ✗ | ☑ |
| Thousands of open source libraries | ☑ | ☑ | ✗ |
| Requires manual setup | ✗ | ☑ | ✗ |
| Supports dynamic and static frameworks | ☑ | ☑ | ☑ |
| Faster build time | ✗ | ☑ | ☑ |
| Dependent dependency management | ☑ | ☑ | ☑ |

Apple supports and recommends Swift package, and Xcode provides ease with integrating it.

> **Note**: If you're interested in learning about creating your own Cocoapods or Carthage, check out the documentation on Cocoapods (https://guides.cocoapods.org/making/making-a-cocoapod.html) and Carthage (https://github.com/Carthage/Carthage#supporting-carthage-for-your-framework).

Now that you've gained enough theoretical knowledge about Swift packages, it's time to get cracking with some practicals.

# Creating and configuring a Swift package

Start by selecting **Package** from **File ▸ New**.

*Creating a package.*

Name the package **PetSaveOnboarding**. Then, select **create Git repository on my Mac** and click **Create**.

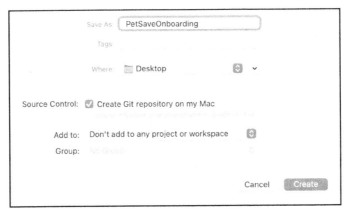

*Adding name of the package.*

This opens a new window. In the project navigator, you see:

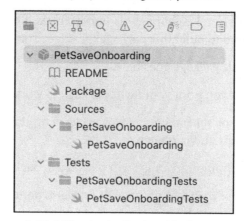

*Initial files in the Project Navigator.*

Open **Package.swift** and replace the content with:

```
// 1
// swift-tools-version:5.5
// The swift-tools-version declares the minimum version of
// Swift required to build this package.

import PackageDescription

let package = Package(
  // 2
  name: "PetSaveOnboarding",
  // 3
  platforms: [.iOS(.v15), .macOS(.v10_15)],
  // 4
  products: [
    .library(
    name: "PetSaveOnboarding",
    targets: ["PetSaveOnboarding"]),
  ],
  // 5
  dependencies: [],
  // 6
  targets: [
    .target(
    name: "PetSaveOnboarding",
    resources: [.copy("Resources/Assets.xcassets")]),
  ]
)
```

Here's a breakdown:

1. The **swift-tools-version:5.5** comment is important as it tells Swift the minimum Swift version required to build this package.

2. The name of the Swift package goes here.

3. Define the platforms you want your Swift package to work on.

4. It defines the library or executables a Swift package produces. It also makes it available to other apps and packages.

5. Add any third-party frameworks the Swift package depends on.

6. It defines the target of the Swift package. It may also define other test targets or packages this target depends on.

Then, delete the group **Tests** as it's not needed.

## Adding code and resources

Now, using Finder, replace **Sources/PetSaveOnboarding** in your package with the **PetSaveOnboarding** framework.

The package's project navigator now looks like this:

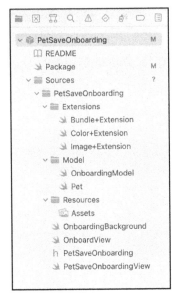

*After copying the framework from the starter project.*

Remove the file **Bundle+Extension.swift** since the Swift package contains its own `module` property. Then, remove **PetSaveOnboarding.h** because you don't need it anymore.

To avoid any Mac-related compilation errors, set the build schema as any **Any iOS Device** or choose any iPhone simulator. Then, build the project.

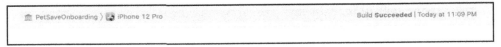

*Swift package built successfully.*

Super! The Swift package is now ready for publishing.

## Publishing the Swift package

**Note**: To follow the rest of the chapter you'll need a Github account. If you don't have one already, create one by going to https://github.com/signup.

Now that you created a Swift Package, it's time to publish it to GitHub. Log in to your GitHub (https://github.com) account or create one if you don't have one.

Then, create a public or a private repository named **PetSaveOnboarding**. You'll see a screen similar to this:

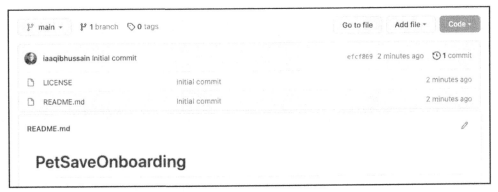

*Repository screen on GitHub.*

Now follow the steps below:

1. Go to the directory that contains your package files using the terminal.

2. Execute the following command to add the newly created remote repository as the origin:

```
git remote add origin https://github.com/<----github-user-name----
>/PetSaveOnboarding.git
```

3. Execute the following command to add all those files to the repository, commit and push them:

```
git add --all
git commit -m "Add package sources"
git push --set-upstream origin main
```

And it's done! Congratulations, you published your package to GitHub. Now, it's time to test if you can consume the package in your project.

# Consuming the Swift package

Open the **PetSave** app with the framework you created earlier. Now, you'll replace the framework with the published GitHub package.

Select **File ▸ Add Packages**:

*Managing Swift package.*

In the search bar, paste the repository link that you created. Then click **Add Package**.

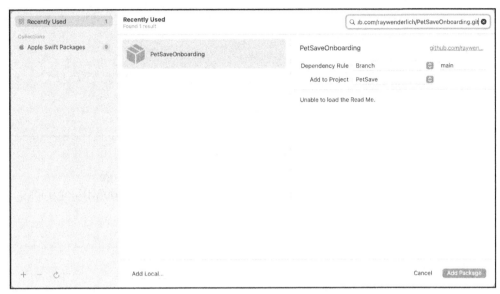

*Searching and adding Swift package.*

Soon after, Xcode will verify the Swift package and prompt you with the following:

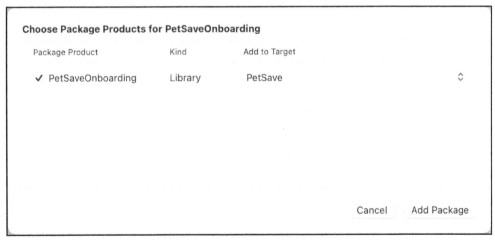

*Choosing package.*

Click **Add Package** and voilà!. In the **PetSave project ▸ PackageDependencies**, you'll see the name and location of the project like this:

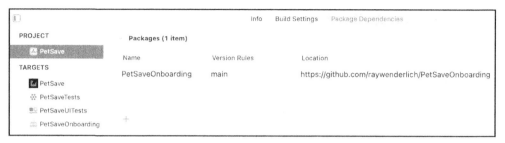

*Package details.*

Also, in the Project navigator, you'll see your package under **Package Dependencies**. Right-clicking **Package Dependencies** provides you with options like updating to the latest packages versions later if need be.

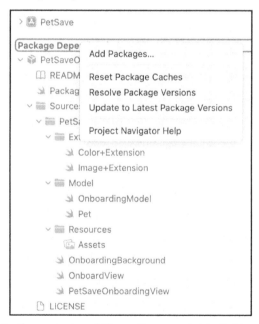

*Swift package added to the project and the options on right-clicking Package Description.*

Finally, delete the **PetSaveOnboarding** framework from the project.

Build and run. You'll see the onboarding screen, this time using Swift packages.

That's so cool, right? You did a great job.

# Key points

- **Modularization** leads to time and cost savings, reusability and faster build times.

- A **framework** is an encapsulated and modularized piece of reusable bundle.

- **Static** frameworks link code at compile time. **Dynamic** frameworks link code at runtime.

- `@AppStorage` is a SwiftUI property wrapper for saving values in `UserDefaults`.

- **Swift Packages** are repositories that enable developers to create, publish and maintain a package. They are managed using **Swift Package Manager (SPM)**.

- Cocoapods and Carthage are alternatives to SPM, which you can use to create and use libraries.

# Where to go from here?

This marks the end of this chapter. You got familiarized and grasped a lot of concepts related to modularization. You learned how modularization can play a vital role in making your overall development faster.

If you want to learn more about creating a framework in iOS with Creating a Framework for iOS tutorial (https://www.raywenderlich.com/17753301-creating-a-framework-for-ios#toc-anchor-002). You can also check out screencasts on Reusable iOS Frameworks (https://www.raywenderlich.com/10318291-reusable-ios-frameworks) and Swift packages (https://www.raywenderlich.com/4167538-sharing-and-editing-swift-packages-with-swift-package-manager). Learn more concepts like local and remote packages with the tutorial on Swift Package Manager (https://www.raywenderlich.com/7242045-swift-package-manager-for-ios).

You can check Apple's documentation on Swift Packages (https://developer.apple.com/documentation/swift_packages). Moreover, go to the official Swift Package Manager (https://www.swift.org/package-manager/) website to read more about it.

In the next chapter, you'll learn all about the ins and outs of SwiftUI's **Navigation**. You'll go over all the possible ways you can perform navigation in SwiftUI.

Ready to navigate your way to the next chapter? Vamos! :]

# Chapter 8: Navigation

By Aaqib Hussain

Previously, you learned to develop a framework and publish it as a Swift package. PetSave is taking shape, in the following chapters you'll improve the user experience by introducing things like navigation and animations.

Navigation allows you to create experiences for your users. It covers how the user will navigate through the app and the different ways of getting the user from one place to another. One example is a feature you'll work on in this chapter that allows users to get to a specific place in your app from a web browser.

> Please note that this chapter is optional. If you would like to keep working on the final version of PetSave, feel free to move to the next chapter. Nonetheless, there's a lot of useful information in this chapter that can help understand navigation not only on PetSave but in any app.

In this chapter, you'll learn in detail about:

- Navigation view

- Types of navigation

- Passing data between views

- Navigating using a router

- Navigate between SwiftUI and UIKit views

- Presenting views

- Tab view

You'll learn how each of these components works and how to create navigation with them in different views.

It all starts with the **navigation view**.

# Navigation view

`NavigationView` lets you arrange views in a navigation stack. Users can navigate to a destination view via a `NavigationLink`. The destination view is pushed into the stack. Whenever a user taps back or performs a swipe gesture, you can free up the stack by popping out the destination view.

You style the `NavigationView` with `navigationViewStyle(_:)`. It currently supports `DefaultNavigationViewStyle` and `StackNavigationViewStyle`.

- `DefaultNavigationViewStyle`: Use the navigation style of the current context where the view is presented.

- `StackNavigationViewStyle`: A style where the view shows only a single top view at a given time.

> **Note:** `DoubleColumnNavigationViewStyle` is now deprecated. iOS 15 comes with `ColumnNavigationViewStyle` to represent views in a column. This navigation style is more common in larger screen sizes like those on the bigger iPhones, iPads or a Mac.

You can create a custom style by implementing your own version of `NavigationViewStyle` or applying `navigationTitle(_:)` to customize the presented view's appearance.

# Navigation link

A `NavigationLink` is a view that controls a navigation presentation. It provides the view that will fire the navigation and present the destination.

NavigationLink can reside directly inside a NavigationView. It's commonly used with a List or Button or on some action performed by the user.

Open **AnimalListView.swift** and take a look at body:

```
var body: some View {
  // 1
  List {
  // 2
    ForEach(animals) { animal in
      // 3
      NavigationLink(destination: AnimalDetailsView()) {
        AnimalRow(animal: animal)
      }
    }

    footer
  } // 4
  .listStyle(.plain)
}
```

Here's a code breakdown:

1.  The top-level view is List.

2.  List nests a ForEach to render the animals.

3.  NavigationLink takes in the destination view you want to show. When the user taps this view, the destination view gets nested inside the current view.

4.  The list style is plain.

To render only the text that the user taps to go to the destination view, use a convenience initializer that takes in a string and creates the Text view. Replace the entire ForEach with:

```
ForEach(animals) { animal in
  NavigationLink(
    animal.name ?? "",
    destination: AnimalDetailsView()
  )
}
```

**Note**: In Xcode, double-click *any* curly opening brace to select the entire code block within the curly opening and closing braces. You can also use **Command-/** to comment the entire code block or press **delete** to delete the entire code block.

Build and run. You'll see this render:

*Animals near you view with just animal names.*

Alternatively, you can do navigation programmatically, using the navigation link like this:

```
@State var shouldShowDetails: Int? = -1
var body: some View {
  List {
    ForEach(Array(animals.enumerated()), id: \.offset)
{ index, animal in
        NavigationLink(
          animal.name ?? "",
          destination: AnimalDetailsView(),
          tag: index,
          selection: $shouldShowDetails
        )
    }

    footer
  }
  .listStyle(.plain)
}
```

You use the navigation link's initializer with `selection` and `tag` parameters. Here, the navigation view presents the destination view when the `index` matches the bound property `shouldShowDetails`.

# Types of navigation

Navigation plays a vital role in giving the user a seamless experience. You must implement navigation so that the app works smoothly. Apple provides three styles of navigation:

- Hierarchical Navigation

- Flat Navigation

- Content-Driven or Experience-Driven Navigation

## Hierarchical navigation

In hierarchical navigation, the root view is the navigation view. You go from one screen to another. The navigation view pushes these screens into a navigation stack. You'll find this navigation style in the **Settings** and **Mail** apps.

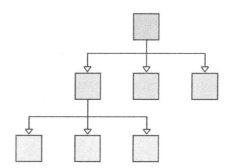

*Hierarchical navigation diagram.*

## Flat navigation

Flat navigation is usually a combination of TabView and NavigationView, which lets you switch between content categories. The **Music** and **App Store** apps are examples of such navigation.

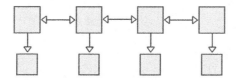

*Flat navigation diagram.*

# Content-driven or experience-driven navigation

Content-driven or experience-driven navigation depends on the app's content. Navigation may also depend on a user navigating to a particular screen. The **Games** and **Books** apps are examples of Content-Driven navigation.

*Content-driven or Experience navigation diagram.*

It's not written in stone that you can only use one of these navigation styles in a given instance. For example, you may combine flat with hierarchical. Many apps use multiple navigation styles.

However, it's important to always give the user a clear path for navigation. Users must know where they are in your app at all times. Make sure you provide users with the minimum number of taps or swaps to reach their destination.

# Passing data between views

There are four ways to pass data:

- Use a property.

- Use@State and @Binding.

- Use @StateObject and @ObservedObject.

- Use view's environment.

## Using a property

Take it step by step. First, how do you use a property to pass data between views? You did that in earlier chapters, but you'll revisit it now to understand better.

Take a look at this code example:

```
struct AnimalDetailsView: View {
  var name: String
  var body: some View {
    Text(name)
  }
}
```

The name property is of type String and passes into the Text view.

Then, consider this:

```
NavigationLink(
  destination: AnimalDetailsView(
  name: animal.name ?? "")
){
  AnimalRow(animal: animal)
}
```

The AnimalDetailsView takes in the name of an animal object. If an animal isn't given a name, it takes in a default empty string.

## Using @State and @Binding

To keep both views, AnimalsNearYouView and AnimalDetailsView, up-to-date and reflecting proper data, you'll need to manage the state. The sender view holds the data in a property marked with @State. The receiver receives the latest data with @Binding. This type of data passing assures both views stay updated. No matter where the data changes, both views get notified.

To better understand this concept, you'll make a small tweak to the code. You'll add a button to the list to enable or disable the user interaction of the navigation link on AnimalsNearYouView, this time using @State and @Binding. You'll add two buttons in the views AnimalListView and AnimalDetailsView to control the state from both views.

First, open **AnimalDetailsView.swift** and replace `AnimalDetailsView` implementation with:

```
struct AnimalDetailsView: View {
  var name: String
  // 1
  @Binding var isNavigatingDisabled: Bool
  var body: some View {
    Text(name)
    // 2
    Button(isNavigatingDisabled ? "Enable Navigation" : "Disable
Navigation") {
        isNavigatingDisabled.toggle()
    }
  }
}
```

1.  You add the receiver view that gets the `@Binding` property wrapper to listen to/ return the changes from/to the sender.

2.  A button to toggle the `isNavigatingDisabled` to either `true` or `false`.

Update your `AnimalsView_Previews`, so you pass the new parameter to `AnimalDetailsView`:

```
AnimalDetailsView(name: "Snow",
  isNavigatingDisabled: .constant(false))
```

Here you pass a constant to `isNavigatingDisabled`, so the view can be rendered in Xcode previews.

Now, open **AnimalListView.swift** and add a `@State` variable to the navigation state in the sender view:

```
@State var isNavigatingDisabled = false
```

Then, add a button nesting `List` before the `ForEach`:

```
Button(isNavigatingDisabled ? "Enable Navigation" : "Disable
Navigation") {
  isNavigatingDisabled.toggle()
}
```

This button will toggle the state of the navigation.

Still in **AnimalListView.swift** replace the `ForEach` with:

```
ForEach(animals) { animal in
```

```
  // 1
  NavigationLink(
    destination: AnimalDetailsView(
      name: animal.name ?? "",
      isNavigatingDisabled: $isNavigatingDisabled
    )
  ) {
    AnimalRow(animal: animal)
  }
  .disabled(isNavigatingDisabled) // 2
}
```

Here, you are:

1. Passing the navigation state to `AnimalDetailsView`.

2. Depending on the state enabling or disabling the user interaction.

Build and run. You'll see a view like this:

*Animals near you view enabled using @State and @Binding.*

Tap **Disable Navigation**. You'll see disabled navigation.

*Animals near you view disabled using @State and @Binding.*

Similarly, enable navigation and select any animal. On `AnimalDetailsView`, you'll see a **Disable Navigation** button.

*Animal details view using @State and @Binding.*

Tap **Disable Navigation** and go back. You'll see disabled navigation on
`AnimalsNearYouView` like this:

*Animals near you view disabled again using @State and @Binding.*

# Using @StateObject and @ObservedObject

`@StateObject` holds the object responsible for updating the UI. You use it to refer to
a class-type property in a view. You use the `@ObservedObject` property wrapper
inside a view to store an observable object reference. Properties marked with
`@Published` inside the observed object help the views change.

One difference between `@State` and `@StateObject` is that the first one works with
value types and the latter with reference types.

Back in **AnimalsNearYouView.swift**, add the following code:

```
class NavigationState: ObservableObject {
  @Published var isNavigatingDisabled = false
}
```

With this, you created `NavigationState` which has one `@Published` property called
`isNavigatingDisabled`. `isNavigatingDisabled` observes the value and maintains
the state of the navigation view.

Now, open **AnimalDetailsView.swift**. Add a property navigationState with property wrapper @ObservedObject like this:

```
@ObservedObject var navigationState: NavigationState
```

Here using the @ObservedObject so the UI updates when the state changes. Also, remove the following property, as it's no longer needed:

```
@Binding var isNavigatingDisabled: Bool
```

Then, update body to:

```
var body: some View {
  Text(name)
  Button(
    navigationState.isNavigatingDisabled ?
    "Enable Navigation" :
    "Disable Navigation"
  ) {
    navigationState.isNavigatingDisabled.toggle()
  }
}
```

Here, the button action uses the published property isNavigatingDisabled in NavigationState to toggle the state.

Then, in the preview code, update AnimalDetailsView to:

```
AnimalDetailsView(
  name: "Snow",
  navigationState: NavigationState()
)
```

This code updates the preview with the latest changes in AnimalDetailsView.

Open **AnimalListView.swift** and add:

```
@StateObject var navigationState = NavigationState()
```

@StateObject keeps the current state of the observable object.

Then, delete isNavigatingDisabled as it's no longer in use.

```
@State var isNavigatingDisabled = false
```

Update the button in the `List` to:

```
Button(
  navigationState.isNavigatingDisabled ?
  "Enable Navigation" : "Disable Navigation"
) {
  navigationState.isNavigatingDisabled.toggle()
}
```

The button now uses the updated `@StateObject`.

Then, update `ForEach` in the `List` to:

```
ForEach(animals) { animal in
  NavigationLink(
    destination: AnimalDetailsView(
      name: animal.name ?? "",
      navigationState: navigationState
    )
  ) {
    AnimalRow(animal: animal)
  }
  .disabled(navigationState.isNavigatingDisabled)
}
```

You pass the state object to the `AnimalDetailsView` initializer.

Build and run.

*Animals near you view enabled using @StateObject and @ObservedObject.*

Tap any animal to go to the animal's details view.

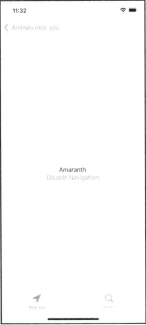

*Animal details view using @StateObject and @ObservedObject.*

You'll find that everything works as before.

## Using view's environment

Environment objects can help you synchronize views. It catches the objects that are injected into the SwiftUI environment.

Back in **AnimalDetailsView.swift**, update the `navigationState` like this:

```
@EnvironmentObject var navigationState: NavigationState
```

This snippet captures the object that is injected into the environment.

Then, in the preview, update `AnimalDetailsView` to:

```
AnimalDetailsView(name:
"Snow").environmentObject(NavigationState())
```

The preview is now in-sync with the latest changes made to the view.

In **AnimalListView.swift,** make sure the `navigationState` is a `@StateObject`:

```
@StateObject var navigationState = NavigationState()
```

Next, update the `ForEach` to:

```
ForEach(animals) { animal in
  NavigationLink(
    destination: AnimalDetailsView(name: animal.name ?? "")
    .environmentObject(navigationState)
  ) {
    AnimalRow(animal: animal)
  }
  .disabled(navigationState.isNavigatingDisabled)
}
```

Here, you inject the `navigationState` from the sender view in the environment.

Now, build and run.

*Animals near you view enabled using @StateObject and @EnvironmentObject.*

Select an animal and go to the details view.

*Animal details view using @StateObject and @EnvironmentObject.*

Play around with the app. Everything works smoothly as it previously did.

Now that you have a sense of how to pass around data. You'll use that and learn another different way of doing navigation.

## Navigating using a router

Having multiple navigation links can make your view complex. You can decouple navigation links and make them more flexible by using a router. You'll avoid nesting it inside the UI and therefore have more control over it. Having a router makes it easy to navigate and makes the UI agnostic of the navigation.

You can customize the view a lot before navigating to that screen. A router provides a layer of abstraction. If you navigate to a `UIViewController`, your SwiftUI view won't be affected in any way.

To gain a better understanding, try this quick exercise.

Under **Core/utils**, create a new file named **NavigationRouter.swift** and add:

```swift
import SwiftUI
protocol NavigationRouter {
  // 1
  associatedtype Data
  // 2
  func navigate<T: View>(
    data: Data,
    navigationState: NavigationState,
    view: (() -> T)?
  ) -> AnyView
}
```

Here's a code breakdown:

1. During the implementation of this protocol, you need to provide the data type you want to pass to the destination view.

2. Calling this method inside the view with the appropriate data returns a destination view. It also requires you to pass the state.

Now open **AnimalDetailsView.swift** and add:

```swift
struct AnimalDetailsRouter: NavigationRouter {
  // 1
  typealias Data = AnimalEntity

  func navigate<T: View>(
    data: AnimalEntity,
    navigationState: NavigationState,
    view: (() -> T)?
  ) -> AnyView {
    AnyView( // 2
      NavigationLink(
        destination: AnimalDetailsView(name: data.name ?? "")
        .environmentObject(navigationState) // 3
      ) {
        view?()
      }
    )
  }
}
```

AnimalDetailsRouter implements NavigationRouter with the implementation for navigating between views.

1.  Data type is AnimalEntity.

2.  This returns an AnyView within a NavigationLink with AnimalDetailsView as the destination view.

3.  Passing the navigationState towards the AnimalDetailsView.

Now picking up the previous example about enabling/disabling the user interaction on navigation using buttons in both views.

Back in **AnimalListView.swift**, add the following properties to the struct:

```
let router = AnimalDetailsRouter()
```

Here, you add a router object to initiate navigation.

Then inside the ForEach, replace NavigationLink with:

```
router.navigate(
  data: animal,
  navigationState: navigationState
) {
  AnimalRow(animal: animal)
}
.disabled(navigationState.isNavigatingDisabled)
```

The router returns a view nested with a navigation link and performs the required navigation.

Now, build and run. You'll see:

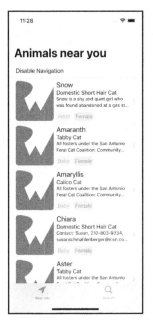

*Animals near you view enabled using navigation router.*

Select an animal, and you'll see the `AnimalDetailsView`:

*Animal details view using navigation router.*

Then, select the **Disable Navigation** button and go back to `AnimalsNearYouView`. You'll see a disabled navigation.

*Animals near you view disabled using navigation router.*

It works as expected. That's great!

# Navigating using a router to a UIViewController

You learned how to use a router. Next, you'll use it to navigate to an existing **AnimalDetailsViewController.swift** in **UIKit**.

Open **AnimalDetailsViewController.xib**.  You'll see a screen with a UILabel and a
UIButton.

*xib file with a UILabel and a UIButton.*

To make the UIViewController talk to the SwiftUI view, you'll implement a bridge
between them. SwiftUI provides a protocol, UIViewControllerRepresentable, and
requires you to provide the UIViewController to which you want to connect. You
also need to provide a method to reflect the changes you want to make to this view
controller.

Under **AnimalDetails/views**, create **AnimalDetailsViewRepresentable.swift**.
Then add:

```swift
import UIKit
import SwiftUI

struct AnimalDetailsViewRepresentable:
UIViewControllerRepresentable {
  // 1
  var name: String
  // 2
  @EnvironmentObject var navigationState: NavigationState
  // 3
  typealias UIViewControllerType = AnimalDetailsViewController
  // 4
  func updateUIViewController(
```

```
    _ uiViewController: AnimalDetailsViewController,
    context: Context) {
      // 5
      uiViewController.set(
        name,
        status: navigationState.isNavigatingDisabled
      )
      // 6
      uiViewController.didSelectNavigation = {
        navigationState.isNavigatingDisabled.toggle()
      }
  }
  // 7
  func makeUIViewController(context: Context)
    -> AnimalDetailsViewController {
      let detailViewController =
      AnimalDetailsViewController(
          nibName: "AnimalDetailsViewController",
          bundle: .main
        )
      return detailViewController
  }
}
```

Here's what the code is doing:

1.  Creates a variable to receive the name of the animal from the
    `AnimalsNearYouView`.

2.  Gets the state of the navigation in the current environment.

3.  Assigns the type of the destination view controller. Here, it's the
    `AnimalDetailsViewController`.

4.  This method is from the `UIViewControllerRepresentable`. Here, you update
    the changes coming from the SwiftUI view.

5.  You set the name of the animal and the status of the navigation here.

6.  This closure listens to the button inside the `AnimalDetailsViewController` and
    toggles the navigation state.

7.  This method is also from `UIViewControllerRepresentable`. Here, you return
    the view controller you want SwiftUI to make renderable.

SwiftUI requires both of these methods' implementation to make and update the
views.

Now, open **AnimalDetailsView.swift**. Then, in `AnimalDetailsRouter`, update `navigate` method as:

```
func navigate<T: View>(
  data: AnimalEntity,
  navigationState: NavigationState,
  view: (() -> T)?
) -> AnyView {
  AnyView(
    NavigationLink(
      destination: AnimalDetailsViewRepresentable(
        name: data.name ?? ""
      ).environmentObject(navigationState)
    ) {
      view?()
    }
  )
}
```

Here, you replace the `AnimalDetailsView` with the new representable view.

Now, build and run. Select an animal and go to the `AnimalDetailsView`. The navigation works fine.

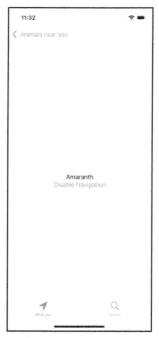

*Animal details view using UIViewControllerRepresentable.*

You can't even tell the difference in the look and feel, right? That's how cool SwiftUI is.

# Presenting views

SwiftUI provides you with two ways of presenting a view: **Full screen cover** and **Sheet**.

## Full screen cover

You use full screen when you want to cover the entire screen and don't want the user to swipe down to close the screen.

## Sheet

Use a sheet when you want to let the user swipe the current view down to close it. This swiping to close feature is something you can disable as well.

Open **AppMain.swift**. You'll see that ContentView uses .fullScreenCover. Now, to see how .sheet view modifier behaves, replace:

```
ContentView().fullScreenCover(
  isPresented: $shouldPresentOnboarding,
  onDismiss: nil
)
```

With:

```
ContentView().sheet(
  isPresented: $shouldPresentOnboarding,
  onDismiss: nil
)
```

Delete the app, so the onboarding screens show again. Build and run. You'll see this view:

*Onboarding screens using a sheet view modifier.*

Both of these ways present the view in a bottom-to-top fashion.

## Using tab view

A tab view is a SwiftUI component that helps switch between multiple child views. It's an example of **flat navigation**. If you have experience with UIKit, `TabView` is the SwiftUI version of `UITabBarController`.

To create a user interface with TabView, you place views inside the TabView. Then you add `.tabItem(_:)` to the view contained inside the `TabView`, which helps toggle between the views.

To get a better understanding, open **ContentView.swift** and look at the following code:

```
var body: some View {
  TabView {
  // 1
    AnimalsNearYouView(
      viewModel: AnimalsNearYouViewModel(
        animalFetcher: FetchAnimalsService(
          requestManager:
            RequestManager()
        ),
        animalStore: AnimalStoreService(
          context:
PersistenceController.shared.container.newBackgroundContext()
        )
      )
    )
    .tabItem {
      Label("Near you", systemImage: "location")
    }
    .environment(\.managedObjectContext, managedObjectContext)
  // 2
    SearchView()
      .tabItem {
        Label("Search", systemImage: "magnifyingglass")
      }
      .environment(\.managedObjectContext, managedObjectContext)
  }
}
```

This code creates two child views inside a `TabView`.

1.  The first tab item selection displays `AnimalsNearYouView`.

2.  The second tab item selection shows `SearchView`.

> **Note**: `.tabItem(_:)` only supports a `Text` or an `Image`, a `Text` with an `Image`, or a `Label`. Adding another type of view results in empty tab item.

To assign a badge on your tab item, add `.badge(2)` before the **Near you** `tabItem`:

```
.badge(2)
```

Now, you'll see **2** on the **Near you** tab.

Build and run. You'll get the following result:

*Near you tab with a badge of 2.*

You can also use the `selection` initializer to perform navigation in `TabView`. The cool thing about `selection` is that it's not limited to `Int` data type. You can pass in any object that conforms to `Hashable`.

Imagine you want to toggle between the child views within the `TabView`, `AnimalsNearYouView` and `SearchView` programmatically.

Start by creating **PetSaveTabType.swift** under **Core/views**. Then add:

```
enum PetSaveTabType {
  case nearYou
  case search
}
```

Since there are two child views in the `TabView`, you add two cases in the `enum`.

Under the same group, create **PetSaveTabNavigator.swift** and add:

```
class PetSaveTabNavigator: ObservableObject {
  // 1
  @Published var currentTab: PetSaveTabType =  .nearYou
  // 2
  func switchTab(to tab: PetSaveTabType) {
    currentTab = tab
  }
}
// 3
extension PetSaveTabNavigator: Hashable {
  static func == (
    lhs: PetSaveTabNavigator,
    rhs: PetSaveTabNavigator
  ) -> Bool {
    lhs.currentTab == rhs.currentTab
  }

  func hash(into hasher: inout Hasher) {
    hasher.combine(currentTab)
  }
}
```

Here's an explanation to the code:

1.  The `@Published` property informs the UI as soon as its value changes.

2.  A method to set the different types of tabs.

3.  Since you'll be using a custom type you need to conform to `Hashable`.

Now, back in **ContentView.swift**, create an object of `PetSaveTabNavigator` inside the `ContentView`:

```
@StateObject var tabNavigator = PetSaveTabNavigator()
```

The `@StateObject` creates the object and maintains its state. It refreshes the entire UI based on this object.

You'll also update the `TabView` with its selection initializer and add tags to the views. Replace the body with:

```
var body: some View {
  // 1
  TabView(selection: $tabNavigator.currentTab) {
    AnimalsNearYouView(
      viewModel: AnimalsNearYouViewModel(
        animalFetcher: FetchAnimalsService(
          requestManager:
```

```
              RequestManager()
          ),
        animalStore: AnimalStoreService(
          context:
PersistenceController.shared.container.newBackgroundContext()
        )
      )
    )
    .badge(2)
    // 2
    .tag(PetSaveTabType.nearYou)
    .tabItem {
      Label("Near you", systemImage: "location")
    }
    .environment(\.managedObjectContext, managedObjectContext)

    SearchView()
      .tag(PetSaveTabType.search) // 3
      .tabItem {
        Label("Search", systemImage: "magnifyingglass")
      }
      .environment(\.managedObjectContext, managedObjectContext)
  }
}
```

Here's a code breakdown:

1. You pass in the `currentTab` from the `PetSaveTabNavigator` object to the selection initializer.

2. Then, you apply a tag to `AnimalsNearYouView`.

3. Finally, you apply a tag to `SearchView`.

Now you can change the tabs programmatically. How? call `switchTab(_:)` which resides inside `PetSaveTabNavigator`. Then you'll see the tabs switch.

> **Note**: You can achieve similar results by using the `selection` on `NavigationView`.

# Deep link navigation with tab view

Now that you understand how to switch TabView programmatically. You'll use this to navigate your way with a deep link.

Select the **PetSave** target and click **info**. Then unfold the **URL Types**.

*Add URL Types.*

Click the small **+**, add *petsave* to the **URL Schemes** and press **return**.

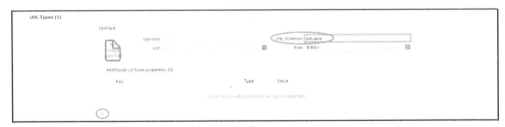

*Add URL Schemes.*

Now, open the **PetSaveTabType.swift** and add the following method to the enum:

```swift
static func deepLinkType(url: URL) -> PetSaveTabType {
  if url.scheme == "petsave" {
    switch url.host {
    case "nearYou":
      return .nearYou
    case "search":
      return .search
    default:
      return .nearYou
    }
  }
  return .nearYou
}
```

This checks if the scheme is *petsave*. Then it checks if the host is either **nearYou** or **search** and returns the respective type. To keep things simple, the default type is .nearYou if the scheme doesn't match *petsave*.

Then, open **ContentView.swift** and add the following modifier at the end of the TabView:

```swift
// 1
.onOpenURL { url in
  // 2
  let type = PetSaveTabType.deepLinkType(url: url)
  // 3
  self.tabNavigator.switchTab(to: type)
}
```

Here, you:

1.  Receive the opened url.

2.  Get the correct tab type using url.

3.  Call switchTab(_:) to present the right tab depending on type.

Build and run. In the simulator, tap **Home icon** and open Safari browser. Type `petsave://search` in the browser and press **return**. You'll see the following alert.

*Deep link alert.*

On the alert, tap **Open**, which takes you to the app's search view.

*PetSave's search opened using deep link.*

Go back to the browser, type petsave://nearYou and tap **go**. When you see the alert, tap **Open**, and you'll see:

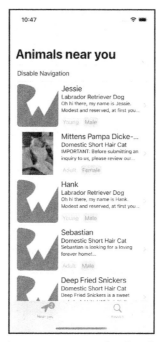

*PetSave's near you opened using deep link.*

Wooooohoooo! The deep link works, and so does the programmatic switching of views. You did a great job!

# Key points

- You can use a router to decouple the code and do navigation.

- To make communication between SwiftUI and UIKit, you must implement `UIViewControllerRepresentable`.

- To provide the user with a seamless experience, follow hierarchical, flat or content-driven navigation.

- You can pass the view specific data using `@State` and `@Binding`.

- You can pass custom data types using `@StateObject` and `@ObservedObject`.

- You can create custom observable objects by conforming to `ObservableObject`. Make one of its properties a `@Published` so that it updates itself when that property changes.

- You can use `@Environment` to read the system objects injected using `.environment()`.

- `@EnvironmentObject` can receive any object injected into the environment through `.environmentObject(_)`.

# Where to go from here?

That brings the end of this chapter. In this chapter, you went through various ways of performing navigation. Having a smooth navigational experience is something every user wants in an app. So when implementing navigation, you should always be mindful of that.

Moreover, go and check out our tutorial on SwiftUI navigation (https://www.raywenderlich.com/5824937-swiftui-tutorial-navigation). You can also read the navigation tutorial from Apple (https://developer.apple.com/tutorials/swiftui/building-lists-and-navigation). Also, you can read more in detail from Apple about the Types of Navigation (https://developer.apple.com/design/human-interface-guidelines/ios/app-architecture/navigation/).

In the next chapter, you're going to add some more fun to the app. You'll learn about adding animations and custom controls to the app's UI while also abiding by Apple's Human interface guidelines.

# Section IV: Enhancing the User Interface & Experience

A successful user experience can be the difference between a 1-star and 5-star app on the App Store. Lively and responsive user interfaces, interactive controls, customization, localization, and accessibility all contribute to whether a user will re-engage with your app after their first use.

In this section, you'll enhance the user interface with animations and custom controls. Also, you'll start to get your app ready for the broad set of users in the world by applying human interface guidelines and accessibility features.

# Chapter 9: Adding Animations & Custom Controls

By Josh Steele

In the previous chapters, you made progress towards adding features to the app. That's good! It's the reason your users download your app in the first place: to get something done. For this app, that means finding a potential future pet.

With the primary functionality in place, it's time to ask how you can:

- Customize your app to improve user engagement?

- Make your app available to as many potential users as possible?

- Lower or eliminate any real or perceived barriers to using your app?

> **Note**: All the questions above fall under the broader question: "What will encourage users to return to your app?" That's the overarching topic for this section of the book.

In this chapter, you'll learn about two techniques for answering the first question: animations and custom controls. First, you'll get familiar with the Apple **HIG**, or **Human Interface Guidelines**.

# Apple Human Interface Guidelines

Apple's HIG, or Human Interface Guidelines for iOS (https://developer.apple.com/design/human-interface-guidelines/ios/overview/themes/) are a set of guidelines, *not requirements*, that you can reference when designing your app's user interface. Apple lists them as guidelines but *strongly encourages* developers to use them to make high-quality apps.

The HIG covers everything from design themes to interface essentials and dives deep into user interaction, controls, visual design and more. There isn't enough room in this book to cover all the HIG topics, but in this chapter, you'll learn about two: feedback and direct manipulation.

# Feedback

The last thing you want users to feel when using your app is uncertain. Your app should respond to user interactions. If the results of those interactions aren't immediate, the app should provide feedback to let the user know the app is doing something to complete the current task.

Of course, feedback shouldn't get in the way of the app's main purpose and should be quickly identifiable without much work on the user's part.

## Feedback use case: Animations

Animations can help bring your app to life by giving a sense of connection between your user and your app. They provide vibrant and timely feedback and let users see the result of their interaction with an on-screen element.

Animations can also provide a sense of fun in your app's interactions. Tapping a heart to favorite an item is a great interaction, but making that heart grow and change color makes the interaction *pop* in the user's eyes.

Animations, however, shouldn't be *overused*. Keep in mind the following guidelines when deciding whether to add an animation to your app.

### When not to use animations

Don't use animations, or any feedback, unless it conveys essential, timely or actionable information. Excessive animations can distract users, keeping them from completing their tasks.

Here's an example. Your app's logo is in a prominent location of the user interface, the upper left-hand corner. That's fine because branding is important.

But, your designer comes by and says they're adding some reflective elements to the logo. They suggest you add an animation so the logo pops and gets the user's attention.

This is *not* a good case to use an animation. Here's why:

- **Drawing attention**: The animation would indeed catch the user's eye, but it would **draw them away** from their main task when using your app.

- **No actionable information**: Users can't do anything with the logo: It isn't **actionable**. Drawing the user's attention to the logo may indicate a false premise that interacting with it will do something.

- **Not important**: Since the animation has no actionable information and draws the user's attention away from their task, you can conclude that it is **not important** when using your app. Therefore, you shouldn't add it.

However, animations **can** be useful. So, when should you use them?

## When to use animations

When used properly, animations can add flair to your app. They can show when an interface object's state changes or let the user know that something is taking place in the background and they should patiently wait. Here are a few examples:

- **Animating view attributes**: Tapping a favorite button animates the icon's color, size or shape.

- **Animating a real-life action**: Tapping send on an email dialog brings up an animation of a mail envelope closing and flying away.

- **Denoting background behavior**: You can unobtrusively display a simple spinner animation to show that a background process is taking place.

Animations make your app more enjoyable, but they shouldn't be a requirement.

## Animations are always optional

There are features like **reduced motion** that can affect (and even disable) effects or animations in your app. Knowing this you should always think of animations as optional. Therefore, don't make animations an integral part of your app.

Here's how you can minimize the animations above but still keep feedback in the app:

- **Favorite button**: Simply change the color and size immediately, instead of animating it over a period of time.

- **Mail envelope**: Tapping send instead updates a text status area after the OS sends the mail.

- **Background processes**: Replace the spinner with a text label that describes any feedback to the user.

With those guidelines in mind, it's time to add a few animations to PetSave.

## Adding an animation to PetSave

Animations can convey various feedback to the user. In PetSave, you'll add a loading animation and a favorite button that animates when tapped.

## Building animated GIFs

When apps fetch data from the network, there's always a possibility of delays. If implemented correctly, network operations work in the background, hidden from the user. Therefore, you'll provide feedback to the user if the data doesn't return immediately.

Here, *immediately* is typically two to three seconds. Beyond that, the user may start to get frustrated that the app isn't responding or showing the data they requested.

Something as simple as an animated view can let the user know work is going on and let them know they don't need to get so *animated* while waiting for the task to finish.

Open **Core/views** and create a **new SwiftUI view** called **LoadingAnimation.swift**. Replace the code in the file with:

```
// 1
struct LoadingAnimation: UIViewRepresentable {
  let animatedFrames: UIImage
  let image: UIImageView
  let squareDimension: CGFloat = 125

  // 2
  init() {
    var images: [UIImage] = []
    // 3
    for i in 1...127 {
      guard let image =
```

```
          UIImage(named: "dog_\(String(format: "%03d", i))")
          else { continue }
        images.append(image)
      }
      // 4
      animatedFrames = UIImage.animatedImage(with: images,
        duration: 4) ?? UIImage()
      // 5
      image = UIImageView(frame: CGRect(x: 0, y: 0, width:
squareDimension, height: squareDimension))
    }

    // 6
    func makeUIView(context: Context) -> UIView {
      let view = UIView(frame: CGRect(x: 0, y: 0,
        width: squareDimension, height: squareDimension))
      image.clipsToBounds = true
      image.autoresizesSubviews = true
      image.contentMode = .scaleAspectFit
      image.image = animatedFrames
      image.center = CGPoint(x: view.frame.width / 2,
        y: view.frame.height / 2)
      view.backgroundColor = .red
      view.addSubview(image)

      return view
    }

    func updateUIView(_ uiView: UIViewType, context: Context) {
      // no code here; just for protocol
    }
  }

// 7
struct LoadingAnimationView: View {
  var body: some View {
    VStack {
      LoadingAnimation()
    }
  }
}


// 8
struct LoadingAnimationView_Previews: PreviewProvider {
  static var previews: some View {
    LoadingAnimationView()
  }
}
```

A lot going on here, but it breaks down into the following major components:

1. `LoadingAnimationView` is a `UIViewRepresentable`. There isn't a good SwiftUI set of widgets to use here, so you'll use a UIKit component and wrap it in a `UIViewRepresentable` so SwiftUI can use it.

2. The `init` method gets this image ready to use.

3. This loop fills the `images` array with the images required to make the animation. The string format `%03d` constructs an integer with three digits and leading zeroes. `i` is the value passed in to construct the integer.

4. To set up `animatedFrames` you used `animatedImage(with:duration:)`. This is a static method of UIKit's `UIImage` that takes in an array of `UIImages` and a `duration` and returns an animated image.

5. Set up `image`. This is an `UIImageView` that will act as the container for your animated image.

6. `makeUIView` places the animated image in a `UIImageView`. The `UIImageView` goes in a `UIView` for the `UIViewRepresentable` to present on screen.

7. This is the actual SwiftUI View that uses a `LoadingAnimation()` inside a `VStack`.

8. The preview provider for your SwiftUI View. So you can see it on Xcode Previews.

As mentioned earlier, an animation like this is useful when loading data from the network.

Open **AnimalsNearYouView.swift**. Look for the `ProgressView` implementation passed in a closure to the `AnimalListView`, inside then `NavigationView`, and replace it with:

```
// 1
HStack(alignment: .center) {
  // 2
  LoadingAnimation()
    .frame(maxWidth: 125, minHeight: 125)
  Text("Loading more animals...")
}
// 3
.task {
  await viewModel.fetchMoreAnimals()
}
```

Here's what you did:

1.  You used an `HStack` and set `alignment` to be `center`.

2.  Inside the `HStack` is the new `LoadingAnimation` and a `frame` modifier that sets the max width and height. Also, you added a `Text` to display the message "Loading more animals…"

3.  Put the asynchronous call to `fetchMoreAnimals` inside a `task(priority:_:)` modifier. You need to do this because the method is `async`. This code is called when the view appears.

Build and run the project in the simulator. Scroll down to the available set of data in the Animals Near You View tab:

*The Animals Near You view.*

Don't blink or you might miss the animation! The network operation for finding animals near you is pretty quick, so the animation barely has a chance to appear on screen.

You'll need a slow connection to test this. To help you with this Apple provides a tool called **Network Link Conditioner**.

If you haven't already downloaded it, you'll need to grab the Additional Tools for Xcode (https://developer.apple.com/download/all/?q=xcode) from the Apple Developer website.

To install it open **Additional_Tools_for_Xcode_13.3_beta_3.dmg**. Inside the **Hardware** folder double-click **Network Link Condition.prefPane**.

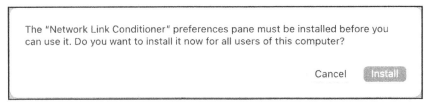

*Dialog confirming the Network Link Conditioner Installation.*

A message asking for confirmation will appear. Click **Install**.

> **Note**: If you're on macOS Big Sur, you may need to get the Additional Tools for Xcode 12.5 (https://download.developer.apple.com/Developer_Tools/Additional_Tools_for_Xcode_12.5/Additional_Tools_for_Xcode_12.5.dmg) if you have trouble installing the Network Link Conditioner preference pane for Xcode 13.

Once installed, open **System Preferences** and open the **Network Link Conditioner**. Turn it on, and set **100 % Loss** for the **Profile**, this will simulate a low or absent network:

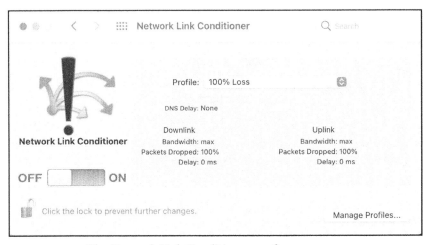

*The Network Link Conditioner preference pane.*

Now build and rerun the app. This time, when the app searches for pets near you, you'll see an animated progress indicator that's appropriately themed for your app!

*The custom animation now appears next to the informative text (best viewed in your simulator or device).*

Disable the network link conditioner, and the app will download new animals to display as usual.

> **Note**: The Network Link Conditioner impacts your **entire** system, so don't forget to turn it off when you're done testing. Otherwise, your next trip to the web will be a slow one!

## Animation modifiers in SwiftUI

You can also add animations to your app by using SwiftUI's built-in animation capabilities. SwiftUI uses both implicit and explicit animations:

- **Implicit Animations**: Implicit animations work via modifiers that take in one or more values. When those values change, the SwiftUI rendering system smoothly animates those changes for you with an `.animation` modifier.

- **Explicit Animations**: Explicit animations aren't tied to a particular view via a modifier but instead operate directly on the change you want to make. This change appears within a `withAnimation` block.

For PetSave, you'll use an implicit animation to animate the heart's color when the user taps the favorite button for a pet.

Open **AnimalHeaderView.swift** and add this lines right below `HeaderTitle` view:

```
// 1
Image(systemName: favorited ? "heart.fill" : "heart")
  .font(.system(size: 50))
  .foregroundColor( favorited ? Color(.systemRed) :
Color(.black))
  .frame(minWidth: 50, maxWidth: 50, minHeight: 50, maxHeight:
50)
  // 2
  .animation(favorited ? .interpolatingSpring(
    mass: 5,
    stiffness: 3.0,
    damping: 1.0,
    initialVelocity: 1) :
    .default,
    value: $favorited.wrappedValue)
  .onTapGesture {
    $favorited.wrappedValue.toggle()
  }
}
```

Here's what's going on:

1. The `Image` has some modifiers that depend on the state of the `favorite` property, such as the `foregroundColor`.

2. The `animation` modifier also responds to changes in `favorited` and uses a spring animation when the user taps the heart. The modifier uses a simple default animation when unfavorited. Because you use the `animation` modifier, this is an implicit animation.

Open **AnimalDetailsView.swift** and, if necessary, click **Resume** in the preview canvas. Click **Play** to activate the live preview. When it becomes active, tap the favorite button. You'll see the heart icon change its fill color smoothly when you tap on it.

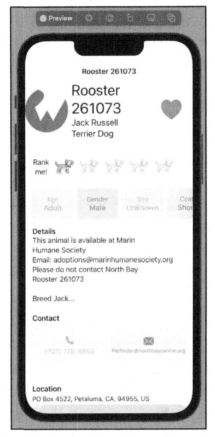

*Animal Details View with animation (best viewed in your simulator or device).*

> **Note**: Try removing the `.animation(_:value:)` modifier and tapping on the heart icon, so you can appreciate how it looks without animation.

Feedback is a great way to send information back to the user. But something must trigger that feedback, usually in the form of interaction with your app. One of the most common interactions is direct manipulations of UI elements.

# Direct manipulation

Direct manipulation is the most, well, *direct* way a user can interact with your app. Users can reach out with their fingers and interact with your app.

Users can control the various views and controls in your app with tapping, swiping and gestures. You can take that a step further by introducing something into your app that has all three.

# Direct manipulation use case: Custom Controls

Developers can go beyond the built-in controls in iOS and make their own **custom controls**. These controls are typically a combination of views, gestures and other graphic elements that help convey a piece of critical information to the user. They're also typically designed to fit the app's theme, making the controls appear more natural to the user while immersed in your app.

Like animations, be judicious in your use of custom controls.

## When not to create custom controls

Apple's set of controls is fairly expansive, and more importantly, familiar to users. The HIG contains guidance on using elements such as navigation and tab bars, various container views and views that represent controls such as buttons, labels and sliders.

Therefore, the guidance on when to **not** create custom controls is when that control already exists!

Apple optimizes the built-in controls and tests them to make sure they work well. For example, UIKit's `UITableView` contains two delegate objects to help populate and style the table. Developers don't know how that table gets rendered on-screen: Apple handles that behind the scenes. It's highly optimized to render well and includes many built-in controls, such as swipe to delete. If you tried to replicate all the capabilities **and** optimizations of UITableView, you'd waste a lot of time!

But custom controls can come in handy!

## When to create custom controls

iOS contains plenty of optimized controls for you to use during development. However, there are some reasons you might develop your own control:

- **Custom Interaction**: Your app may have specific interaction needs. For example, an internet radio app might try to emulate a typical car radio for its controls. This would require spinning a dial, which is not a built-in control in iOS.

- **Custom Behavior**: When a user interacts with a control, you may want to include custom behaviors that better fit your app's look and feel.

- **Custom Appearance**: iOS exposes a fair amount of APIs that let developers customize the appearance of the built-in controls. But, if those APIs don't provide **exactly** what you need, or the control has a presentation bug, you may need to customize the control. You can also customize controls to apply themes that match the app's overall aesthetic.

When you make a custom control, it'll probably be for at least one of the reasons above. You'll most likely use a combination of existing iOS functionality, such as animation, gestures and custom views with UIKit or SwiftUI.

With those guidelines in mind, it's time for you to add a custom control to PetSave.

## Adding a custom control to PetSave

You'll add a ranking control that lets users provide feedback on pet details and specify how likely they are to adopt that pet. To accomplish this, you'll use the following techniques:

- **SwiftUI Views**: The overall view is a series of Image views in an HStack.

- **Gestures**: When a user taps on a single Image, it'll adjust the opacity of the other Images where appropriate and update the current ranking.

Open **Core/views** and create a new SwiftUI view called **PetRankingView.swift**. Replace the current implementation for PetRankingView with:

```swift
import SwiftUI

struct PetRankingView: View {
  // 1
  @ObservedObject var viewModel: PetRankingViewModel
  var animal: AnimalEntity

  // 2
  init(animal: AnimalEntity) {
```

```
      self.animal = animal
      viewModel = PetRankingViewModel(animal: animal)
    }

  // 3
  var body: some View {
    HStack {
      Text("Rank me!")
        .multilineTextAlignment(.center)
      ForEach(0...4, id: \.self) { index in
        PetRankImage(index: index, recentIndex:
$viewModel.ranking)
      }
    }
  }
}
```

Here's what this code does:

1. `PetRankingViewModel`, which is an `@ObservedObject`, responds to changes in the published elements of the model.

2. The `init` method sets the `animal` and initializes the `PetRankingViewModel`.

3. The body consists of a `Text` label in front of five `PetRankImages` arranged in an `HStack`.

Add the following code below `PetRankingView`:

```
struct PetRankImage: View {
  let index: Int
  // 1
  @State var opacity: Double = 0.4
  @State var tapped = false
  @Binding var recentIndex: Int

  var body: some View {
    // 2
    Image("creature_dog-and-bone")
      .resizable()
      .aspectRatio(contentMode: .fit)
      .opacity(opacity)
      .frame(width: 50, height: 50)
      .onTapGesture {
        opacity = tapped ? 0.4 : 1.0
        tapped.toggle()
        recentIndex = index
      }
      .onChange(of: recentIndex) { value in
        checkOpacity(value: value)
      }
```

```
      .onAppear {
        checkOpacity(value: recentIndex)
      }
    }

    // 3
    func checkOpacity(value: Int) {
      opacity = value >= index ? 1.0 : 0.4
      tapped.toggle()
    }
  }
}
```

The PetRankImage view encapsulates the Image of a dog holding a bone. It also controls the image's opacity, which helps show the enabled state. Here's what the PetRankImage code does:

1.  opacity and tapped are @State properties. They track whether this particular image is enabled, contributing to the overall ranking. The recentIndex @Binding comes in from the parent control and determines whether this image is enabled.

2.  The Image has opacity, onTapGesture and onChange modifiers to help change the state based on user interaction.

3.  checkOpacity updates the image's opacity based on the passed in recentIndex.

Below the PetRankImage struct, add:

```
final class PetRankingViewModel: ObservableObject {
  var animal: AnimalEntity
  // 1
  var ranking: Int {
    didSet {
      animal.ranking = Int32(ranking)
      objectWillChange.send()
    }
  }

  // 2
  init(animal: AnimalEntity) {
    self.animal = animal
    self.ranking = Int(animal.ranking)
  }
}
```

PetRankingViewModel monitors the current ranking the user chose, and sets that value to the animal's ranking property. Items of note in the PetRankingViewModel:

1.  The ranking property has didSet that publishes the change to listeners of the model using objectWillChange.send().

2.  The init method initializes the animal and ranking properties based on the passed in animal property.

Update the PetRankingView_Previews struct to use a test animal entity to populate PetRankingView and add a padding and previewLayout modifier to customize the preview:

```
struct PetRankingView_Previews: PreviewProvider {
  static var previews: some View {
    if let animal = CoreDataHelper.getTestAnimalEntity() {
      PetRankingView(animal: animal)
        .padding()
        .previewLayout(.sizeThatFits)
    }
  }
}
```

In the preview pane, click **Resume**. You'll see your control:

*The PetSave custom ranking control.*

This is looking pretty good. 5/5 dogs, would create again!

Play the preview, and tap the low opacity dogs in the control to set the rating for this animal.

*The PetSave custom ranking control has a 5 out of 5 ranking!*

Finally, it's time to add the custom control to the app. Open **AnimalDetails/view**. In **AnimalDetailsView.swift**, add PetRankingView between the first `Divider` and `AnimalDetailRow` add the following code:

```
PetRankingView(animal: animal)
  .padding()
  .blur(radius: zoomed ? 20 : 0)
```

Here you're adding add `PetRankingView` passing the `animal` you want to rate. In addition, you added two modifiers to the new view: `padding(_:_:)` to add some separation and `.blur(radius:opaque:)` which, depending on the state of `zoomed`, could be 20 or zero.

Build and run the app. Now, interact with the custom control to rank the pets you view:

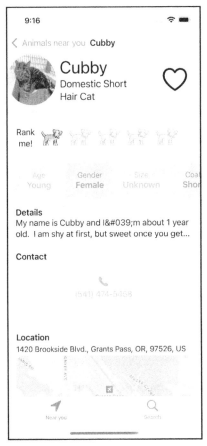

*The completed Animal Details view!*

# Key points

- **Apple's Human Interface Guidelines** are a great resource for ensuring your app has a great look and feel and fits alongside other apps in the store.

- **Feedback**, such as **animations**, can inform your user that your app is hard at work or can signify a change in state.

- **Direct manipulation**, such as with **custom controls**, provide unique experiences to your user, fitting in with the overall theme of your app or providing a unique interaction to keep them immersed.

# Where to go from here?

Congratulations! You took your first dive into the Apple Human Interface Guidelines. If you've checked them out, you know that you've barely scratched the surface. You'll read about a few more areas in the later chapters of this section.

You also learned important "Dos and Don'ts" for when to use animations and custom controls. Both can help a user feel connected with your app, but be careful not to **overuse** them.

If you're interested in learning more about the world of iOS Animations, check out iOS Animations by Tutorials (https://www.raywenderlich.com/books/ios-animations-by-tutorials).

You're not done taking advantage of the wealth of information in the HIG! In the next chapter, you'll learn how to make your app accessible to a broader set of users by learning about Accessibility in iOS.

# Chapter 10: Implementing Accessibility

By Josh Steele

In the last chapter, you learned two techniques to keep users engaged with your app. Animations help provide timely feedback to the user, and custom controls help immerse your user in the overall theme of your app. Both are part of Apple's HIG, or Human Interface Guidelines for iOS (https://developer.apple.com/design/human-interface-guidelines/ios/overview/themes/).

**Accessibility** is a broader technology that applies to all the Apple operating systems and has a dedicated section under the HIG website (https://developer.apple.com/design/human-interface-guidelines/accessibility/overview/introduction/).

In this chapter, you'll learn how the Accessibility technologies in iOS help make implementing those guidelines available to more users.

But what exactly is Accessibility, and why should you use it in your app?

# Why design for accessibility?

Here are two statistics that may surprise you:

1. According to the CDC, one in four adults in the United States has some type of disability (https://www.cdc.gov/media/releases/2018/p0816-disability.html).

2. Current estimates state that one in 12, or 8%, men (https://en.wikipedia.org/wiki/Color_blindness) are color blind.

If that first number surprises you, you're not alone. Many people have invisible disabilities, such as color blindness.

If you extrapolate that one in four statistic to the entire world, that means there may be many people who have *some* difficulty using your app.

When you use Accessibility technologies, your app:

1. **Becomes more accessible**: This one may seem obvious since it's right there in the name. A larger number of people can download and use your app.

2. **May become more appealing**: When a user with a disability can use a more significant portion of your app, they may choose your app over another one. Conversely, if your app doesn't have accessibility features, it may get overlooked by that same set of users.

Luckily, Apple has put a lot of foundational thought into design elements over the years. There *were* some hits and misses along the way. Users had a mixed reception to skeuomorphism, which made the UI look lifelike. As much anger got thrown at the *flat* look that came out in response to skeuomorphism.

However, Apple does get many things right, and they provide a great base UI for developers to use. They also describe those in, you guessed it, the Apple HIG.

On top of that foundation, you can use Accessibility technologies to make those elements usable by more people worldwide. Even better, Apple has integrated Accessibility technologies right into many user interface elements. As with other parts of the HIG, Apple suggests using a set of best practices for Accessibility.

# Best practices in the Apple Human Interface Guidelines

Each iOS user interface component has its own best practices for design and accessibility. Before learning about those, you should be aware of three overarching principles, as highlighted in the HIG (https://developer.apple.com/design/human-interface-guidelines/accessibility/overview/best-practices/).

## Designing for accessibility

Software engineering principles place design early on (https://en.wikipedia.org/wiki/Waterfall_model) in the development process. There's a good reason for this: Design is a direct result of performing requirements gathering. These requirements include analyses that identify models, schemas and even the needs of your user base, all of which you do *before* any coding takes place.

Typical design processes focus on the usability of your user interface, including making sure the user can accomplish various tasks within your app. When you incorporate accessibility into your design process, your goal is to make your app usable for not only people with disabilities but **as many people as possible**. The HIG highlights two focus areas here:

- **Simplicity**: Familiar interactions that keep tasks simple and straightforward to perform.

- **Perceivability**: Users can engage with your app with several of their senses, including sight, hearing and touch.

You'll see both of these areas pop up from time to time in this chapter.

## Supporting adaptability

One of the best things about using Apple's built-in user interface elements is that you *automatically* get the accessibility support for those elements. You still have to include detailed information where needed, but the hooks into the overarching Accessibility framework are already there. Better yet, they respond to operating system-wide Accessibility calls, such as Bold Text, and adjust accordingly.

You can also easily add accessibility features to your custom user interface elements. This lets tools such as **VoiceOver** recognize that element and present it to the user. You'll learn about VoiceOver later in this chapter.

## Test, test, test and did we mention test?

Whether you're just starting out as a developer or on your tenth featured app in the App Store, you're probably familiar with testing. Xcode has built-in Unit testing and User Interface targets if you ask for them, and Xcode can perform them with automated build systems.

When you integrate Accessibility technologies into your app, you have to go a step further. Once you turn accessibility features on, you can explore alternative methods users can use to interact with your app. You'll discover areas that need improvement from an accessibility standpoint and may even find areas to improve your app's overall user experience.

You should run each use case for your app with an accessibility feature, such as VoiceOver, turned on. You'll see how the app behaves and if a user can accomplish that use case easily. **Accessibility Inspector** in Xcode can help you with this.

You'll learn more about VoiceOver and Accessibility Inspector later in this chapter.

With these guidelines in place, it's time to go deep into some key user interface elements in iOS. There's a mix of general design guidelines and accessibility technologies in each area. So, time to get started!

## Text

Whatever language you use, your app uses text to convey important information to your users. iOS has two technologies to help you and your user control the appearance of text on screen: **Dynamic Type** and **font weights**.

### Dynamic Type

In iOS 7, Apple added **Dynamic Type** to the iOS SDK. Dynamic Type has a few interesting features:

- **Adjustable text size**: Users can enable Dynamic Type to adjust the on-screen text size **system-wide**. Those who want to see more text on screen can make the font smaller. Others, with vision difficulties, for example, can increase the font size to make the text more *accessible* to them.

- **Apps must add support**: Although the toggle for Dynamic Type is system-wide, only systems that use Dynamic Type fonts will respond to that call from the OS.

You can enable Dynamic Type by going into the Accessibility settings and turning it on. Under Settings in iOS, the Accessibility settings include a **Display & Text Size** category of settings. Within that group of settings, you can toggle on **Larger Text** and choose the text size you prefer.

*The Dynamic Type size selection screen in iOS 15.*

You can also enable Dynamic Type in the Preview Canvas by using the .environment modifier on your preview:

```
ContentView()
    .environment(\.sizeCategory, .extraLarge)
```

You use the \.sizeCategory key path to access the Dynamic Type size for the preview. The value .extraLarge sets the text size.

You still need to enable Dynamic Type support in your app before taking advantage of this feature. Here's how the text in PetSave looks without Dynamic Type support, specifically, the PetRankingView view:

*PetRankingView without Dynamic Type.*

You've seen this screen if you've followed along in building the project to this point. PetSave uses several built-in iOS technologies, including the Text SwiftUI widget for displaying text in the app. By default, this widget uses a Dynamic Type font.

The starter project also uses font modifiers on some of the Text views to change to other font sizes such as .caption or .headline. This is a great example of taking advantage of the built-in features iOS provides. You can see this in action in the Preview Canvas.

Open the starter project and go to **PetSave/Core/views** and open **PetRanking.swift**.

Update the previews block at the bottom of the file:

```
struct PetRankingView_Previews: PreviewProvider {
  static var previews: some View {
    if let animal = CoreDataHelper.getTestAnimalEntity() {
      Group {
        PetRankingView(animal: animal)
          .padding()
          .previewLayout(.sizeThatFits)
          .environment(\.sizeCategory, .extraSmall)
          .previewDisplayName("Extra-Small")

        PetRankingView(animal: animal)
          .padding()
          .previewLayout(.sizeThatFits)
          .previewDisplayName("Regular")

        PetRankingView(animal: animal)
          .padding()
          .previewLayout(.sizeThatFits)
          .environment(\.sizeCategory, .extraLarge)
          .previewDisplayName("Extra-Large")
      }
    }
  }
}
```

This code adds a few more previews to the canvas to show the `.extraSmall` and `.extraExtraLarge` Dynamic Type sizes.

Click **resume** on the preview canvas, if necessary, and you'll see the various font sizes:

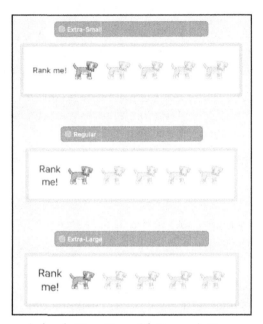

*Animals Near You with Dynamic Type.*

There are some things you need to keep in mind when using Dynamic Type in your app:

- **Avoid truncation**: As your user increases the Dynamic Type size, the text size increases, but the device size doesn't increase along with it. So your text runs the risk of becoming truncated if it becomes too large. Using the `numberOfLines` property in a label lets the system automatically grow the label vertically.

- **Adjust layout if needed**: If your user interface is complex, larger text sizes may make several regions of the interface hard to read. You may need to adjust the layout of your user interface to larger text sizes. For example, shifting horizontal layouts, such as HStack, to a VStack can keep certain elements from getting truncated.

- **SF Symbols is dynamic**: Text isn't the only thing that responds to Dynamic Type. SF Symbols can grow and shrink right along with the text on screen, keeping the interface uniform. This is another reason to use built-in technologies such as SF Symbols!

## Font weights

Your font choice is important when you design your app's user interface. Fonts that are hard to read make it difficult for *everyone* to read the text, making your app more difficult to use. Once you choose a font for your app, there are some best practices to keep in mind:

- **Use regular or heavy fonts**: For the best user experience, avoid thin or light fonts and use regular or heavy weighted fonts. These fonts are easier to read.

- **Ensure bold text is readable**: Users can activate bold text under the **Display & Text Size** section of the Accessibility preferences pane. Ensure that text in your app looks good with this feature enabled.

# VoiceOver

VoiceOver is a built-in screen reader in iOS. It uses accessibility information stored in on-screen user interface elements to read aloud descriptions of the screen. With it, you can:

- **Speak the name of elements**: You can drag your finger across the screen to have VoiceOver read the names of the item you're currently touching.

- **Use VoiceOver gestures to interact**: You can use special VoiceOver gestures to interact with the elements since the main interaction with the elements causes VoiceOver to read the names.

- **Adjust speaking rate and pitch**: You can adjust the rate and pitch of the voice that VoiceOver uses to your liking.

Later in this chapter, you'll learn how to ensure your app has the information VoiceOver needs. You'll also learn how to preview what VoiceOver will say for each element by using the Accessibility Inspector.

# Navigation

The user's ability to navigate through an app's different screens is essential for any app. Navigation becomes more important when considering accessibility.

Here are some best practices to follow:

- **Ensure navigation is possible**:  Make sure VoiceOver can navigate to every element.

- **Provide alternate text**: By adding alternative text labels to user interface elements, you ensure VoiceOver provides users a more detailed description of that element. Both custom elements and system-provided controls support alternative text labels.

- **Support the VoiceOver rotor**: The VoiceOver rotor lets a user navigate between various section types of a document or webpage. Make these elements visible to the rotor so VoiceOver can present them to the user.

# Color and contrast

How you use color in your app can convey a great deal of information to your user. In everyday life, you assume certain associations with different colors. For example, red means stop and green means go.

If you recall the statistic from the beginning of the chapter, estimates state that roughly 8% of all men have a red-green color blindness disability, meaning they have difficulty telling red and green pigments apart. You may be thinking, "But what about traffic lights?". Good question. Luckily, there's a paradigm for this:

*Depiction of a railroad traffic light.*

It's a worldwide paradigm that vertical traffic lights have red at the top, green at the bottom and amber in the middle.

Unfortunately, there aren't worldwide paradigms for iOS development. However, there are some best practices:

- **Use glyphs**: You can use recognizable glyphs, such as those from SF Symbols, in addition to the colors to convey information.

- **Use text labels**: Even without color, text is important, and you can still use it to convey information.

- **Use standard colors**: Be sure to take advantage of iOS's built-in features. System colors respond properly to accessibility features such as Invert Colors.

- **Respond to Invert Colors**: Speaking of **Invert Colors**, if you have custom colorings, make sure your app responds appropriately when your user enabled Invert Colors.

The contrast between colors is another powerful tool to make parts of your user interface *pop*. If a foreground object and a background object are too similar in color, it can be hard to distinguish them.

Go to **AnimalDetails/views** and open **AnimalDetailCard.swift**:

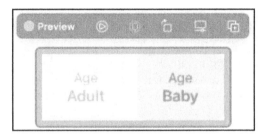

*Poor contrast ratio.*

The green-on-green and blue-on-blue color combinations don't provide the best contrast. Similar shades on top of each other don't stand out well.

The Institute for Disability Research, Policy and Practice at Utah State University has an online contrast checker (https://webaim.org/resources/contrastchecker/), so you can look up contrast values if you know the colors' hex values. The current guidelines, which Apple also recommends in the HIG, are:

- **Normal Text (<= 17 pt)**: Ensure a contrast ratio of 4.5:1.

- **Large Text (> 17 pt)**: Ensure a contrast ratio of 3:1.

Use the calculator above to check your ratios and ensure your elements pop on the screen. The contrast ratio for the green block is 1.88:1, which is less than the requirements above. A proper contrast ratio can turn the above image into this one:

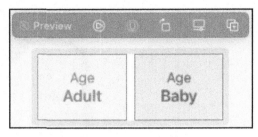

*Great contrast ratio.*

The text stands out a bit more now with the greater contrast ratio. You should check all areas of your app where contrast ratio issues may arise. Fortunately, Xcode has **Accessibility Inspector** to help accomplish that.

# Using the Accessibility Inspector

The best way to learn about accessibility features in iOS is to apply them to an app. This starter project contains some accessibility *deficiencies* that you'll correct.

Run and build the starter project. Then, in the Xcode menu, go to **Xcode -> Open Developer Tool -> Accessibility Inspector**.

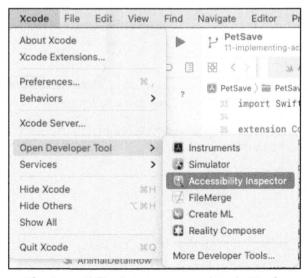

*The Accessibility Inspector menu item in Xcode.*

Put the Simulator and Accessibility Inspector window side by side. In the upper left-hand corner, select the simulator as the item to inspect, then click **target selector** at the top right and click over the animals' list. You'll see something like this:

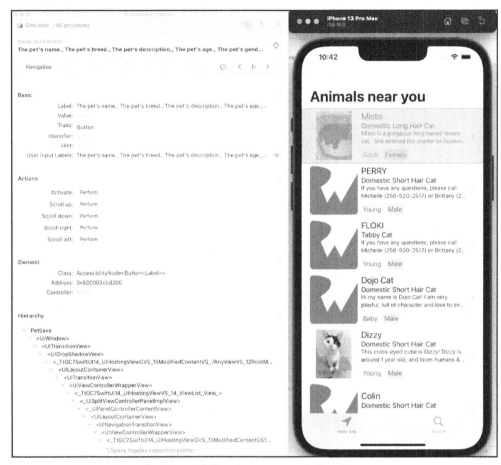

*The Accessibility Inspector and Simulator.*

The Accessibility Inspector has three areas you can use to help test your app, the first of which is the **Inspection Tool**.

# Inspection tool

**Inspection Tool** is the default tool when the Accessibility Inspector launches. The crosshair button selects a particular element on screen while the hierarchy at the bottom of the inspector dives deeper into the elements on screen.

With the first row selected, scroll down in the hierarchy and choose the first element in the row. Then click the arrow to the right of the element to dive in:

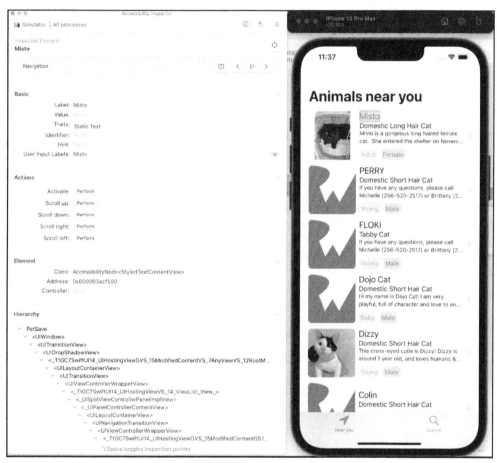

*Details from inspecting an element in the on screen view.*

The **Basic** section at the top lists some information about the element under inspection. It's static text and lists the text of the Text view in the **Label** section.

That label comes into play when using VoiceOver. Tap the **Speak** button, and you'll hear what VoiceOver would say for this element:

*The speak button allows you to hear what VoiceOver would say for this element.*

Speaking the text of the Text element is useful. But, it's not *informative* to someone who can't see the screen and depends on the descriptions from VoiceOver to help them. Later on, you'll see how to improve this label to give VoiceOver more informative content.

If you have a complex app, it can be time-consuming to go through each and every element and inspect it by hand. Fortunately, the **Audit Tool** can do that for you.

## Audit tool

You can use the **Audit Tool** to generate a report of possible Accessibility violations from the user interface elements currently on screen.

Select the Audit Tool, the middle button in the upper right-hand corner of the Accessibility Inspector.

*Audit Tool icon.*

Run an audit with the **Animals Near You** view showing:

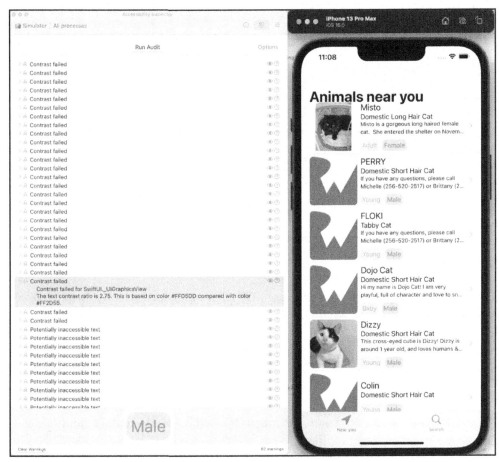

*Results of an audit of the Animals Near You screen.*

There are several contrast-related warnings. Fix these by using a darker color for the text to make it stand out from the background.

Go to **PetSave/Core/AnimalDetails/views/** and open **AnimalDetailCard.swift**. Add
the following extension to `Color`:

```
extension Color {
  func darken(_ amount: Double) -> Color {
    let uiColor = UIColor(self)
    var red: CGFloat = 0
    var green: CGFloat = 0
    var blue: CGFloat = 0
    var alpha: CGFloat = 0
    uiColor.getRed(&red, green: &green, blue: &blue, alpha:
&alpha)
    let darkenedUIColor =
      UIColor(
        red: min(red - amount / 100, 1.0),
        green: min(green - amount / 100, 1.0),
        blue: min(blue - amount / 100, 1.0),
        alpha: 1.0)
    return Color(darkenedUIColor)
  }
}
```

This method extracts the color's current RGB values and darkens it by the passed in
amount. `Color` has a limited API, so the code converts `Color` to a `UIColor` to help
get the component values.

In the foreground modifier later in the file, use a darker color:

```
.foregroundColor(color.darken(40.0))
```

This will take the passed in color and darken it by 40%. Use this darker color in the
`AnimalAttributes` view modifier.

Open **AnimalAttributesCard.swift** and update the modifier:

```
struct AnimalAttributesCard: ViewModifier {
  let color: Color
  func body(content: Content) -> some View {
    content
      .padding(4)
      .background(color.opacity(0.2))
      .cornerRadius(8)
      .foregroundColor(color.darken(+40))
      .font(.subheadline)
  }
}
```

Again, the foreground color's darkness increases by 40% to increase the contrast ratio.

You can address the **Potentially inaccessible text** warnings in the audit report by including .accessibility modifiers on your Text fields. For example, in **AnimalContactLink.swift**, add a modifier to the title's Text element:

```
Text(title)
  .font(.callout)
  .accessibility(label: Text("The contact information for this
pet: " + title))
```

Adding this label also helps with the VoiceOver issue from earlier. VoiceOver now has a more complete label to read aloud and gives the user the on screen information and the *context* in which it exists.

> **Note**: Go and check **AnimalRow.swift**, the Text views already have accessibility(label:) in place.

Update the other Text elements in the app. With these corrections in place, build and rerun the app. Then rerun the audit:

*The updated audit result.*

The report shows that many of the contrast warnings are gone, but not all of them. These are from native iOS elements, specifically the disclosure indicator, which means Apple has some work to do to make their own elements accessible!

The **Potentially inaccessible text** warnings are still in this report, even though you added accessibility labels to the Text views. This seems to be a bug in Accessibility Inspector, possibly because it doesn't completely understand SwiftUI.

The Accessibility Inspector is a powerful tool, but it would be nice to have tools built right into Xcode that give you more insight into the accessibility of your UI elements. Fortunately, Xcode 13 and macOS Monterey put such a tool into developers' hands.

## The Xcode accessibility inspector

It's time for a quick detour from the Accessibility Inspector *app* to the similarly named Accessibility Inspector *property pane* in Xcode:

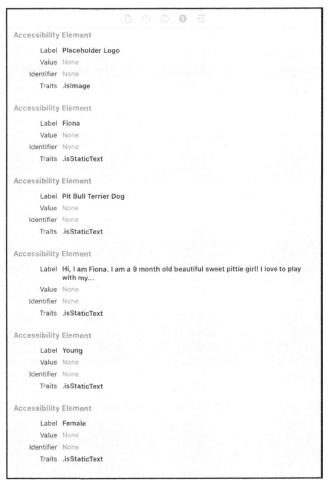

*The Accessibility Inspector property pane in Xcode 13.*

The image above shows the `AnimalRow` view accessibility information. To see this in action, open **AnimalRow.swift** and click `AnimalRow(animal: animal)` in the previews struct at the bottom of the file. Then click the accessibility tab: It's the second icon from the right in the Inspectors tab, showing a person inside a circle.

The Accessibility Inspector property pane now shows all of the relevant accessibility elements within `AnimalRow`, which as a reminder looks like this:

*The AnimalRow view in the Petsave app.*

The Accessibility Inspector pane shows the accessibility information for each element. It also lists the elements in the order in which VoiceOver would read them out.

When VoiceOver reads this view, it says: "Fiona, Pit Bull Terrier Dog, Hi, I am Fiona. I am a 9-month-old beautiful sweet pittie girl. I love to play with my. Young. Female. Button."

That's a *lot* for someone to deal with. SwiftUI has some new accessibility modifiers that can help developers provide important information first and give the user the choice to reveal more content.

You'll simplify the VoiceOver details in three steps:

1. **Combine accessibility**: Treat the entire row as one unit from an accessibility perspective.

2. **Hide existing labels**: Hide some accessibility labels so that only certain ones show by default.

3. **Add custom fields**: Add the remaining accessibility labels as custom accessibility entries.

First, combine the accessibility entries of the internal views of the `HStack` by using a modifier:

```
HStack {
//...
}
.accessibilityElement(children: .combine)
```

Make sure you add this modifier to the topmost `HStack`, the one that contains all the children views.

This code combines the accessibility entries of the children into one listing for the container. This modifier changes the entry for the `HStack` in the accessibility inspector to look like this:

*The AnimalRow view in the Petsave app.*

While that's better, it's still pretty verbose. Hide some accessibility labels that shouldn't be there by default.

Except for the name and gender, add the following modifier to the `Text` views throughout this view:

```
.accessibilityHidden(true)
```

Here, you disable VoiceOver's ability to read these entries. Now the accessibility inspector looks like this:

*Some accessibility labels are now hidden.*

Much more to the point! You still need to give the user the chance to access the other information. Add the following modifiers after `accessibilityElement(children:)`:

```
.accessibilityCustomContent("Age", animal.age.rawValue,
  importance: .high)
.accessibilityCustomContent("Breed", animal.breed)
.accessibilityCustomContent("Type", animalType)
.accessibilityCustomContent("Description", animalDescription)
```

The Accessibility Inspector now shows this:

*Now the HStack has custom accessibility fields*

To properly test this, you need to deploy the app to a device. Then:

1.  **Enable VoiceOver**: Enable VoiceOver in Settings via the **Accessibility->VoiceOver** menu item.

2.  **Go to PetSave**: Ask Siri to **Open PetSave**.

3.  **Select a row**: In the Animals Near You view, select a row. VoiceOver will speak the important parts and tell you there is more content.

4.  **Activate the VoiceOver Rotor**: Make a twist motion on the screen with two fingers. The VoiceOver rotor will appear. Keep twisting until it says **More Content**.

5.  **Flick up to hear more**: Once you choose **More Content**, lift your fingers. Then immediately flick up to hear the first custom accessibility element. Continue flicking to hear more content.

6.  **Turn off VoiceOver**: When you're done, ask Siri to **Open Settings**. Turn off VoiceOver from there with a double-tap the switch.

# Accessibility settings

Once you've made corrections from the audit, you still have work ahead. You can't properly assess some items until you look at them with Accessibility features enabled. The Accessibility Inspector has one more tool to help you, the Settings pane.

The Setting pane lets you toggle settings on and off from the Accessibility Inspector instead of having to go into the Simulator settings:

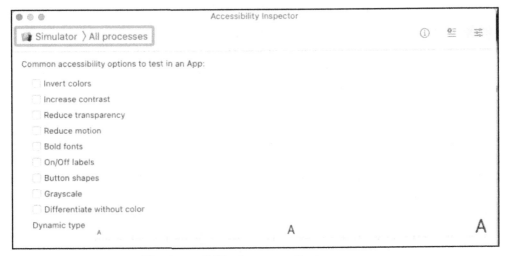

*The Accessibility Inspector Settings pane.*

Using these settings depends on your app and the features it supports. Take advantage of the *accessibility* of these settings and use them to test your app thoroughly!

# Key points

- Using **Accessibility** technologies in your app makes your app more accessible to a larger audience.

- Incorporate accessibility **early in the design of your app**.

- Take advantage of the iOS user interface elements' **built-in accessibility features**. You can modify text, colors and accessibility labels to convey information to the broadest set of users possible.

- **Testing is vital** when working with accessibility technologies. You may not actively use these features in your day-to-day app use. Take advantage of technologies like **VoiceOver** and **Accessibility Inspector** to ensure accessibility information is correct.

# Where to go from here?

Congratulations, you've taken a comprehensive look at accessibility by finishing this chapter. Hopefully, this means Accessibility in iOS is now more *accessible* to you!

For a deeper look at implementing Accessibility in your app, there are several (https://www.raywenderlich.com/20656613-adapting-to-user-accessibility-settings-in-swiftui) tutorials (https://www.raywenderlich.com/7180554-ios-accessibility-in-swiftui-tutorial-part-1-getting-started) available (https://www.raywenderlich.com/6827616-ios-accessibility-getting-started) at raywenderlich.com.

Apple's HIG, or Human Interface Guidelines for iOS (https://developer.apple.com/design/human-interface-guidelines/accessibility/overview/introduction/) has a specific section that covers Accessibility, which supplements the information presented in this chapter.

There are also several (https://developer.apple.com/videos/play/wwdc2021/10121/) sessions (https://developer.apple.com/videos/play/wwdc2021/10119/) from WWDC (https://developer.apple.com/videos/play/wwdc2021/10122/) 2021 (https://developer.apple.com/videos/play/wwdc2021/10023/) that are worth looking at in regards to accessibility and the new features introduced in iOS 15.

There's one more area to cover in this section of the book. In the next chapter, you'll learn some ways to customize your app's look and feel to give it a unique identity.

# Chapter 11: Customizing the Look & Feel of Your App

By Josh Steele

In the previous chapter, you learned about implementing accessibility in your app. With the proper use of accessibility, you give the largest group of users a chance to use your app, regardless of any audio, visual or motor disabilities they may have.

Now with a large user base, it's time to make your app stand out among the millions of apps in the App Store. There are different ways to do this. Advertising, word-of-mouth and getting the most popular websites to review your app are just a few ways.

Before you do any of that, it's important to make your app *look* unique. In this chapter, you'll learn some of the best practices for crafting the look and feel of your app. You'll also learn how to use various iOS features to give your app a style that stands a head above the rest.

# Defining look and feel

In this section of the book, you've learned a lot about Apple's Human Interface Guidelines (HIG) (https://developer.apple.com/design/human-interface-guidelines/ios/overview/themes/). This chapter is no different. Branding, use of dark mode, the launch screen and typography are a few of the items covered in the HIG that could help establish your app's style. This style is usually referred to as your app's *look and feel*.

The definition of look and feel can vary, but in this chapter, you'll focus on two areas:

- **Branding**: Your app name, logo and design scheme can help your app stand out from the crowd.

- **Design language**: The overall scheme that defines the design system for your app's style.  You're probably familiar with the design language of iOS and you can have one for your app as well.

You may have noticed an overlap between those two areas. Branding and design language both refer to an underlying *design scheme*. Your design scheme is more evident in your app logo or launch screen. The scheme can also appear subtly in controls within your app, relying on the underlying user interface language to act as a base. Here, the scheme acts as a skin on existing controls.

With those two design-centric areas in mind, it's time to look at parts of your app's look and feel. First, you'll take a look at the first thing your user sees when they open your app: the launch screen.

# Launch Screen

If you have a brand, it's essential to get it to the users' eyes as soon as possible. Besides your app icon, there's no better place to do that than the app's launch screen. The HIG contains important guidance when it comes to the launch screen:

- **Use the built-in storyboard**: Take advantage of your project's `LaunchScreen.storyboard` and avoid using a static image, *if possible*. The storyboard can adapt to the various screen sizes and orientations that iOS devices support.

- **Mimic a fast launch**: If your storyboard looks a lot like your app's initial home screen, it can mimic a fast launch of the app. It's a sleight of hand trick, or maybe a sleight of eye trick, that can keep your user from detecting any slowness in your app's startup.

- **Support Dark Mode**: The launch screen should support dark mode, which you'll learn about later in this chapter.

- **Avoid Localization**: iOS renders launch screen content differently from other storyboards in your project and doesn't change. Therefore, iOS won't localize any text on that storyboard.

Here's what the current PetSave launch screen looks like:

*The PetSave launch screen.*

It's a static image! That helps convey the app's branding. However, according to the HIG, it's not ideal since you should avoid static images if possible. Replace that with something that looks like the main window without the content in the middle.

Open the project in this chapter's **starter** folder, then open
**Launchboard.storyboard**. Bring up the Xcode Library by pressing **Command-Shift-L** and add a View Controller. Be sure to keep the existing view controller with the
image for now:

*Add a new view controller for the LaunchScreen.*

From the library again, drag over a Tab Bar and Navigation Bar, and place them at the
bottom and top, respectively:

*Add a tab bar and a navigation bar.*

Then remove the text from the navigation bar, and set the tab bar item's icons to match what's in the main app: a custom item with the **location** SF Symbol and a custom item with the **magnifyingglass** SF Symbol. Leaving the text out ensures your users will have a consistent experience, regardless of their native language.

*Set the initial state for the bars.*

Set this view controller as this storyboard's initial view controller in the Attributes inspector:

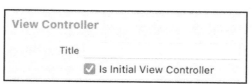

*Set the initial view controller.*

By designating this view controller as the one to use, you can keep both in case your designer changes their mind later.

Build and run the app in the simulator. Now instead of seeing the raywenderlich.com branded launch screen, the simulator presents something that looks similar to your home screen but without content:

*The new interstitial launch screen.*

This new screen gives you a better transition from launch to the actual home page look and feel, but it doesn't work well with the onboarding module that opens on first launch since the background is different.

This could be one of those *good enough* design decisions you may make when designing your app. You and your designer will have to make that decision.

Speaking of onboarding, using onboarding in your app is a best practice, so you'll revisit that next.

## Using onboarding

Using iOS features such as location tracking, HealthKit access and motion of the device requires the user to grant your app permission to access that data. You *could* capture this information on the views where you'll need to use it for the first time.

However, putting those prompts inside an onboarding module is a better technique. While the HIG does suggest avoiding asking for setup information upfront, it says it's permissible on the first launch. When using onboarding, keep in mind:

- **Get to your app quickly**: Your user doesn't want to sit through screen after screen of onboarding material. They'd rather use your app as soon as possible. Get the information you need, and transition into your app once you get it.

- **Avoid licensing agreements**: Avoid displaying licensing agreements and other legalese users have to accept before using your app. If absolutely necessary, it can go somewhere else in your app.

- **Run onboarding once**: The onboarding module should execute on the first launch of the app. Subsequent launches should go straight to the app's home screen. If you can, store settings in the cloud. This way, if the user reinstalls the app on a device, your app can get as much information from the cloud as possible and only reprompt the user for the other information when it needs it.

The onboarding in **PetSave** is in pretty good shape, as you saw earlier in the book:

*The 3 screens of PetSave's onboarding module.*

- **Simple and to the point**: The onboarding doesn't drag the user through many screens and quickly introduces them to the higher-level features of the app.

- **Shows design language**: The background image and the images in the onboarding screens show playful animals drawn in the app's style.

From a design perspective, the onboarding includes the app's branding, which is great. However, you saw earlier that it doesn't *quite* align with the launch screen. Later in this chapter, you'll touch on one more reason you might want to send the onboarding module back to the developer for more work - dark mode.

# Crafting the finer details

Your launch screen and onboarding focus more on the branding aspect of your app. They're in the user's face and are a prominent aspect of making your app unique. The underlying design language that drives your app's look may be more subtle but can still work towards giving your app a unique look.

As with the launch screen and onboarding, built-in features in iOS and Xcode can help you craft this design language with little effort.

## System and custom fonts

Almost all apps have text to convey information to users. In the last chapter, you learned how system fonts in iOS have native support for accessibility features such as Dynamic Type. In addition, system fonts:

- **Are easy to read**: Apple designed both San Francisco (SF) and New York (NY) system fonts to be easy to read in various sizes, weights and styles.

- **Support multiple languages**: When you localize your app, it becomes available to people worldwide. System fonts in iOS have built-in support for over a hundred languages.

The system fonts contain a lot of built-in flexibility. Here are some guidelines about when to take advantage of that flexibility in your app:

- **Emphasize importance**: Just like in the text of this book, you can emphasize the importance of a word or phrase by making it bold or by italicizing it.

- **Use the fewest fonts possible**: If you switch back and forth between different fonts in your app, it can appear disjointed and give the user a less than ideal experience.

- **Check custom fonts**: If you use a custom font, make sure it's legible and adapts to accessibility features. System fonts already support these features out of the box.

You can install a custom font into your Xcode project in a few simple steps. First, add the font file to your project:

*Adding a font to the PetSave project.*

The font here is called **Sheep Sans**. It's available at <u>DaFont.com</u>. The author was kind enough to make it free to use.

Before proceeding, add the font to both the PetSave and PetSaveTests targets:

*Add the font to the appropriate targets.*

Then, you need to specify which fonts to include in the app bundle.

Add a new entry in **Info.plist** called **Fonts provided by application**. Under that entry, set Item 0's value to the name of the font file, `sheep_sans.ttf`:

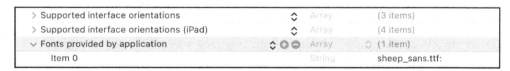

*Add a font to Info.plist*

You can then use the new font with the Font.custom method. Open **AnimalRow.swift** and update the modifiers for the animal name and breed. Type to use the new font:

```
Text(animalName)
  .multilineTextAlignment(.center)
  .font(Font.custom("sheep_sans", size: 18,
relativeTo: .title3))
  .accessibilityLabel(animalName)
Text(animalBreedAndType)
  .font(Font.custom("sheep_sans", size: 15,
relativeTo: .callout))
  .accessibilityLabel(animalBreedAndType)
  .accessibilityHidden(true)
```

The custom method on the Font class includes a relativeTo: argument that lets the font scale adaptively to that text style instead of the default, body.

Use the preview canvas to see how the new font looks:

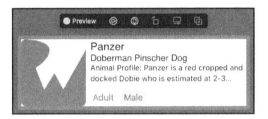

*The Sheep Sans font in the AnimalRow preview.*

This text looks very similar to the built in font, but there is a bit of a flair in the tail of the lowercase "a". Even subtle differences from the built in fonts may be enough to give your app the unique look you want.

A unique font can, of course, help make your design language more unique. However, a font that is *too* unique can impair the user. If the font is hard to read, especially on a small display like the iPhone, your user may be discouraged from using your app.

How you style your font may also have an impact. The discussion about colors in the accessibility chapter comes to mind here. Also, your design language should ensure that a font, especially a custom one, remains legible when it's bold or italicized.

Colors are a vital component of your design language, especially when the entire display inverts itself as it does in Dark Mode.

# Dark mode

Starting in iOS 13, Apple offered users the option of viewing their views in **Dark Mode**. Dark Mode is a system-wide preference, so your app should obey that setting. You have to ensure that your app looks good in *both* light and dark modes.

Chances are, if you didn't plan for Dark Mode support from the start, you probably designed in Light Mode. That's ok! Keep these things in mind when determining how your app will look in Dark Mode:

- **Your current color scheme**: How does your current color scheme look with a darker theme? Are there now dark colors on dark colors?

- **Did you lose contrast?**: With a much darker theme, be sure to check contrast ratios. Don't forget your logos or images.

- **Check your custom colors**: While some colors and other user interface elements, such as Spacer(), automatically handle the switch between Light and Dark Modes, custom colors don't. You'll need a **Color Set** to handle those.

As with many other areas of iOS, there are some nice, built-in defaults in SwiftUI that make Dark Mode convenient to use:

- **Adaptable system colors**: Dark Mode is dynamic, which means that when user interface elements come to the front, their background color shifts slightly to provide a visual difference between the foreground and background. Custom colors don't support this dynamic quality, so stick with system background colors.

- **High contrast colors**: System colors also provide a sufficient amount of contrast, at least 7:1, which is another reason to use them.

- **Label color support**: The primary, secondary, tertiary and quaternary label colors also, you guessed it, naturally respond to changes in Light and Dark Mode. Thanks, Apple!

- **SF Symbols support**: SF Symbols support both Light and Dark Mode, which is another reason to use SF Symbols when possible.

With this knowledge, it's time to look at PetSave and see where it could use some improvements in Dark Mode. You have a few options to see views in Dark Mode.

In your SwiftUI previews, use this modifier to enable Dark Mode:

```
.preferredColorScheme(.dark)
```

That's pretty easy! If you're using the simulator, you'll need to put the entire simulator in Dark Mode. You do this through the Simulator's **Features -> Toggle Appearance** menu item or the **Shift-Command-A** keyboard shortcut.

Here's what the preview canvas for the PetSave home page looks like:

*The PetSave home screen in Dark Mode.*

At a high level, this looks good. The text has automatically flipped from black to white, courtesy of the OS. The same is true for the background of the List and the rows within the list. Even the colors that list the age and gender look ok against the darker background.

Once you tap a row to see details, however, you'll see a problem:

*The list row in Dark Mode.*

The tag field that shows the pet's coat has a contrast issue! The now dark background sits behind the dark tag background and lighter text color.

Color sets provide a solution to this problem. You can specify a color set that uses different colors based on whether the app is in light or dark mode.

To make a color set, open the **Assets Catalog** in the project. Right-click the existing colors folder and choose **New Color Set**:

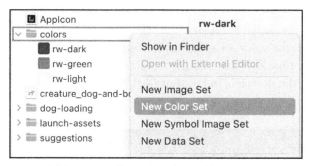

*Add a new color set to the project assets.*

A new color entry appears, allowing you to specify a color for **Any Appearance** and **Dark**. Rename the color to **coat-background-color**. In the **Any Appearance** swatch, supply the current color for the background, which is systemBrownColor. Update the attributes panel to reflect this:

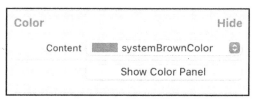

*Use the system brown color for Light Mode.*

For the **Dark Mode** swatch, you need to choose a color that stands out well against the darker background. Choose systemYellowColor from the dropdown menu:

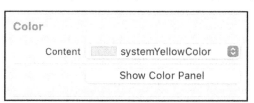

*Use the system yellow color for Dark Mode.*

This color acts as a good contrast to the brown from Light Mode.

In **AnimalDetailRow.swift**, update the block that displays the coat:

```
if let coat = animal.coat {
  AnimalDetailCard(
    title: "Coat",
    value: coat.rawValue,
```

```
    color: Color(UIColor(named: "coat-background-color") ??
      .systemBrown)
  )
}
```

This update makes the color an appropriate color from the `coat-background-color` set, along with a fallback if that color is `nil`. iOS determines the correct color to load based on whether the device is in Light or Dark Mode.

Refresh the preview canvas to see the result:

*The coat tag is much easier to see.*

While Dark mode is easy to take advantage of, it may require a little work on your end to make sure your design language is compatible. When you implement your changes for Dark Mode, try to maintain a uniform look and feel throughout the app to the greatest extent possible to help maintain a sense of consistency through your app.

## Maintaining consistency

Consistency is an essential quality of your design language. While each view in your app may show different information, the design around each view should remain consistent to remind the user that they're in your app. They'll associate your unique look and feel with using your app.

The iOS's existing design language is well known and is *mostly* adhered to throughout Apple's apps. Take advantage of this design language by building upon it with your customizations.

Earlier, you learned that fonts should remain consistent. It's the same with color. Your design language may dictate, for example, that headers should always be particular shades of green whether you're in light or dark mode.

Iconography is an important part of your design language. You can use SF Symbols (https://developer.apple.com/sf-symbols/) to not only provide icon consistency *within your app*, but with other apps on your user's device. Therefore, the guidance for iconography is to use SF Symbols whenever possible.

As usual, SF Symbols have built-in features to help you:

- **Tinting**: SF Symbols look great when tinted. If you choose an app-wide tint color, any SF Symbols you use will automatically adjust.

- **Hollow vs. filled**: Many SF Symbols come in two formats: hollow and filled. Depending on your background and overall design scheme, you may want some symbols hollow and others filled.

- **Built-in Dark Mode**: Apple designed SF Symbols to look great in Dark Mode.

Surprise! You've been using SF Symbols the whole time you've been reading the book! The icons in the `TabView` are common SF Symbols and should be familiar to most iOS users:

*The icons in the TabView.*

There's another bit of iconography that the app uses. Longtime readers of raywenderlich.com books may recognize it:

*The raywenderlich.com logo is part of PetSave's branding.*

That's right! The raywenderlich.com logo is the placeholder for the table row images and provides subtle branding inside the app.

Xcode and iOS features help bring your app's design scheme elements to life. There's one more set of tools that will help widen your app's reach and enhance the look and feel at the same time.

# Internationalization and localization

You might not associate look and feel with internationalization and localization. **Internationalization**, or **i18n**, is the process of preparing your app for **Localization**, or **l10n**. Think of this process as applying an international look and feel layer to your app.

This process can take place in several areas of your project:

- **Localized resources**: Xcode supports localized resource bundles for text and images and maintains them separately from the rest of the project. This way, you can localize them separately and bring them into your project later in the development cycle.

- **SF Symbols**: SF Symbols seem to have a never-ending list of capabilities, including supporting localization.

- **Foundation APIs**: The APIs in Foundation provide a great deal of functionality for dealing with different dates, prices, currencies, lengths and more. Now you don't have to write a date converter for the millionth time!

- **Layout support**: SwiftUI and UIKit have built-in support for localization features such as right-to-left text.

Once you know which locales and languages you want to support, configuring your project is straightforward. For this example, you'll apply a Spanish localization to **PetSave**.

# Making a localizable Strings file

Before localizing the project, add **Localizable.strings** to the project. Right-click the project, select **New File** and choose **Strings File**:

*Adding a Strings file to the project.*

Call it **Localizable.strings**, this file stores key-value pairs representing the text in your app and the translation for the given language.

iOS will automatically look for localizable strings files like these when run in associated languages. To tell iOS that the app supports other languages, you need to add a locale to Xcode.

# Adding a locale to Xcode

Now with the localizable Strings file in place, it's time to localize your project!

Open the project file. Under **Localizations**, click the + button and add the Spanish locale:

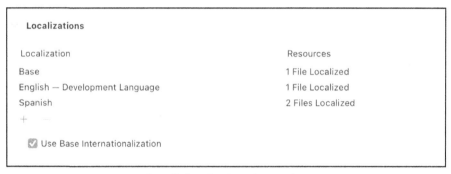

*Localizing PetSave in Xcode.*

A dialog will pop up asking what you want to localize. Only the **LaunchScreen.storyboard** is available, so click **Finish**:

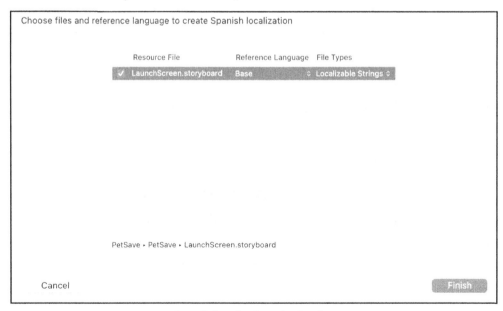

*Localizing PetSave in Xcode.*

You need to make sure the **Localizable.strings** you made is localizable. Select that file, and in the File Inspector in Xcode, click the **Localize** button:

*Localizing PetSave in Xcode.*

From the dialog that appears, choose **Spanish**:

*Localize the file for Spanish.*

You want to specify entries for English as well, so enable English localization as well in the File inspector:

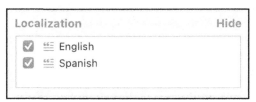

*Add English to the localization options.*

## Adding localization entries

Add the following entries to the English file **Localizable(English)**:

```
"Age" = "Age";
"Gender" = "Gender";
"Size" = "Size";
"Coat" = "Coat";
"Adult" = "Adult";
```

```
"Male" = "Male";
"Female" = "Female";
"Unknown" = "Unknown";
"Short" = "Short";
"Details" = "Details";
"Contact" = "Contact";
"Location" = "Location";
"Rank me!" = "Rank me!";
"Animals near you" = "Animals near you";
"Near you" = "Near you";
"Search" = "Search";
"Young" = "Young";
```

The values here match the keys because English is the project's base language. Now, add the following translations to the Spanish file **Localizable(Spanish)**:

```
"Age" = "Edad";
"Gender" = "Género";
"Size" = "Talla";
"Coat" = "Pelo";
"Adult" = "Adulta";
"Male" = "Masculina";
"Female" = "Femenino";
"Unknown" = "Ignoto";
"Short" = "Corta";
"Details" = "Detalles";
"Contact" = "Contacto";
"Location" = "Posición";
"Rank me!" = "Clasificarme!";
"Animals near you" = "Animales cerca de usted";
"Near you" = "Cerca de usted";
"Search" = "Búsqueda";
"Young" = "Menor";
```

# Configuring your scheme's locale

To properly test your localization, you'll need to update your project's scheme. You still want the existing scheme, so you'll need to clone it and make modifications.

Open the scheme dropdown and choose **Edit Scheme**. In the dialog that appears, choose **Duplicate Scheme**:

*Duplicating a scheme in Xcode.*

After clicking **Duplicate**, rename the scheme **PetSave (Debug, Spanish)**:

*Renaming a scheme in Xcode.*

Under the **Run** entry in the side column, find the **Options** tab. Change the App Language to **Spanish**:

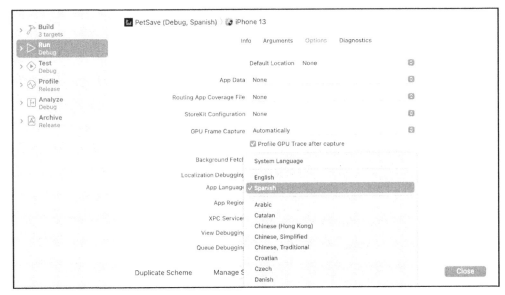

*Changing the App Language to Spanish.*

## Testing your project

From the scheme picker, choose the **PetSave (Debug, Spanish)** scheme, and run the app in the simulator.

*PetSave's home screen in Spanish.*

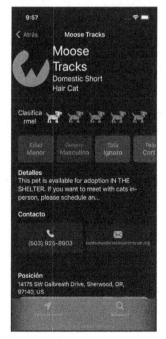

*The animal detail view in Spanish.*

iOS doesn't translate all of the words. Much of the data used by the app comes from the remote API, and that text is only available in English.

But, Xcode can translate other items like headers, fixed string values and the tab bar item titles ahead of time. With these translations available, you've added another layer of look and feel to your app. You've also taken another step in expanding your app's reach to more people around the world!

## Key points

- **Branding** and your app's **design language** are the major components of your app's look and feel.

- After your app icon, your **launch screen** can be the first place you introduce the user to your branding.

- Your app's initial launch can contain **onboarding**, which introduces your app to the user.

- Onboarding should be brief but informative.

- **Fonts** help define the text-based portion of your app's look and feel.

- Fonts, especially custom ones, should be accessible and easy to read.

- Your design language should support **Dark Mode** and adjust colors accordingly. **Color Sets** are useful when adapting your app for Dark Mode.

- Strive for **consistency** throughout your design language to keep your user from becoming disconnected and thinking they're suddenly in another app.

- **Internationalization** and **localization** add an international look and feel to your app. Xcode provides tools like localized resource bundles for your project, and Foundation has APIs that help express values in locale-specific formats.

# Where to go from here?

Congratulations! You've finished this chapter and this section of the book. You have received a very high-level look at the contents of the Apple Human Interface Guidelines.

In this section of the book, you learned how animations, custom controls, accessibility features and look and feel customizations can all contribute to making your app unique in the vast sea of apps in the App Store.

There's always more to learn, though. As before, check out the rest of Apple's Human Interface Guidelines (HIG) (https://developer.apple.com/design/human-interface-guidelines/ios/overview/themes/) for other topics not covered in this section. Apple has some guidance on Localization (https://developer.apple.com/localization/), and they also provide a deeper dive into using SF Symbols (https://developer.apple.com/design/human-interface-guidelines/sf-symbols/overview/).

Using a translation API to perform dynamic translation is one way to translate text coming from a source that's outside of your control, such as Petfinder's API. If you're interested in this approach, you could look into using such a translation API. There are free and paid options available.

In the next chapter, you'll learn about maintaining users' privacy when they use your app.

# Section V: App Privacy, Maintenance & Deployment

As you approach deployment more and more things come to mind: am I protecting that user's data and privacy? Do I have any edge cases in my code that I haven't seen? How do I get beta testers, and why won't my Code Signing work? All these questions can be summarized into three topics: Privacy, Debugging and App Distribution.

In this section you'll dive deeper into these topics, getting you ready to send your app to the App Store.

# Chapter 12: App Privacy

By Renan Benatti Dias

The iPhone completely changed the way people use phones. A phone is no longer just a device for making calls: It's a whole **computer in your pocket**, full of features and capabilities.

With it, the **App Store** transformed the way developers deliver their experience to customers. Developers create apps and submit them to the App Store. Apple reviews them, and then they become available to users. Potential users can browse and find many different kinds of apps, and they trust **Apple's review** to guarantee the minimum quality of that app.

However, with all the new capabilities developers can access, privacy has become a real concern to everyone. The conversation about who owns your data and how companies can use it is an issue that triggers a never-ending debate.

Apple has taken a strong position on this: People's privacy is important and they should decide if they want to share any data with developers.

With that in mind, Apple built new features into iOS and the App Store to make developers more transparent and iOS more private.

In this chapter, you'll learn about:

- iOS's many **privacy features**.

- **Requesting location** data from users.

- Sending the user's location in the request to Petfinder's API to find pets near that location.

- How apps **adapt UI** to account for users' privacy choices.

- The App Store's **Privacy section**.

Before you start, take a closer look at why privacy is important.

# Why privacy is important

Apple takes people's privacy very seriously. It understands that people don't want to share every detail of their lives. People have the right to choose what and how much they share. That's why Apple has worked hard to make privacy features: to give people a choice in what they want to share.

Apps may want to collect data to drive a specific feature, make a more targeted advertisement or even improve released features.

Apple understands that developers may need access to this data to build better features, but that doesn't mean people don't have a choice. **Transparency**, letting users understand what they are sharing and why, is a critical aspect of privacy.

That's why Apple has built features that allow developers to ask for authorization to access those capabilities and make users aware of when and why.

# iOS privacy features

Many of iOS's privacy features focus on apps and developers being transparent.

iOS's camera and microphone indicator are great examples. iOS displays a **green circular dot** at the top-right corner of the screen whenever an app uses either camera.

*iOS app using camera.*

You'll also find an indicator at the top of **control center**, showing the name of the app that recently used the camera.

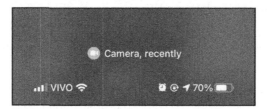

*iOS control center.*

Similarly, when an app accesses the microphone, an **orange circular dot** appears in the top right-hand corner.

*iOS app using microphone.*

Much like the green light near the MacBook's camera, these indicators try to call the users' attention and show them an app is using those capabilities.

iOS has many other privacy features like the **clipboard prompt**, which shows a banner displaying an app is pasting text from the clipboard, or the permission to access the user's gallery, contacts or location data.

# The privacy view modifier

SwiftUI also has a couple of **view modifiers** to keep sensitive data private. Lock screens can access a widget without unlocking the iPhone, which is a potential problem if a widget shows sensitive information.

Apple introduced the `redacted(reason:)` and `privacySensitive(_:)` view modifiers and the environment variable `redactionReasons` to help with this problem. With these view modifiers, you can protect sensitive content given the context.

Take a look at the following code:

```swift
struct CreditCardView: View {
  var body: some View {
    VStack(alignment: .leading, spacing: 82) {
      VStack(alignment: .leading) {
        HStack {
          Text("Ray Bank")
            .font(.title2)
          Spacer()

          Text("platinum")
            .font(.caption2)
        }
        Text("Credit Card")
          .font(.caption)
      }

      VStack(alignment: .leading) {
        HStack(alignment: .bottom) {
          Text("1234 5678 9123 456")
          Spacer()
          Image(systemName: "flag.square.fill")
            .font(.title)
            .imageScale(.large)
        }
        HStack {
          Text("Exp: 02/20")
          Text("Valid: 02/21")
          Text("Security Code:")
          Text("123")
        }
        .font(.caption2)
      }
    }
    .padding()
    .background(.green)
    .foregroundColor(.white)
    .mask(RoundedRectangle(cornerRadius: 8))
```

```
      .padding()
    }
  }
}
```

This view shows a virtual credit card from a banking app.

*Example of displaying sensitive information.*

Credit cards contain sensitive information like the card number, security code and even the user's name. If you were to use this view in a widget, the cards number and security code could be accessible to anyone through the lock screen.

Even with the iPhone unlocked, people might want to redact those pieces of information so that those around them can't see.

That's where redacted(reason:) and privacySensitive(_:) come into play. By adding privacySensitive(_:) to the sensitive views and redacted(reason:) in a top hierarchy view, SwiftUI redacts that information.

```
Text("1234 5678 9123 456")
  .privacySensitive()

Text("Security Code:")
Text("123")
  .privacySensitive()
```

privacySensitive marks the credit card's number and security code Text as private and sensitive data. Now, using this view in a private context will redact those fields.

```
struct WidgetView: View {
  var body: some View {
    CreditCardView()
      .redacted(reason: .privacy)
  }
}
```

WidgetView is a sensitive context, and the lock screen can display it. You can redact these fields by adding redacted(reason:) with the reason of .privacy to CreditCardView.

*Example of hiding senstitive information.*

You can also use the environment variable redactionReasons to change how you hide the view.

```
if redactionReasons == .privacy {
  Text("Hidden card number")
} else {
  Text("1234 5678 9123 456")
}
```

That way, when the view is presented in a sensitive context, the hidden message replaces the card number.

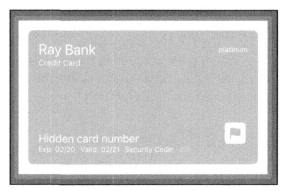

*Example of displaying sensitive information with a hidden message.*

These are a couple of APIs you can use to protect user privacy.

PetSave doesn't display any sensitive data. Even though it uses the user's location to find pets, it doesn't display it in any view, so you won't use these view modifiers.

## Location and privacy

A user's location is very **sensitive data**. It might reveal to developers where the user lives, walks or commutes. So, users should be aware and in control whenever apps have access to their location.

Right now, the **Animals near you** feature does *not* use the user's location to find pets near them. It *randomly* lists pets. However, the whole point of this feature is to find pets that match the user and that are near them.

You'll ask the user's permission to access their location data to improve **Animals near you**.

# Adding location to find pets near you

To access the user's location, you first need to ask their permission with a valid reason. Remember, it's the user's choice to allow access to their private details.

You'll build a new view to ask for permission. With that permission in place, users will get a location-specific list, rather than the default list the app shows when it doesn't have permission to access the user's location.

## Building a view to ask permission

Inside **AnimalsNearYou/views**, create a new **SwiftUI View** and name it **RequestLocationView.swift**.

Add the following property to the new view:

```
@EnvironmentObject var locationManager: LocationManager
```

LocationManager is a class you use to manage the person's location. You'll use it to start monitoring the person's location and ask them for permission to do so.

Since you'll use a single instance of LocationManager throughout the project, you'll use an @EnvironmentObject. @EnvironmentObject is a property wrapper that stores and shares an instance among views of the view hierarchy.

Next, add the following method:

```
func startUpdatingLocation() {
    locationManager.startUpdatingLocation()
}
```

startUpdatingLocation is a method from LocationManager that starts tracking the user's location. Once the user grants permission to their location data, LocationManager will keep track of their location and call the delegate method locationManager(_:didUpdateLocations:) with the updated location.

Next, add the following import at the top of the file:

```
import CoreLocationUI
```

Apple introduced a new CoreLocationUI framework in iOS 15. You'll mainly use it with the CoreLocation, working in a standard, known way, to request access to the user's location data.

Then, replace the code of body with:

```
VStack {
  // 1
  Image("creature_dog-and-bone")
    .resizable()
    .frame(width: 240, height: 240)
  // 2
  Text("""
    To find pets near you, first, you need to
    share your current location.
    """)
    .multilineTextAlignment(.center)
  // 3
  LocationButton {
    locationManager.startUpdatingLocation()
  }
  .symbolVariant(.fill)
  .foregroundColor(.white)
  .cornerRadius(8)
}
.padding()
.onAppear {
  // 4
  locationManager.updateAuthorizationStatus()
}
```

Here's a code breakdown:

1.  Adds an image of a dog as a placeholder.

2.  A Text that explains why the user has to share their current location.

3.  A button to ask the user to share their location. Here, you call startUpdatingLocation to starts tracking the user's location.

4.  An onAppear(perform:) view modifier to update the authorization status when the view first appears.

Next, add the following under RequestLocationView, inside the preview code:

```
.environmentObject(LocationManager())
```

You need this code to make Xcode previews work because you use an @EnvironmentObject inside the view.

# The new Location button

`LocationButton` is a new SwiftUI button that brings a couple of improvements to asking permission to access the user's location. This new button doesn't require you to add a reason text in the **info.plist** that explains why you want to access the user's location data. It already has a default text and alert for asking permission when the user taps the button and doesn't require you to manually call a method.

It also creates a consistent design language between iOS apps while still allowing you to customize their appearance.

## Location status types

iOS has five location authorization statuses:

1. **notDetermined**: iOS returns this status when `CLLocationManager` doesn't yet know if the user has granted or denied access to their location data.

2. **restricted**: This status doesn't mean the user has denied authorization. Instead, it indicates the user has an active parental control restriction. The user can't change the authorization status. However, the user's parent can change it under **Settings ▸ Screen Time ▸ Content & Privacy Restrictions ▸ Privacy ▸ Location Services**.

3. **denied**: This status explicitly indicates that the user has denied authorization for this app to access their location data.

4. **authorizedAlways**: Apple introduced this status in **iOS 8** with `authorizedWhenInUse` to improve user privacy. It indicates the app has access to the location data at any time, even when the user is *not* using the app.

5. **authorizedWhenInUse**: This status indicates the app has access to the user's location data *only* when the user is using the app.

You have to keep track of these statuses when working with location data to handle them in the features using location data.

When you use `LocationButton`, it grants the app a temporary `authorizedWhenInUse` if the user grants permission. This is great for features that require a **one-time** authorization to work.

# Updating Animals Near You to request authorization

Now that you have a view for asking for the user's authorization, it's time to update **Animals Near You** to use it.

Back inside **AnimalsNearYouView.swift**, add:

```
@EnvironmentObject var locationManager: LocationManager
```

This line helps access `locationManager` using `@EnvironmentObject`.

Now, replace the code inside `NavigationView` with:

```
// 1
if locationManager.locationIsDisabled {
  RequestLocationView()
    .navigationTitle("Animals near you")
} else {
  // 2
  AnimalListView(animals: animals) {
    if !animals.isEmpty && viewModel.hasMoreAnimals {
      HStack(alignment: .center) {
        LoadingAnimation()
          .frame(maxWidth: 125, minHeight: 125)
        Text("Loading more animals...")
      }
      .task {
        await viewModel.fetchMoreAnimals()
      }
    }
  }
  .task {
    await viewModel.fetchAnimals()
  }
  .listStyle(.plain)
  .navigationTitle("Animals near you")
  .overlay {
    if viewModel.isLoading && animals.isEmpty {
      ProgressView("Finding Animals near you...")
    }
  }
}
```

Here's what's happening:

1. First, you use `locationIsDisabled` to check if you have access to the user's location. It's a computed property of `LocationManager` that checks the app's location status. If the app doesn't have permission to access the user's location data, you show the new `RequestLocationView` to ask for authorization.

2. If the app has access to location services, you show the list of animals, just like before.

Finally, inside the preview at the bottom of the file, add the following line at the end of the view:

```
.environmentObject(LocationManager())
```

This code makes Xcode previews work since you're using an `@EnvironmentObject` inside `AnimalsNearYouView`.

Before you build and run, go back to **ContentView.swift** and add the following property:

```
@StateObject var locationManager = LocationManager()
```

Here, you use `@StateObject` to store an instance of `LocationManager`. Then, at the end of tab view, add the `environmentObject`:

```
.environmentObject(locationManager)
```

You then pass the `locationManager` to the environment of the view.

`@StateObject` is a property wrapper that works like `@State`, except it creates a single instance only once, even if the view is invalidated and recreated.

Before you build and run, update the preview code with the following line under `ContentView`:

```
.environmentObject(LocationManager())
```

This code makes preview work.

Build and run.

*Requesting user's authorization to access their location.*

Tap **Current Location**.

*Current Location button alerting user.*

Tapping the button presents an alert requesting the user's authorization to access their location. The user may or may not allow it. If the user taps **Not Now**, the same alert shows till the user taps **OK**. Thus, it becomes clear to the user that the location-based feature will *only* work when they allow access.

Tapping **OK** shows the list of animals once again.

*Pet list.*

# Sending location data in the request

Now, PetSave asks for authorization to access the user's location. However, it's not doing anything with this data yet.

You'll add this data in the body of the request to fetch animals.

Open **AnimalsNearYouViewModel.swift** and find the following code inside `AnimalsFetcher`:

```
func fetchAnimals(page: Int) async -> [Animal]
```

Update this line with:

```
func fetchAnimals(
  page: Int,
  latitude: Double?,
  longitude: Double?
) async -> [Animal]
```

This code updates the protocol method to accept latitude and longitude as parameters.

Now, open **services/FetchAnimalsService.swift** and update `fetchAnimals(page:)` to conform to `AnimalsFetcher`:

```
func fetchAnimals(
  page: Int,
  latitude: Double?,
  longitude: Double?
) async -> [Animal] {
```

Next, find the following two lines inside `fetchAnimals(page:latitude:longitude:)`:

```
latitude: nil,
longitude: nil
```

And replace them with:

```
latitude: latitude,
longitude: longitude
```

This updates `FetchAnimalsService` to accept `latitude` and `longitude` to pass them as parameters to the request.

Sending a latitude and longitude to Petfinder's API makes it search and return pets in a 100 miles radius of that location.

Back inside **AnimalsNearYouViewModel.swift**, import `CoreLocation` and replace:

```
func fetchAnimals() async {
```

With:

```
func fetchAnimals(location: CLLocation?) async {
```

This code updates fetchAnimals to take a CLLocation instance with the user's current location.

Next, replace the contents of fetchAnimals(location:) with:

```
isLoading = true
do {
  // 1
  let animals = await animalFetcher.fetchAnimals(
    page: page,
    latitude: location?.coordinate.latitude,
    longitude: location?.coordinate.longitude
  )

  // 2
  try await animalStore.save(animals: animals)

  // 3
  hasMoreAnimals = !animals.isEmpty
} catch {
  // 4
  print("Error fetching animals... \
(error.localizedDescription)")
}
isLoading = false
```

Here, you:

1. Pass the user's **latitude and longitude** from location to the request to fetch animals.

2. Store the animals from the response just like before.

3. Set hasMoreAnimals to false if the response returned no animals.

4. Catch and print the error fetching animals may cause.

You also have to update fetchMoreAnimals to pass the location data.

Find fetchMoreAnimals and replace it with:

```
func fetchMoreAnimals(location: CLLocation?) async {
```

Next, replace:

```
await fetchAnimals()
```

With:

```
await fetchAnimals(location: location)
```

fetchAnimals(location:) will now fetch pets with the user's location.

Before you move on, update **AnimalsNearYouView.swift** to get the user's location and pass it to the view model call.

Find the following line:

```
await viewModel.fetchMoreAnimals()
```

And replace it with:

```
await viewModel.fetchMoreAnimals(location:
locationManager.lastSeenLocation)
```

Also, find:

```
await viewModel.fetchAnimals()
```

And replace it with:

```
await viewModel.fetchAnimals(location:
locationManager.lastSeenLocation)
```

The view model uses the location manager's lastSeenLocation to fetch the pets.

Finally, you also have to update **AnimalsFetcherMock.swift** to conform to AnimalsFetcher.

Open **AnimalsFetcherMock.swift** and replace fetchAnimals(page:) with:

```
func fetchAnimals(
  page: Int,
  latitude: Double?,
  longitude: Double?
) async -> [Animal] {
```

Again, the mock method uses latitude and longitude to fetch animals.

Build and run. Tap **Current Location** to list animals near you.

*AnimalsNearYou view using user's location.*

Great, `AnimalsNearYouView` now uses the user's location to list pets near them.

However, every time you close the app and relaunch it, you'll have to tap **Current Location** again.

*Tapping Current Location button again on relaunching the app.*

That's because `LocationButton` only grants the app a temporary `authorizedWhenInUse`. So, every time you open the app, you'll have to tap **Current Location** again.

> **Note**: When the user taps **OK**, the alert asking for their permission is *not* displayed again.

That's not a good user experience, at least not for this type of feature.

You'll change the implementation of `LocationManager` to request a permanent `authorizedWhenInUse`.

# Requesting authorization when in use

Open **LocationManager.swift** and add the function below to `LocationManager`:

```
func requestWhenInUseAuthorization() {
  cllLocationManager.requestWhenInUseAuthorization()
}
```

`requestWhenInUseAuthorization` is a method from `CLLocationManager` that asks the user's permission for their location data. This method prompts an alert to the user asking permission to access their location.

> **Note**: This method requires adding a reason text, inside **info.plist**, explaining why your app needs the user's location while using the app. You use the key **Privacy - Location When In Use Usage Description** and a text explaining how you'll use the user's location. The sample project already comes with this text inside its **info.plist**.

Back in **RequestLocationView.swift**, inside the action of `LocationButton`, find:

```
locationManager.startUpdatingLocation()
```

Replace it with:

```
locationManager.requestWhenInUseAuthorization()
```

Now when the user taps **Current Location**, it'll prompt the new alert to ask for a permanent `authorizedWhenInUse`.

Finally, delete **PetSave** from the device or simulator you're using for more accurate results. Then, build and run. Tap **Current Location**.

*Asking user for permanent location authorization, when the app is in use.*

The user can **Allow Once**, **Allow While Using App** or **Don't Allow**. If the user taps **Allow Once**, the app will have the same one-time `authorizedWhenInUse` as `LocationButton`. If the user taps **Allow While Using App**, the app will have a permanent `authorizedWhenInUse`.

If the user taps **Don't Allow**, the app won't have access to their location, and tapping the button won't do anything.

Go ahead and tap the different options to test the behavior. You can delete PetSave from the device or simulator to get a fresh start every time.

# Location accuracy

iOS also has a neat feature for protecting people's privacy. Most features that request the user's location don't need their accurate location. They only require an approximate location to recommend or find places nearby them.

When allowing an app access to their location, people can choose whether it's their precise location or not.

*User's precise location on.*

So, instead of giving the app their full location, users can choose to disable precise location, giving the app an approximate range where they are. The app can still use this data to drive features, and the user's precise location is still private.

## Adapting the UI depending on accuracy level

Dealing with location accuracy means the app has to adapt to some situations. Take **Apple Maps** for example. When the user allows the app to use a precise location, a **blue dot** in the map represents their location.

*Apple Maps example displaying a blue dot when precise location is on.*

However, if the user disables precise location, a **shaded circular area** represents their approximate location.

*Apple Maps example displaying a shaded circle when precise location is off.*

This example shows how an app's behavior can change depending on the user's choice.

Another way Apple Maps adapts is the **Favorites** section. If precise location is off, it doesn't show an **Estimated Time of Arrival** for each place since calculating this value requires more precise data.

*Apple Maps favorite section.*

You can use `requestTemporaryFullAccuracyAuthorization(withPurposeKey:)` to request a precise location temporarily to increase the accuracy until the next app launch.

While designing your app, it's important to pay attention to your users' privacy and your app needs. If you don't need to use precise location data, there's no need to ask for it.

`AnimalsNearYouView` requires a location to work, but it doesn't matter if it's precise. The API still finds pets within a 100 miles radius.

## Updating the tests

Before you finish this feature, you have to update your tests to take into account the new location manager property.

Inside **AnimalsNearYouViewModelTestCase.swift**, find the following line inside `testFetchAnimalsLoadingState` and `testFetchAnimalsEmptyResponse`:

```
await viewModel.fetchAnimals()
```

And replace it with:

```
await viewModel.fetchAnimals(location: nil)
```

Next, inside `testUpdatePageOnFetchMoreAnimals`, replace:

```
await viewModel.fetchMoreAnimals()
```

With:

```
await viewModel.fetchMoreAnimals(location: nil)
```

And finally, inside `testFetchAnimalsEmptyResponse`, replace:

```
await viewModel.fetchAnimals()
```

With:

```swift
await viewModel.fetchAnimals(location: nil)
```

In these tests, `AnimalsNearYouViewModel` initializes the location with `nil`.

Finally, inside `EmptyResponseAnimalsFetcherMock` at the bottom, update
`fetchAnimals(page:)` with:

```
func fetchAnimals(
  page: Int,
  latitude: Double?,
  longitude: Double?
) async -> [Animal] {
```

This test now uses latitude and longitude to fetch animals.

Build and run the tests.

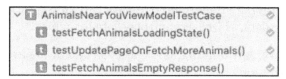

*Test is successful.*

# App Store's Privacy section

When launching an app in the App Store, Apple makes every developer provide a list
of data their app collects. **App Store's Privacy Section** ensures developers explain
to their users what kind of data they're collecting.

Whenever a developer wants to release an app in the App Store, they must provide a
list of the data they and third-party partners collect. This information allows users to
better choose and understand what kind of data they'll be giving the developer
before they download the app.

## Understanding different types of data

Apple categorizes the many types of data an app may collect. It requires you to
understand which kind of data you collect and disclose them under the following
categories:

1. **Contact Info**: Data that may contain the user's name, email, phone, physical
   address or any other information that could be used to contact them.

2. **Health & Fitness**: Data related to the user's health and fitness, including data
   from HealthKit API or the Fitness API.

3. **Financial Info**: Any data related to payments and purchases inside the app or related to the user's assets and financial information.

4. **Location**: The precise location data and course location information of any route the user may take, including approximate location.

5. **Sensitive Info**: Sensitive info may include personal information data such as racial or ethnic data, sexual orientation, political opinion and biometric data.

6. **Contacts**: The app may access users' contacts with names, phone numbers and email.

7. **User Content**: Any data that users create like text messages, email, photos and videos and audio data, as well as gameplay data for games.

8. **Browsing History**: Any information regarding content the user has viewed online outside the app.

9. **Search History**: Search information like search queries inside the app.

10. **Identifiers**: Any data that may identify the user like a screen name, handle or ID, including Device IDs, such as the device's advertising identifier.

11. **Purchases**: Tracking a user's purchases or purchase tendencies.

12. **Usage Data**: Any device interactions such as taps, clicks and scrolling. Any other information related to how the user interacts with the device and app, including information about advertisements the user may have seen or interacted with.

13. **Diagnostics**: Any performance, crash and log data.

14. **Other Data**: Any other type of data related to the user.

These categories describe the type of data developers may want to collect. Users can see the whole list and what data the app collects.

When you open an app in the App Store and scroll down, you'll find the **App Privacy** section with the data the developer has provided.

*App Store displaying App Privacy section.*

For example, the raywenderlich.com app collects the user's **Search History**, **Usage Data** and **Identifier**. It also collects **Diagnostics** data not linked to users.

Tapping the section will open the details of the data that it collects.

*App Privacy details.*

# Key points

- Users' **privacy** is very important. Always design your app with privacy in mind.

- **Location data** is also private data, and developers must handle it with care.

- You can use `LocationButton` for features that require the person's location on a **one-time** basis.

- Use `requestWhenInUseAuthorization` to request the person's location whenever they use your app.

- Not all apps require precise location data. When designing your app, remember people may not want to share their precise location.

- App Store's App Privacy section is the place where you'll disclose what kinds of data your app collects.

# Where to go from here?

In this chapter, you went over what's privacy and why you should care. Also, you added the functionality to get the current location so users of PetSave can enjoy a more personalized experience.

To learn more about privacy, iOS's latest privacy features, and requesting location data, check out our article What's New With Privacy? (https://www.raywenderlich.com/24738637-what-s-new-with-privacy).

You can also learn more about app privacy on Apple's App privacy details on the App Store (https://developer.apple.com/app-store/app-privacy-details/) page.

In the next chapter, you'll learn some techniques to find bugs in your app. Debugging is part of the software development process, so it makes sense to go over it while creating a real-world app.

# Chapter 13: Debugging

By Aaqib Hussain

Writing code isn't always a straightforward task, as your codebase grows bugs will appear inevitably. Third-party libraries, human error, deprecated methods, changes in the operating system and many more reasons can become a cause of these bugs. Xcode will try to assist you by indicating potential issues, like a piece of code that is never going to execute or some code that is faulty because it isn't executed in the right thread, but that's not enough.

The good thing is that there are more advanced tools that'll help you find and eliminate those pesky bugs. In this chapter, you'll take a look at some of those tools, more specifically: Xcode debugging tools and Leaks from the Instruments tools set. Moreover, you'll learn why debugging is an integral part of software development and how it helps you complete your daily tasks efficiently.

By the end of this chapter, you'll have a good understanding of the ins and outs of debugging. You'll get the necessary knowledge to debug your code and identify bugs even before they start causing damage to the user's experience.

> Please note that this chapter is optional. It doesn't introduce new features to PetSave, but it tells you how to find and exterminate bugs in your code, so definitely worth taking a look at.

Are you ready to squash some bugs? Here you go!

# Debugging

Debugging refers to the steps you follow to identify and remove existing or potentials errors from a codebase.

## Why do you need to debug your code?

Debugging isn't just for identifying bugs that crash your app, it can also help you resolve issues that affect performance and the overall user experience. Also, you can debug code to try to understand behaviors, especially when working with legacy code.

## Xcode debugging tools

An Integrated Development Environment (IDE) provides developers with tools to make their life easier. Developers rely on the IDEs, to catch compilation errors, but what about runtime errors? Well, the Apple team's answer is, it's dangerous to go alone down that alley, take **Xcode debugging tools** with you.

Xcode has a wide variety of tools to pull you out of these entanglements. Debugging tools is how you refer to the group formed by the following tools:

- Breakpoints

- Method call stack

- Debugging views

- Memory graph

More generically, you can say **Instruments** are also part of this toolset. You'll learn more about Instruments later in this chapter.

Each tool provides its own set of benefits. Start by getting into these tools and learning about breakpoints.

# Breakpoints

**Breakpoints** is the first and most basic tool in the Xcode tool belt. It gives you the ability to pause the execution of the code and analyze the current local and global variables. With the help of breakpoints, you can analyze code line by line.

Open this chapter's starter project and build and run. You'll notice a minor bug:

*Displaying a list of animals.*

Did you notice something wrong? Everything looks fine. Nothing's wrong there, right?

Wait, hold on.

If you remember correctly, you designed the tags to have their view color correspond to the animal's age. Here you see the same age but different colors of tags. Something is wrong with the code that needs debugging.

*Identifying and highlighting the bug.*

Start with **AnimalsNearYouView.swift**. Inside `NavigationView`, place a breakpoint on:

```
AnimalListView(animals: animals)
```

To place a breakpoint, go to the line and click the margin or the line number on the left.

> **Note**: To see the line number on the left, go to **Xcode ▸ Preferences**. Select **Text Editing**. Under **Display**, check **Line numbers**.

You'll see a blue rectangular arrow like this:

```
54    AnimalListView(animals: animals) {
55        if !animals.isEmpty && viewModel.hasMoreAnimals {
56            ProgressView("Finding more animals...")
57              .padding()
58              .frame(maxWidth: .infinity)
59              .task {
60                await viewModel.fetchMoreAnimals()
61              }
62          }
63      }
```

*Applying breakpoint.*

Build and run. Notice the code execution stop at the breakpoint. In the image below, you'll see some buttons on the **Debug bar**:

```
54    AnimalListView(animals: animals) {
55        if !animals.isEmpty && viewModel.hasMoreAnimals {
56            ProgressView("Finding more animals...")
57              .padding()
58              .frame(maxWidth: .infinity)
59              .task {
60                await viewModel.fetchMoreAnimals()
61              }
62          }
63      }
1    2    3    4    5
```

PetSave ⟩ Thread 1 ⟩ 0 closure #1 in AnimalsNearYouView.body.getter

*Getting to know about breakpoint buttons.*

So, what's the purpose of these buttons? They make the breakpoints more powerful. Take a look at each button, from left to right:

1. **Deactivate breakpoints**: If you don't want to debug anymore, toggle this button to disable all the breakpoints in the app.

2. **Continue program execution**: Jumps to the next breakpoint if there are any. Otherwise, it runs the app normally.

3. **Step over**: Takes you to the next line of execution, ignoring the current context.

4. **Step into**: Takes you inside the current context of the line of execution.

5. **Step out**: Takes you outside the current context of the line of execution.

Click **Step into**. This will let you into `AnimalListView(animals:footer:)`. Now, inside `NavigationLink`, place a breakpoint on:

```
AnimalRow(animal: animal)
```

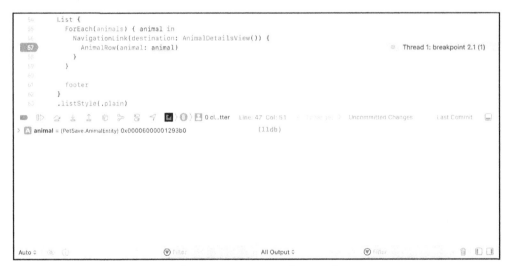

*Using step into.*

Then, click **Continue program execution**. Now code execution stops at `AnimalRow(animal: animal)`.

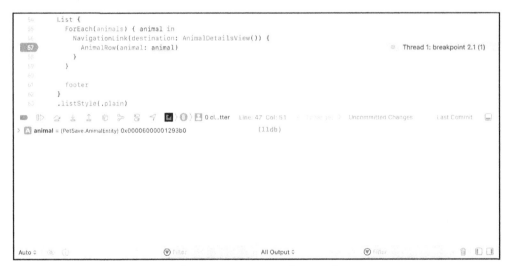

*Breakpoint stopping at the next line.*

It's time to investigate the animal model. Ensure you see the **Variables View** window by clicking **Show the Variables view** at the bottom right.

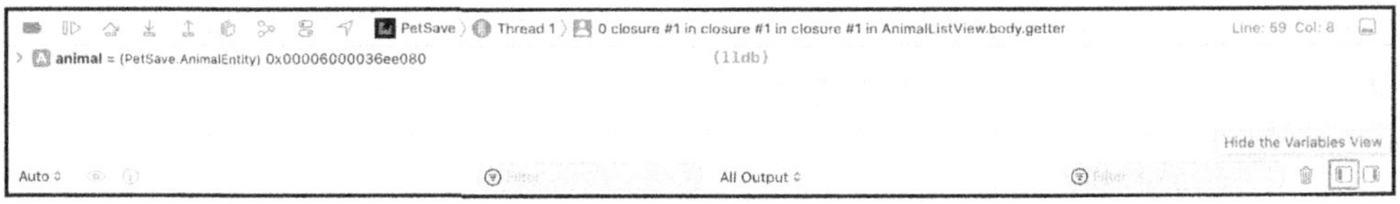

*Variables view window.*

Select animal in **Variables view**.

*Inspecting animal.*

Then, click ⓘ, that is the **Print Description**, located at the bottom-left bar.

*Printing description using the ⓘ.*

There's another way you can print the object description. In the **Console**, type po
animal and press **enter**. **po** extends to print the object. You'll see a similar result.

*Printing description using po.*

Click **Continue program execution** again, so you can check more animals as the
breakpoint pauses the execution. You'll see the animal's **age** parses correctly. That
means there's something wrong with presenting the data.

Open **AnimalRow.swift**, that takes care of presenting the data. Inside body, find this
line:

```
Text(NSLocalizedString(Age.baby.rawValue, comment: ""))
```

The age is hardcoded here, that's the problem! Replace the hardcoded age with the
age from the model. Update the line to:

```
Text(NSLocalizedString(animal.age.rawValue, comment: ""))
```

Now you take age from the `AnimalEntity`. Deactivate the breakpoints, then build and run again. The bug is gone!

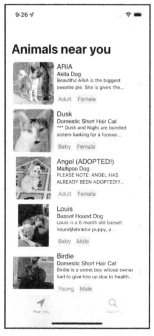

*The bug fixed.*

Woohooo! You did it. You squashed the bug that's been *bugging* the app. ;]

You can also use breakpoints to add expressions, making your breakpoint stop only if a condition is met.

Open **AnimalListView.swift** and place a breakpoint on:

```
AnimalRow(animal: animal)
```

Double-click the breakpoint, and you'll see:

*Breakpoint window.*

Here's a breakdown:

1.  You can enable or disable this breakpoint by checking this box.

2.  Enter the name of the breakpoint.

3.  Add the condition that stops the breakpoint.

4.  You can ignore the breakpoint as many times as you indicate.

5.  Use **Add Action** to add some actions, like running the debugger command po animal.name or executing a shell command.

6.  Check **Options** to continue after actions are evaluated.

Click **Add Action** and you'll see:

*Knowing about add action.*

1.  Use the + or - buttons to add more actions.

2.  Enter the debugging commands here. Commands like po animal.name will execute during debugging.

Now add the following data:

- In the **Name** field, add `LookingforAnimal`.

- Enter `(animal.name?.count ?? 0) > 5` in the **Condition** field. Xcode's code completion is available in these text fields to help you avoid typos.

- Leave **Ignore** at 0.

- The drop-down in **Action** adds different actions that Xcode provides. For simplicity, you'll use **Debugger Command** here, but you can also use:

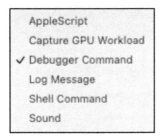

*Action options.*

- Enter `po animal.name` in the text field below the action drop-down.

- Leave **Options** unchecked.

The breakpoint expression dialog looks like this:

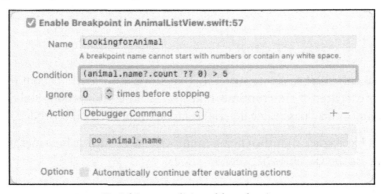

*Finishing conditional breakpoint.*

Build and run. You'll see the breakpoint stops when the animal's name has more than five letters. Xcode also runs the action and prints the animal name in the console:

*Testing the conditional breakpoint.*

Notice that continuing the breakpoint doesn't stop on any animal that has less than five letters. This can be a useful mechanism when you need to debug iterative code.

# Method call stack

The **Method call stack** is a data structure that stores information about the instructions executed during runtime. It keeps the order of methods and their states in the memory. It also passes local variables to another method if needed.

Each thread has a stack that the OS maintains. The OS controls how methods are called and pass the variables between methods.

You can use the method call stack when you're debugging to find the places where the error is happening and understand the flow that caused the issue.

Enable the breakpoint in **AnimalsNearYouView.swift** on the following line:

```
AnimalListView(animals: animals)
```

Build and run. When the app stops at the breakpoint, check the **Debug navigator** on the left, it should look similar to this:

*List of methods in the callstack.*

Here, you'll see the call stack. Go ahead and navigate to each method. You can also find what's triggering a specific method by retracing the steps.

# Debugging views

Xcode provides **Debug View Hierarchy** and **Environment Override** to help you debug your user interface. Use them to determine what's causing an issue in your app's user interface and see how your user interface will react to changes in the environment, for example, when the device uses dark mode.

Look at the buttons next to **Step out**. You'll see a view like this:

```
54    AnimalListView(animals: animals) {
          if !animals.isEmpty && viewModel.hasMoreAnimals {
            ProgressView("Finding more animals...")
              .padding()
              .frame(maxWidth: .infinity)
              .task {
60              await viewModel.fetchMoreAnimals()
              }
          }
```
```
              1   2   3
    ID    PetSave  Thread 1   0 closure #1 in AnimalsNearYouView.body.getter
```

*More Xcode features.*

Take a closer look at these buttons:

1. **Debug View Hierarchy**: Use this button to visualize your entire screen *sometimes* even component by component.

2. **Debug Memory Graph**: Helps you visualize all the active objects in the app.

3. **Environment Overrides**: This button can help you override some of the apps' environment properties. For example, you can change the appearance or test accessibility features in real-time.

## Debug view hierarchy

With the app still running, click **Debug View Hierarchy**. You'll see a new bar appear on top of the Debug bar:

*Debug View Hierarchy bar.*

Here you see the app's debug view of the current screen:

*Studying view hierarchy.*

Here's a breakdown of this screen:

1. On the left, in the **Debug navigator**, you see the entire view hierarchy.

2. Use this slider to increase or decrease spaces between the views and observe each view closely.

3. Use the **Show Clipped Content** to see any views going out of the view bounds.

4. **Show Constraints** displays the layout constraints of the views.

5. Use **Adjust view mode** to select **Contents**, **Wireframes** or **Wireframes and Contents**. The default is **Wireframes and Contents**.

6. You can change the background color of the Canvas that shows the views. Use the **Change canvas background color** to switch between either light or dark mode, depending on the Xcode theme.

7. **Orient to 3D** presents the views in a 3D manner.

8. Zooms out the views on canvas.

9. **Actual Size** brings the view to the actual size of the device.

10. To zoom in on the views, click **Zoom In**.

11. You can **Adjust the range of visible views** by altering the slider. It'll show you only the views you want to see at a given moment.

12. The **Object inspector** window shows you the properties of a selected view.

Select the first **Label** in the Debug navigator. You'll see its properties on the right in the **Object inspector**. Also, increase the spaces between the views using the slider. You'll see:

*Using the slider.*

Then, select any view in the canvas, and click and drag the view like this:

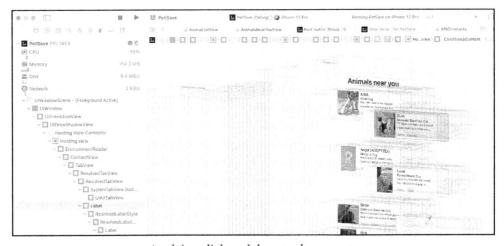

*Applying click and drag to the canvas.*

Now, click **Orient to 3D**. The button now appears as **Orient to 2D**. Your view orients itself in 2D.

*Orientation mode.*

To check the constraints, click **Show Constraints**. You'll see:

*Looking at the constraints.*

Inspect everything closely to check your constraints. If you click the same button again, you'll see your normal view.

*Orientation mode.*

Click **Adjust view mode** and you'll see a drop-down:

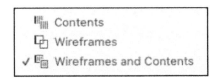

*Adjust view mode options.*

Currently, the default option is **Wireframes and Contents**. Select **Contents**, and you'll see the views without wireframes.

*Seeing the content.*

You can also play around with the range to focus *only* on the views of interest.

*Using the range slider.*

Move the range to its default position again. Now, click **Show Clipped Content**. You'll see all the views that are going out of bounds.

*Examining the clipped content.*

Isn't that great? You can have a deep look at how your views are rendered and identify user interfaces bugs, without using an external tool.

## Memory graph

**Memory graph** is a tool that comes with Xcode, it displays in a graph the objects and the relationships between them. Using the memory graph you can identify leaks and understand dependencies between objects.

To see the memory graph of the objects, on the Debug bar, click **Debug Memory Graph** :

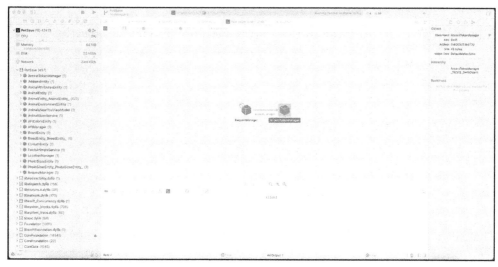

*Object memory graph with references.*

**Note:** Click **Zoom in** to see the names of the objects.

Check the Debug navigator on the left. You can view all the objects in memory. When there are memory issues or leaks, Xcode shows a purple triangle with an exclamation mark in front of the object.

Expand the graph by using the two-way arrow button shown on the object:

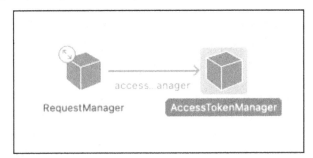

*RequestManager object referencing to AccessTokenMananger.*

That button shows the objects referencing this `RequestManager`. Click it, and you'll see:

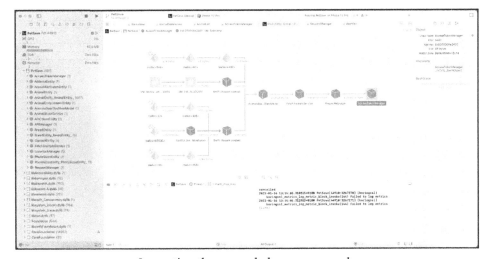

*Inspecting the expanded memory graph.*

These are all the objects pointing to `RequestManager` and their addresses in the memory. You can even expand these further. It also shows the amount of space it's taking in the memory.

Also, note the two buttons you see here:

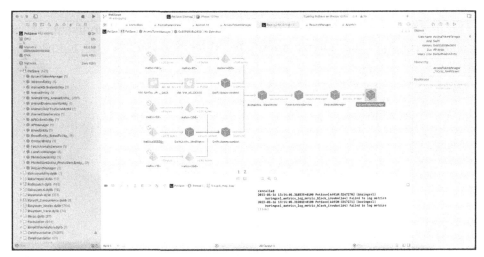

*Buttons in memory graph.*

1. **Jump to the definition** takes you to the code that defines the selected object.

2. **Print the description** prints the object description in the console.

Click the **AnimalsNearYouViewModel** object. You'll see another button enabled next to the print description object button. This button, **Focus on this instance**, helps further focus on the selected object.

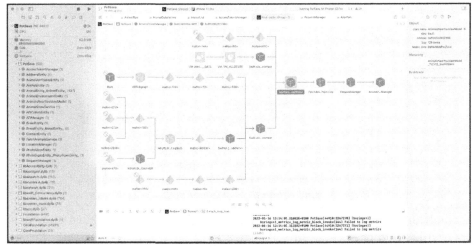

*Focusing on a selected object.*

# Environment overrides

Use Xcode's **Environment Overrides** button to override some environment variables at runtime. Click **Environment Overrides**, and you'll see the following popup:

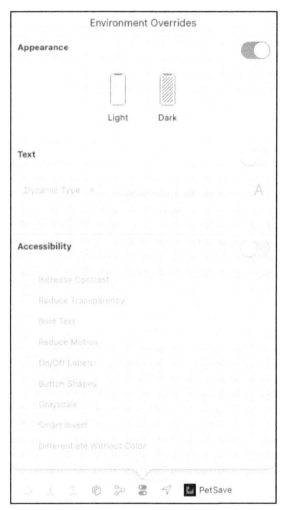

*Environment override popup.*

By default, all the variables are off. You can select the corresponding switch to enable **Appearance**, **Text** or **Accessibility**.

Play around with these variables to see how they affect the app.

# Instruments

**Instruments** is one of the most essential tools Xcode provides. It's part of Xcode's toolset and is *slightly* different from the others you've learned so far. From Xcode, Instruments opens as an app on its own.

Instruments depends on giving results based on trace data, also referred to as **trace**. The tool collects traces from important parts of apps that are harder to debug, like the app's internal infrastructure, processes and operating system. You can also save all the profiling traces and share them with your team or colleagues.

Open Instruments by selecting **Xcode ▸ Open Developer Tool**.

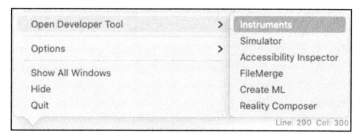

*Instruments.*

Select **Instruments**. A window appears:

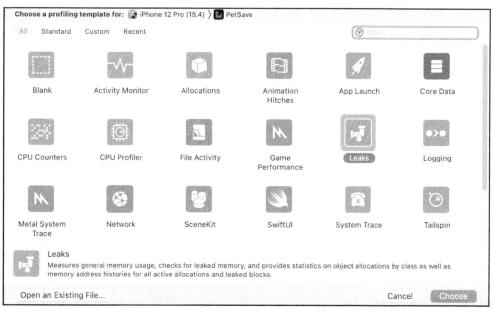

*Main window of the instruments tool.*

Instruments bundles in several profiling templates. Each profile works according to your needs. Here is the complete list:

- Blank
- Activity Monitor
- Allocations
- Animation Hitches
- App Launch
- Core Data
- CPU Counters
- CPU Profiler
- File Activity
- Game Performance
- Leaks
- Logging
- Metal System Trace
- Network
- SceneKit
- SwiftUI
- System Trace
- Tailspin
- Time Profiler
- Zombies

Now that's a nice set of tools! Here you have a wide set of templates, from **Core Data** that helps investigate core data related bugs, like faults or problems when saving records, to **SwiftUI** a tool you can use to identify issues like slow frames affecting your user experience. Also, more agnostic tools like **Logging** or **Activity Monitor** to monitor system-level processes. For now, you'll focus on one of these tools, **Leaks**.

# Leaks

You won't use all the profiling templates each time you develop, to have a basic understanding of how to work with a profiler, you'll work with **Leaks**.

**Leaks** measures memory usage in general and detects leaked memory. It also records all the allocations by a class and other references to memory addresses, including active allocations and leaked code blocks.

On the Instruments window, select **Leaks** and click **Choose**. You'll see:

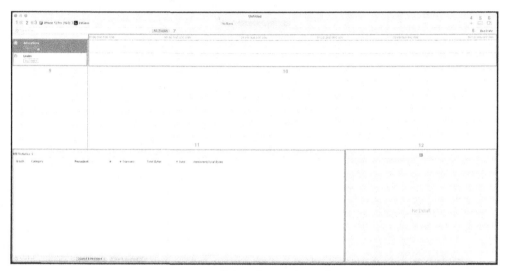

*Demystifying the Leaks tool.*

Here's a breakdown of what's on the screen:

1.  With **Start an immediate mode recording**, you can start recording the trace.

2.  Use this button to pause the started profiling.

3.  This button selects the simulator or the process.

4.  You can add more instruments with this button.

5.  This button helps you hide or show the detail area.

6.  Use this button to hide or show the inspector area.

7.  To focus on one instrument at a time. You can put an instrument filter.

8.  You can click **duplicate** to save the current traces data.

9. This area shows the list of instruments. The leaks template comes with an **Allocations** instrument. Every newly added instrument gets added here.

10. Displays the app's graph for the instrument selected.

11. You can view the objects in the memory and space they take.

12. Shows you the stack trace.

At the top, select the simulator and **PetSave**, then click **Start an immediate mode recording**. It opens the app on the simulator, and you'll see something like this:

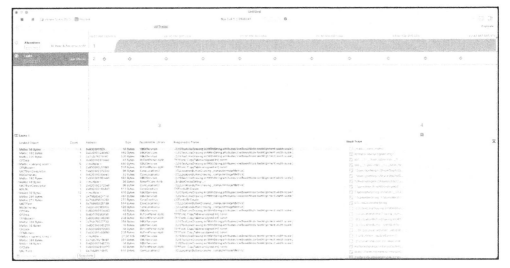

*Profiling the app.*

Here, it:

1. Shows the app's memory allocation.

2. Shows all the leaks. A green checkbox means no leaks. A red cross means new leaks. A gray dash means no new leaks.

3. Displays all the objects causing a memory leak. Notice that **Leaks** is selected in Instruments, and the filter is set to **Leaks** just below.

4. Shows the stack trace for the object selected in the left pane.

Double-click the red icon to display all the leaks in the section below.

*Leaks data.*

The leaks you see here are system-generated.

# Retain cycle

A **retain cycle** occurs when two objects hold references to each other. Both objects stay in memory and aren't released. You can check for these in the Leaks instrument or debug memory graph.

To eliminate this problem, you make the dependent object weak. By default, these references are strong. There's also another type of reference, unowned. The main difference between weak and unowned is that weak can be nil whereas unowned can't be nil throughout its lifecycle.

Look at the example below:

```
// 1
class PetOwner {
  var name: String?
  var pet: Pet?
  deinit {
    print("Petowner removed!")
  }
}
// 2
class Pet {
  var name: String?
  var owner: PetOwner?
  deinit {
    print("Pet removed!")
  }
}
// 3
var pet: Pet? = Pet()
```

```
pet?.name = "Snowfy"
// 4
let petOwner = PetOwner()
petOwner.name = "Ray"
petOwner.pet = pet
pet?.owner = petOwner
```

Here's a code breakdown:

1.  A PetOwner class contains the owner's name and the Pet.

2.  The Pet class contains the pet's name and owner.

3.  This is the Pet object.

4.  The PetOwner object references Pet. Pet references its owner object.

Now, imagine at some point the variable pet becomes nil. In this scenario, you *may* think the object will deallocate and deinit will be called. However, it won't because both objects strongly reference each other. To free the memory, you can make one of them weak, like this:

```
class PetOwner {
  var name: String?
  weak var pet: Pet?
  deinit {
    print("Petowner removed!")
  }
}
```

Now the deinit gets called.

A closure *may* also create a retain cycle. For example, when referencing self in a closure, it's best to mark it with a [weak self] to avoid retain cycles. Take a look at the code below:

```
DispatchQueue.main.asyncAfter(deadline: .now()) {[weak self] in
  self?.doSomeUIUpdates()
}
```

You can also use [unowned self] depending on your requirements.

# Key points

- **Breakpoints** help you debug code line by line.

- Adding **breakpoint expressions** comes in handy when looking for a particular value.

- Use Xcode's **Memory graph** to find retain cycles and leaks in your code.

- **Call stack** shows you all the methods in the memory stack. You can navigate to the initial method using the stack.

- Use **Instruments** to profile your apps. Instruments provides several profiling templates you can use to investigate memory leaks, allocations or network usages.

- Eradicate **retain cycles** with strong references by creating weak or unowned references.

# Where to go from here?

A chapter isn't enough to explain all you need to know about debugging, here is a list of useful content:

- Interested in knowing more about debugging? Start with our video course on iOS Debugging Fundamentals (https://www.raywenderlich.com/18770184-ios-debugging-fundamentals/).

- Looking for an intermediate course? Take a look at Intermediate iOS Debugging (https://www.raywenderlich.com/21191818-intermediate-ios-debugging).

- raywenderlich.com also has a book that covers the advanced topics of debugging. Read Advanced Apple Debugging & Reverse Engineering (https://www.raywenderlich.com/9153-advanced-apple-debugging-reverse-engineering-updated-for-xcode-10-and-ios-12) for some more information.

- To start with Instruments, check out our article on Getting started with Instruments (https://www.raywenderlich.com/16126261-instruments-tutorial-with-swift-getting-started).

- To learn more about Instruments take a look at Monitoring Http Traffic with Instruments (https://www.raywenderlich.com/27390649-monitoring-http-traffic-with-instruments).

This brings you to the end of this chapter. You became familiar with debugging and learned to use breakpoints, visualize views in the view hierarchy and play with Instruments.

Your hard work paid off, and you're *almost* at the end of this *real-world* journey. So far, you've done well, and there's *just* one more milestone to complete. In the next and final chapter, you'll learn about **Deploying an app to the AppStore**.

Excited to complete the last milestone?

# Chapter 14: Deploying to the App Store

By Renan Benatti Dias

You've arrived at the last chapter of this book. It's finally the time you've been working for: sending your app to the **App Store**. This will be the sum of all your hard work. After your time creating, developing, improving and debugging your code, your job will finally pay off.

In this chapter, you'll learn how to submit your app to the App Store and all the steps required to release your app. You'll also learn how to distribute your app to **Beta Testers** and get feedback from them.

More specifically, you'll learn how to:

- Create an **Apple ID** and enroll in **Apple's Developer Program**.

- **Archive** and **upload** a build of your app to Apple.

- Create your app's **Product page** in the App Store.

- Use **TestFlight** to beta test your app and get **feedback** from testers.

Additionally, you'll learn about the **App Store Review Guidelines** and how to submit your app for review.

# Getting Started

Apple has high criteria for apps it allows in the App Store. You're not allowed to have an app in the App Store unless you follow many guidelines Apple created to ensure the quality of software in the App Store. Not only that, but Apple also requires you to be a part of their developer program.

Before you start uploading your apps to the App Store, there are a couple of things you'll need to do and have to continue. The first one is an **Apple ID**.

> **Note**: If you want to follow along with this chapter, you'll have to have these requirements. Otherwise, you may not be able to generate the necessary certificates and profiles or even access App Store Connect. Make sure you have all the requirements to follow along with this chapter.

# Understanding the Apple ID

The Apple ID is your main account in Apple's ecosystem. It's how Apple identifies developers and customers. You use it to access the **App Store**, **Apples Services** and every other Apple portal. Developers also use an Apple ID to access Apple's developer portal, **App Store Connect**.

If you already use any of Apple's products, you most likely have an Apple ID.

This section will teach you how to set up an Apple ID. Even if you already have an Apple ID, it's common practice to create one for your app. That way, it's easier to scale if you end up founding a company for it.

If you already have an Apple ID and want to use it here, you can skip this section.

## Creating an Apple ID

You can create a new Apple ID using an iOS, iPadOS or macOS device by opening the Settings app or when you set up your device. Here, you'll use Apple's **Apple ID portal** to create a new Apple ID.

First, open Apple's Apple ID portal (https://appleid.apple.com) in Safari.

Next, click **Create Your Apple ID** at the top right corner.

Fill out the form with your **first name**, **last name**, **region** and all required information. Pay attention to the **email** you use here because it'll be your new Apple ID.

Follow the steps onscreen to verify your information.

If you have any trouble, take a look at Apple's page How to create a new Apple ID (https://support.apple.com/en-us/HT204316).

## Activating Two-factor authentication

**Two-factor authentication** is an extra layer of security on top of your account's password. It provides a secure way to have trusted devices that allow you to sign in to your account through a **verification code**.

You have to activate two-factor authentication to use your Apple ID to upload your apps. You can activate two-factor authentication on iOS, iPadOS or macOS or use the Apple ID portal.

Go to Apple ID portal (https://appleid.apple.com) and sign in. The page will prompt you to upgrade your account security with two-factor authentication. Click upgrade and enter the phone number you want to receive verification codes when you sign in. Click **Continue** and enter the verification code to verify your phone number and turn on two-factor authentication.

It's highly recommended that you set up your Apple device with two-factor authentication. That way, you have a trusted device to sign in with your account.

Check out Apple's Two-factor authentication for Apple ID (https://support.apple.com/en-us/HT204915) page to learn more about two-factor authentication and how to activate it with a device.

> **Note**: The video course Publishing to the App Store (https://www.raywenderlich.com/11678704-publishing-to-the-app-store) on raywenderlich.com also walks through the process of creating a new Apple ID.

# Apple's Developer Program

Just having an Apple ID isn't enough. Apple is very strict about who and what goes into the App Store. It tries to create the most secure place for its customers. To that end, Apple requires that every developer that wants to publish their app in the App Store enrolls in the **Apple Developer Program**.

This program gives developers access to Apple developer tools like **Xcode**, **CloudKit**, **TestFlight** and **App Analytics**, to name a few. As a member of the developer program, you also have access to **beta software** like iOS and iPadOS beta versions.

The Apple Developer Program costs **$99 per year** and you enroll it using an Apple ID.

To enroll in the Apple Developer Program, open the Developer Portal (https://developer.apple.com) and sign in to your account.

Apple has two types of enrollments: one for individuals and one for organizations. Each has different legal, tax and financial implications, but both have the same access to developer tools.

If you're using your Apple ID, it's ok to enroll as an individual. However, if you're publishing an app in the name of a company, you'll have to enroll as an organization.

Follow the onscreen instructions and fill out the information to enroll in the program. Check out Apple's Enrolling and Verifying Your Identity with the Apple Developer App (https://developer.apple.com/support/app-account/) page to read detailed steps on how to do this.

# Setting up Xcode

When creating a new project in Xcode, you have to choose a few options, including the **Organization identifier**. With it, Xcode also generates the **Bundle Identifier**. Apple uses these to identify the team and app in their system.

PetSave already comes with a **Bundle Identifier**, in this case, **com.raywenderlich.PetSave**. You'll have to change this identifier to one of your own.

## Changing the Bundle Identifier

A **Bundle Identifier** is an app's unique identifier inside Apple's system. You can't change it later, so think carefully about the identifier you want to use.

It's common practice to use the reverse DNS notation of the app's website, and since this is a unique identifier, you can't use identifiers that other apps already use. That's why you can't use **com.raywenderlich.PetSave**.

Open the **starter** project for this chapter and select your target in the project navigator. In the **General** tab, change the **Bundle Identifier** to your identifier.

# Code Signing

In the same target, open **Signing and Capabilities**. Make sure to check the box for **Automatically manage signing**.

This makes Xcode responsible for managing the app's certificates and profiles, removing a rather complex and tedious task from your hands.

> **Note**: If you wish to learn more about app certificates and profiles, check out Chapter 4, Code Signing & Provisioning (https://www.raywenderlich.com/ books/ios-app-distribution-best-practices) of our book **iOS App Distribution & Best Practices**.

A warning may appear in the status section. That's because you have to sign into Xcode with your Apple ID and select the team for your app.

Click **Xcode ▸ Preferences…** and select the **Accounts** tab.

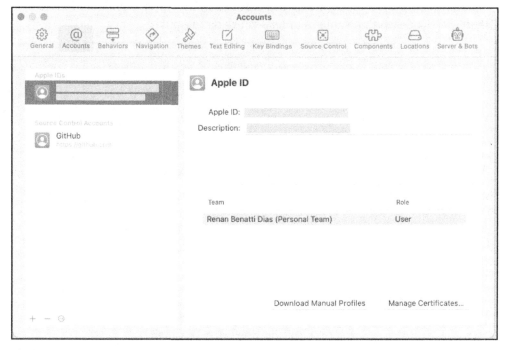

Click the + at the bottom left of the view to add an account.

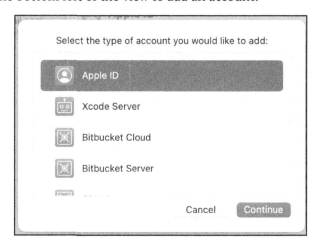

Select **Apple ID** and enter the Apple ID you enrolled in the Apple Developer Program. You must use the Apple ID you enrolled in the Apple Developer Program. Otherwise, Xcode won't be able to upload your app to Apple.

Next, you'll receive a verification code for two-factor authentication. Type the code in the field.

Success! You configured Xcode with your Apple ID account.

Go back to the project navigator and select your team. This will remove the warning in **Signing and Capabilities**.

You're done setting up Xcode. Now, you'll create your app in Apple's portal to upload and send it to review.

## Understanding the App Store app page

It's not enough to just upload your app to Apple. You also have to create your app's page so that Apple can display it in the App Store. Your App page is the face of your app when people browse or search the App Store for apps related to pets.

## Page Structure

In the page, you'll find the app's **name**, **icon**, **subtitle**, **app reviews**, **screenshots**, **description** and much more.

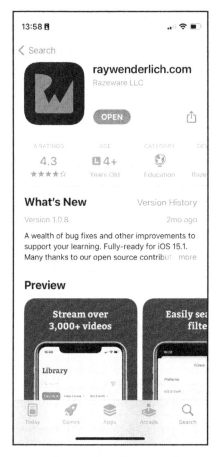

This page is the face of your app to any App Store customer. A good and informative page will engage people and get them to download your app, making it more popular over time.

> **Note**: To learn more about App Store app pages, check out Apple's Creating Your Product Page (https://developer.apple.com/app-store/product-page/).

Next, you'll learn how to set up your app page and good practices to make your app stand out.

## Creating a new App ID

Before creating your app inside Apple's portal, you must create a new **App ID**. Apple uses the App ID to identify your app in its system.

In Safari, open Apple's developer portal (https://developer.apple.com). Click **Account** and enter your Apple ID and password. Next, select **Certificates, Identifiers & Profiles** and click **Identifiers**.

Here, you'll find and manage all the identifiers for your apps.

Click the blue + next to **Identifiers** and select **App IDs** from the list.

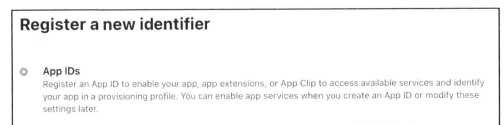

Click **Continue**. On the next page, leave **App** selected and click **Continue** again.

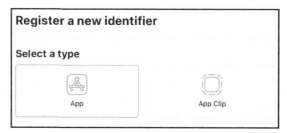

Now, fill out the form with a description and the **Bundle ID**. The description can be anything you wish to use to identify your app, and you can edit it later if you want. The **Bundle ID must be the one you used in Xcode** for your app, and you can't change this later.

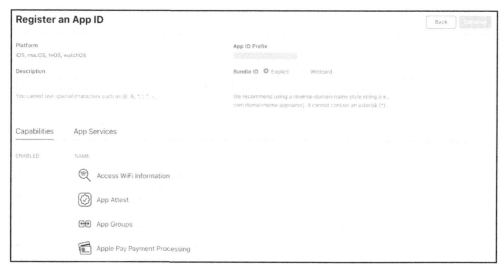

Leave the options under **Capabilities** and **App Services** unchecked because PetSave doesn't use any of those.

Click **Continue**. Review everything and click **Register** to finish.

Fantastic! You've created your new app identifier. Now, off to create your new app page.

# App Store Connect

Still in Safari, open Apple's developer portal (https://developer.apple.com) again.
Next, select **App Store Connect** and click **Go to App Store Connect**.

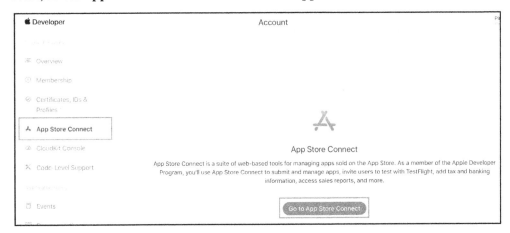

> **Note:** You can also access App Store Connect by using the following link
> https://appstoreconnect.apple.com in Safari.

This is the **App Store Connect** page. It gives you access to multiple tools like **App
Analytics**, **Sales and Trends** and **Payments and Financial Reports** for growing
and managing your apps inside the App Store.

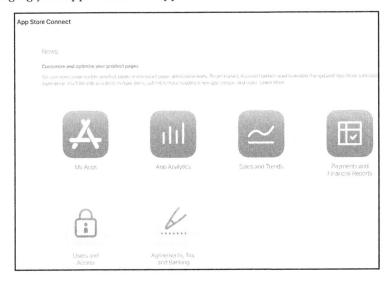

Next click **My Apps**. This page lists all the apps you create under your account and lets you track the status of your apps.

On this page, click the blue + at the top left of the page. Then click **New App** to open a form with the information needed to create your new app.

Under **Platforms**, check the box for **iOS**. Type **PetSave-Test** for the name and select **English (US)** as the primary language. The name you choose here will be the name of your app in the App Store.

Next, select the Bundle ID you just created under **Identifiers** on the **Certificates, Identifiers & Profiles** page. Also, type the same Bundle ID under SKU. **SKU** stands for **Stock-keeping Unit**. This is an internal-facing identifier to match your app to your team.

Your form will look similar to this:

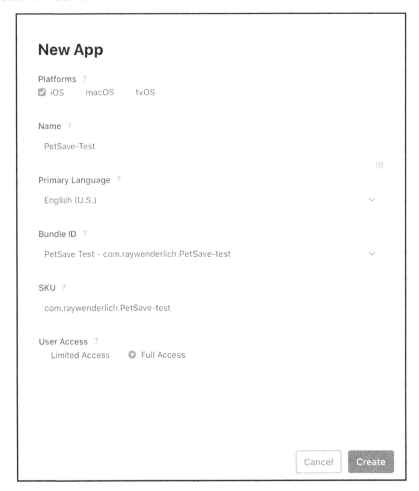

> **Note:** The name you choose has to be unique. If another app already uses your app's name, you can either try to file a claim or change your app's name. Your Bundle ID and SKU should also be different from the image.

Click **Create** to finish.

Great job! You created your app in App Store Connect.

Notice that your app has a **yellow** status on the left.

**iOS App**

⊙ 1.0 Prepare for Submission

That means your app has yet to go through Apple's review process before going to the App Store. You have to fill out some information about your app so that Apple can review it.

But before you do that, you'll upload a build of your app to the App Store Connect.

# Uploading a build

Now that you have your app record set up in App Store Connect, it's time to archive and upload a build of your app.

An **archive** of your app is a build that has all your app's symbols and debug information. With it, you can send your app to Apple and distribute it in the App Store.

You'll use Xcode to archive and upload this build to App Store Connect.

## Build Numbers and semantic versioning

Before you archive your app, it's essential to understand how Apple and developers track software versions.

Open the project navigator and click **General**. Inside the **Identity** section, notice the **Version** and **Build** fields.

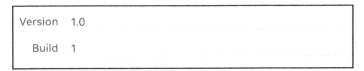

The Version field is a number that represents a version of your app. Usually, developers adopt **semantic versioning**, with a three-component number. The first number represents a **major version**, when the developer adds new features to the app. The second number represents a **minor version**. You change this number when you enhance an existing feature. The last number represents a patch or bug fix.

The Build field is a number that uniquely represents a build of a version. One version can have any number of builds, as long as they have different build numbers.

If you're working on your first version of the app, you might want to upload different builds to the App Store Connect. To do this, bump the build number in the project navigator and upload another archive.

Since you want to upload the first version of PetSave, leave the version number 1.0 and the build number 1.

## Archiving your App

In Xcode, set the build destination to **Any iOS Device (arm 64)**.

This generic target tells Xcode to build your app without a specific device in mind.

Next, click **Product ▸ Archive**.

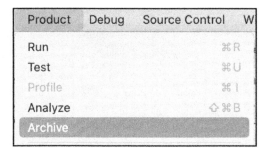

This will trigger a build of PetSave and create an archive of it. After Xcode compiles your code, you'll see the **Organizer** window with your archived app.

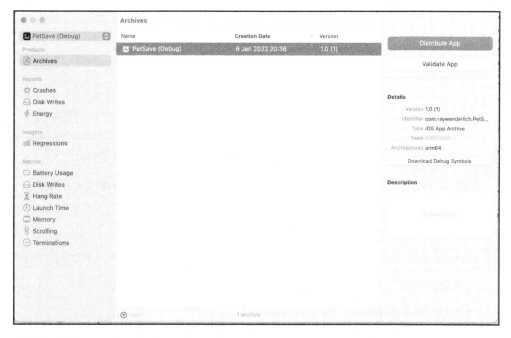

**Note**: If you don't see this window but notice the archive operation has finished, you can open the Organizer window by clicking **Window** in the toolbar, then clicking **Organizer** or by pressing **Command-Option-Shift-O**.

Here, you'll find all the archives of your apps. Select your latest archive, and click **Distribute App**.

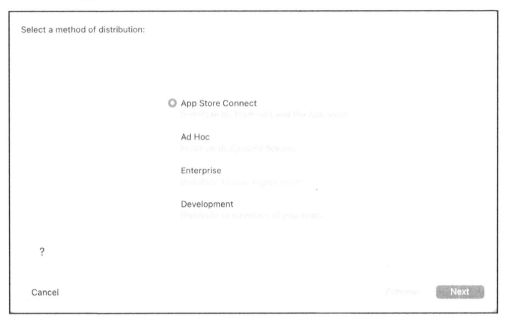

Xcode lets you choose how you want to distribute your app. You can select:

1. **App Store Connect** to distribute your app through **TestFlight** and the **App Store**.

2. **Ad Hoc** to distribute your app to selected devices.

3. **Enterprise** if you want to distribute your app to an organization.

4. **Development** for distributing your app to the development team.

Select **App Store Connect** and click **Next**.

> **Note:** If you want to learn more about other ways that you can distribute apps, check out Chapter 5, Internal Distribution (https://www.raywenderlich.com/ books/ios-app-distribution-best-practices/v1.0/chapters/5-internal-distribution) of our book **iOS App Distribution & Best Practices**.

Leave **Upload** checked to send the app to App Store Connect and click **Next**.

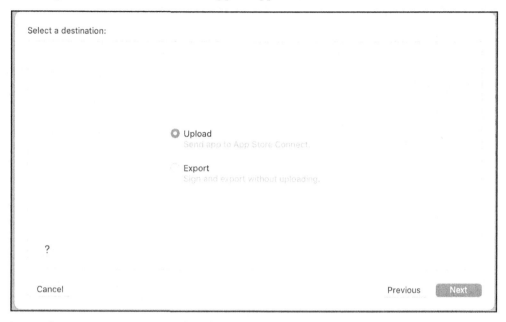

Leave the App Store Connect distribution options checked and click **Next**. You want to upload the debug information of your app as well.

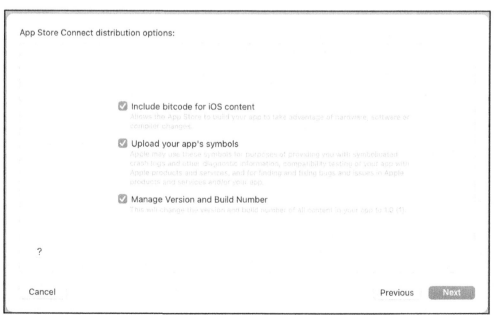

Finally, your app needs to be re-signed for distribution. Leave **Automatically manage signing** checked to let Xcode handle this for you and click **Next**.

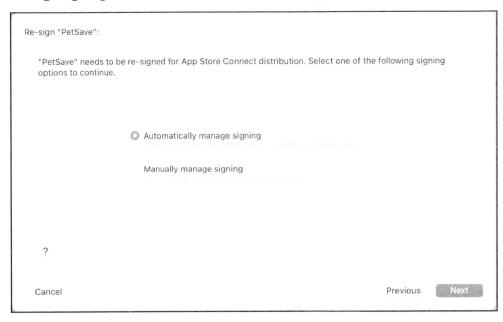

Finally, Xcode shows a review screen for you to review your upload.

Review the information and click **Upload**. Xcode will start uploading your app to App Store Connect.

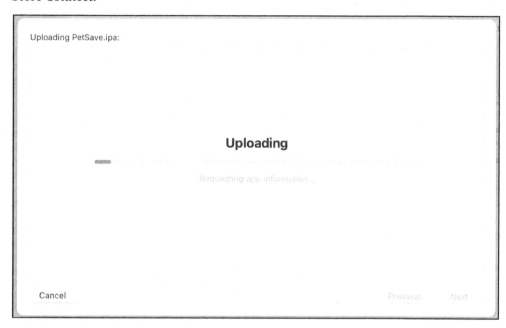

Wait for Xcode to finish uploading your build. This might take a while, depending on your internet connection.

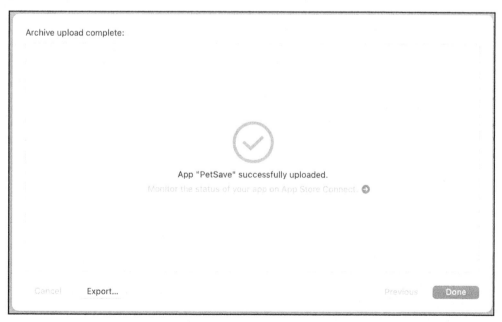

Success! You managed to upload the first build of PetSave.

With that done, it's time to finish filling out information about your app to submit it for review.

# Submitting your app for review

Now you're in the last phase of getting your app to the App Store: submitting it for Apple's review.

Apple reviews every app before it goes to the App Store. Every version you upload has to go for review before your customers can download it. Apple takes its review process seriously and is strict about what it allows in the App Store.

## App Store Review

When you submit your app for review, an Apple employee beta tests your app to make sure it follows the **App Store Review Guidelines** and **Apple Developer Program License Agreement**. They also look for any crashes or issues with your app.

If they find a problem, Apple rejects your app and gives you feedback on what they found. They might find a problem that violates their policies or even a crash.

If Apple rejects your build because of a guideline, you can still plead your case inside the **Resolution Center**. Apple gives you feedback and even screenshots about why they rejected your app. If you disagree with the feedback, you can send a message pleading your case.

> **Note:** To learn more about Apple's App Store Review Guidelines, check out the official documentation (https://developer.apple.com/app-store/review/guidelines/).

## Setting up Metadata

On App Store Connect, select **PetSave** and click **1.0 Prepare for Submission**. Here, you'll set up information to build your app page in the App Store. You can update this information every time you upload a new version to App Store Connect.

You've already provided some information, like the app's name. Now, you'll set up the screenshots and description of PetSave.

## Adding screenshots

Find the folder named **App Store Screenshots** inside the materials folder. Open it and drag and drop the screenshots in the screenshot field.

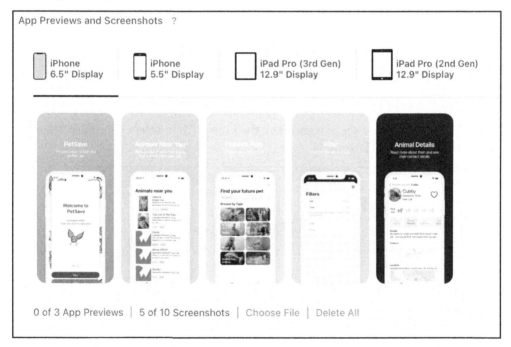

Customers will see those screenshots when they open your app's page in the App Store. Apple requires you to upload screenshots for devices with 6.5" and 5.5" displays. If your app also runs on iPad, you must upload screenshots for the iPad Pro (3rd Gen), the one with a notch, and the iPad Pro (2nd Gen).

You must take good screenshots of the app's features. Most customers go straight to the screenshots section to see if your app does what they think it does.

Below the screenshots, you'll find a couple of empty fields. Fill out each with:

1. **Description**: A description of PetSave, with its features and functionality. This is where you convince users that PetSave is the best app for finding pets.

2. **Keywords**: Keywords are words that make an App Store search more accurate and help find your app. Use words that people would search when looking for an app to adopt a pet.

3. **Support URL**: This is an URL people can use to get help with anything regarding your app.

4. **Marketing URL**: This URL is for people who want to learn more about your app and its features.

## Submitting your app for review

Next, you must select the correct build to submit for review.

Scroll down to the **Build** section and click the blue +. Then select your most recently uploaded build and click **Done**.

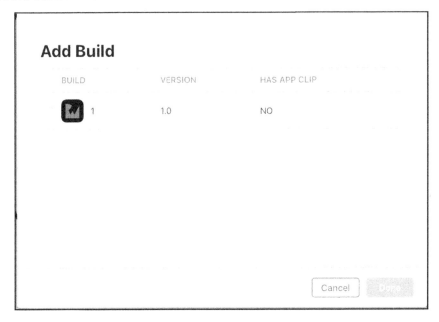

If this is your first time uploading a build, you might face a popup about app encryption.

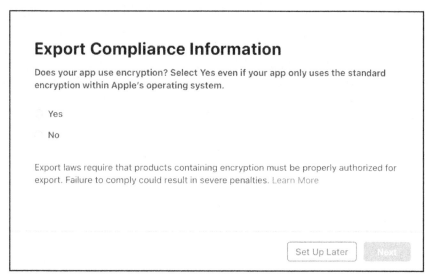

Apple requires you to disclose if your app uses any kind of encryption so that they can review it properly. Since PetSave does not use any particular encryption besides the standard one, simply select **No** and click **Done**.

With that, version 1.0 uses build number 1, and App Store Connect is already smart enough to fill the app's icon.

## App metadata

Before you move on, fill out the **Copyright** field. This field should be the name of a person or organization that owns the app. If you're releasing an app yourself, you can use your name here. However, if you're releasing an app on behalf of a company, you must use their legal name. For example, the Ray Wenderlich app uses **Razeware 2022**.

Next, scroll down to **App Review Information** and uncheck **Sign-in required**.

PetSave doesn't require users to sign in, but you'd have to provide Apple with an account to review your app if it did. You can also fill out the notes field with information about your app the reviewer might find helpful.

Scroll to the top and click **Save** to save all the information you've changed so far.

Finally, it's time to submit to Apple. If you're working on your app, this is when you'd click **Submit for Review**, next to the **Save**. Your app status would then change to **Waiting for Review**.

After Apple approves your build, the status of your app changes to **Ready for Sale**, indicating you can release your app in the App Store. If they find a problem, the status will change to **Rejected**, and you'd have to either respond to the issue in the Resolution Center or upload a new build.

Suppose this was an update to an existing app. Once your new version was marked ready for sale, you'd have the option to distribute it to all users immediately or to have apple distribute it slowly over seven days. This lets you and your team stop the update and fix any **regression** or breaking changes to existing code caused by the update.

# Using TestFlight to beta test your app

Before you finish this chapter, there's one last thing you should learn about App Store Connect: **TestFlight**.

TestFlight is Apple's solution for beta testing your apps. You can use it to distribute builds to developers or internal QA testers. You can even distribute to external testers by creating invite links.

## Why beta test?

All software has flaws. No matter how much you code, test and safeguard your code, software is so complex that there's bound to be a problem somewhere. But that doesn't mean you can't track problems and fix them.

Developers have many tools at their disposal to find and mitigate problems in their code. For example, throughout this book, you've used unit testing to mitigate problems with your code.

But even so, developers may become too familiar with their code and miss a couple of flaws. With beta testing, you allow a fresh pair of eyes to analyze your app and give crucial feedback. People that aren't working on the app may find problems with features, UX and much more.

## Using beta testing to find problems and bugs

**TestFlight** is a powerful tool for beta testing your app and getting valuable feedback before releasing it to the general public. Beta testers can use your app before everyone else and find problems or suggest improvements.

You'll learn how to add people as internal testers to test PetSave.

## Signing testers to beta test

Before you release PetSave for testers, you must invite them for beta testing. Back inside App Store Connect, click **Users and Access**.

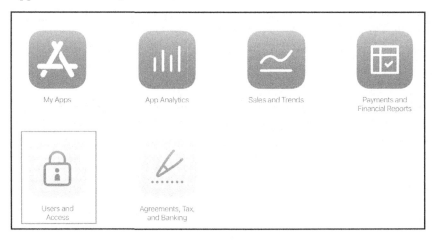

Next, click the blue + under the page's heading. The page will open a form for a new user.

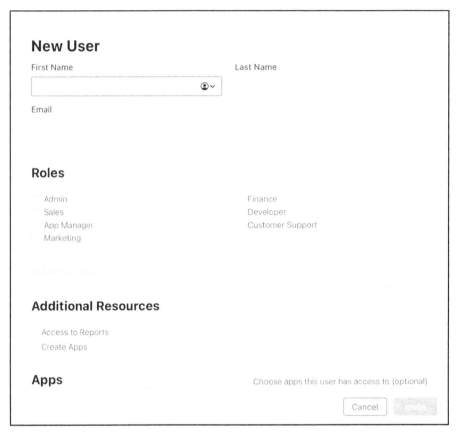

Fill out their first name, last name and email. Then check **Developer**. When adding people to your account, you have to select what kind of role they'll have. Each role has different permissions and access to tools inside App Store Connect.

Finally, click **Invite** at the bottom. Apple sends an email invitation to the people you invite to join your team.

Once the person accepts the invitation, they'll show up as a user under Users and Access.

Back inside App Store Connect, select your app and click **TestFlight** at the top of the page.

Under **Internal Testing**, select **App Store Connect Users** and click the blue + next to **Testers**.

Next, select all the users you wish to add to the **App Store Connect Users** group and click **Add**.

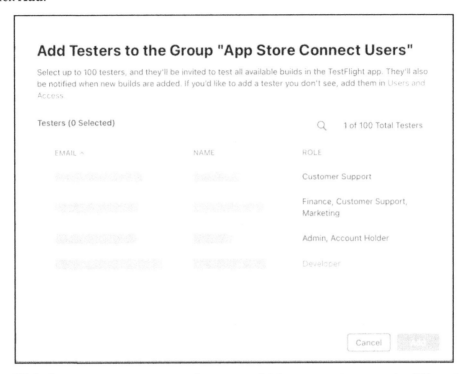

TestFlight lets you create groups and manage which group gets access to different builds and different apps.

App Store Connect sends an email inviting the selected users to download your app inside the TestFlight app. You can even see which users installed the app.

## Adding test Information

Now that beta testers can download your app, you have to let them know what they should focus on when testing the app. TestFlight has a **Test Details** field that lets you write what's new for beta testers to test.

Click the build you just released in TestFlight.

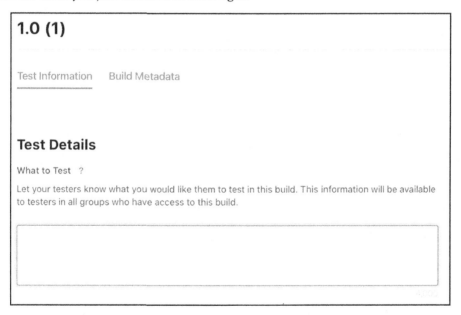

On this page, you can let testers know what to look for in this new build. Write about the initial features of PetSave and click **Save**.

# Getting feedback

After adding a description to Test Details, you'll find the same description in TestFlight under **What to Test**.

Also, when testers first download and open the app, an overlay view shows them the same text.

It also tells testers how to give feedback by taking screenshots.

Testers can go back to the TestFlight app and tap **Send Beta Feedback**, where they can write their feedback and attach a screenshot.

You'll then find this feedback back inside the TestFlight tab under **Feedback** and **Screenshots**.

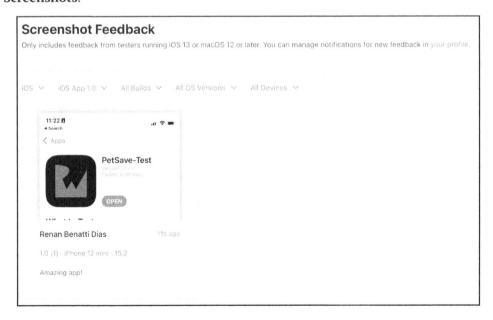

## Key points

- You have to enroll in **Apple's Developer Program** to submit your app to the App Store.

- **Code signing** can be challenging, but you can let Xcode do most of the work for you.

- The **App Store app page** is the face of your app. Build a nice, informative page, and people will be more interested in your app.

- You use Xcode to create **archives** of your app and upload them to Apple.

- Apple **reviews** all builds you submit to the App Store, approving or rejecting depending on their guidelines.

- **TestFlight** is a powerful tool for beta testing your apps.


## Where to go from here?

This is the last chapter of this book, but that doesn't mean there's nothing left to learn about sending your app to the App Store.

If you're interested in learning more about this topic and best practices for distributing your app and beta testing, check out our book iOS App Distribution & Best Practices ([https://www.raywenderlich.com/books/ios-app-distribution-best-practices](https://www.raywenderlich.com/books/ios-app-distribution-best-practices)).

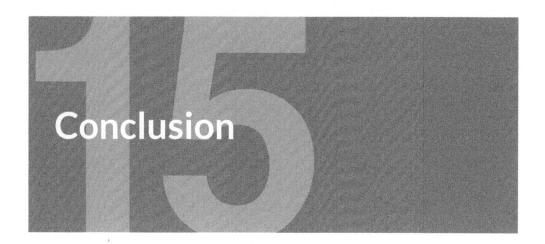

# Conclusion

What a ride! You went from an idea to having an actual app that can be placed on the App Store. We hope you enjoyed this ride and that you learned a lot along the way. We encourage you to use these new techniques and knowledge in your projects. Go out there and create your own real-world apps, and comeback here if you need help.

If you have any questions or comments as you work through this book, please stop by our forums at https://forums.raywenderlich.com and look for the particular forum category for this book.

Thank you again for purchasing this book. Your continued support is what makes the tutorials, books, videos, conferences and other things we do at raywenderlich.com possible, and we truly appreciate it!

— Josh, Renan, Aaqib, Pinal, Kenny and Libranner

The *Real-World iOS by Tutorials* team

Made in the USA
Coppell, TX
22 January 2023